Port Orford
A History

Patrick Masterson

BookPartners, Inc.
Wilsonville, Oregon

BookPartners, Inc.
P.O. Box 922
Wilsonville, OR 97070

Table of Contents

Dedication

This book is a memory in print for the men and women whose lives and character formed the spirit and history of Port Orford. It is impossible to name them all, but they who participated in the Port Orford adventure, past and present, know who they are. May this book give them a broader sense of their contributions.

Foreword

In recalling my childhood on the Hughes Ranch during the Depression Years, only one regret comes to mind. I wasn't old enough to appreciate the information my Uncle Edward could have provided about life in Northern Curry County during his childhood, the late 1860s to the 1880s.

My memories of the 1930s and 1940s are vivid. As a child I romped over every inch of the ranch. My playground, where Indians once roamed, revealed 5,000 years of tribal occupation. I discovered and explored piles of flint fragments scattered on the sand dunes. Across the Sixes River, I searched through extensive shell mounds that marked the site of a large native village.

To the north was Blacklock Point, with Cape Blanco to the south. South of the Cape was an old mine, still being worked in the thirties. Down towards the beach, a pile of old chimney bricks marked the original farmstead near the mouth of the Sixes.

The ranch was isolated, which made it imperative to be self-sufficient. Our lights were kerosene; our neighbors distant. There was a smokehouse full of salmon, jerky and bacon; a barrel of salted butter stood on the back porch; ice-cold buttermilk came to us from the creamery cellar. These were all things I took for granted growing up.

A boy would remember the firearms propped against the weather-worn door frame of the old bunkhouse. One was an octagon barrel .45 caliber rifle; the other, a rusty musket. Above the metal sink hung a white life ring with the name "J.A. Chanslor, San Francisco" stenciled around it.

To the east from the Hughes Ranch was the creamery, filled with idle machinery and butter-making equipment, relics of a 1900 industry. Also on the sprawling spread was a structure I love — a huge barn to shelter tons of hay. Inside were an old buckboard and a buggy. Beneath the eaves of the barn hundreds of swallows' nests were attached to the lofty rafters.

Perhaps, most impressive to a small child standing on the road just before harvest time, were the fields of barley and oats. Strong ocean winds swept across the land creating giant, golden waves. A child could imagine being engulfed and carried out to the sea beyond.

All this, and more, I can recall. It is the earlier years that lack documentation. An occasional news brief, a letter, or two and county records provide some insights, but not nearly enough. Therefore, you, the reader, must forgive the void.

My interest in the history of the Northern Curry County area was whetted by Louis Knapp who for 30 years shared his books, papers and pictures with me. My research has taken me into library stacks and historical archives across the land and I've made contact with people who know the area by mail, phone and in person. The resulting files of material will be made available to the public once this work is printed.

What started out to be a story in photos was altered, somewhat, for the events that composed the history of the Port Orford region demand responsible narrative in addition to photography and sketches.

I hope you enjoy this work as much as I have enjoyed compiling it.

Patrick Masterson
Port Orford, Oregon

1

The First Settlement

Perhaps the likeliest place to start a history of Port Orford is with a man, Captain William Tichenor, who played a major role in the founding of the original white settlement, the first of its kind, on the Southern Oregon Coast. It's proper and informative to learn something about the personal history of the adventurer whose overriding interest in the area was undoubtedly the prospect of finding a fortune in gold in the draws, creeks and rivers of the area that came to be known as Port Orford.

Born June 13, 1813, in Newark, New Jersey, William Tichenor was the youngest of six boys in a family of ten. He began a maritime career at age fifteen, shipping on the vessel *James Perkins* bound for France in 1828. During the next 20 years, Tichenor spent time in the New Orleans-New York trade, shopkeeping and farming in Knox County, Indiana and dabbling in politics. He married Elizabeth Brinkerhoff in January, 1834. In 1837, he moved to Edgar County, Illinois, from there he took a short trip to sea in 1842. Spurred on by tales related to him by an older brother who had visited Yerba Buena (San Francisco) in 1828, Tichenor decided to wend his way west in 1849. In the fall of that year, after several months of successful mining at Tichenor's Gulch on the American River, he wound up in San Francisco with 70 pounds of gold. After recuperating from the grueling trip across the plains and mining hardships, he purchased the schooner *Jacob M. Ryerson*. On March 20, 1850, he sailed from San Francisco with 85 passengers bound for the gold country on the Trinity River. A gale set in on the party and on the 27th he was abreast of Cape Blanco at which point he launched a long boat and explored the roadstead of Port Orford, but did not land due to the presence of "numerous naked savages and their hostile appearance …" Continuing south, the *Ryerson* entered the Eel River where Tichenor "…made a location of the town of Humbolt immediately at the left of the entrance on the south of the bluff…" Pushing on up the Eel with a small exploration party, Tichenor constructed a blockhouse " …below the first of the forks of the river…," the Indians there showing "…good and great hostility…" After nearly a month on the Eel River, the vessel cleared the river bar and on June 24, entered Humbolt Bay where 28 Donation Land Claims were taken including one or two which would eventually become the site for the city of Eureka, named by John Hayward, a mate on the *Ryerson*.

Upon his return to San Francisco, Tichenor sold the *Ryerson* and was given command of the brig *Emily Farnham* in which he carried goods to Union Town (Arcata) and in October, set out from San Francisco with 85 passengers bound for the Columbia River. Upon arriving in Astoria, a dispute arose between the Collector of Customs and Tichenor, who defiantly sailed out of the Columbia River with an army officer (Lt. Wood) on board as an uninvited guest. Tichenor was exonerated by the Customs Officer at San Francisco. He resisted, on the same trip, the attempt of the "doctor's" to come aboard and collect fees of $10 a passenger regardless of their origin, after quarantining the boat thus breaking an organized scam created by corrupt city officials.

Tichenor then accepted command of the 400 ton steamer *Seagull* which he described as "… strongly built, with sufficient power but wrongly applied." Regular trips were made to the Columbia River where he was the second man to be appointed bar pilot. When weather permitted, Tichenor explored and examined the entire coast of Oregon and settled on the roadstead just south of Cape Blanco as a site to locate a Donation Land Claim which led to the landing of nine men recruited in Portland on June 9, 1851, to stake the claim.

On May 12, 1852, Tichenor's wife Elizabeth and their small children arrived at Port Orford on board the vessel *Anson* and they moved in to a well furnished house prepared by Tichenor. Thus, they became the first white settlers in the area. Captain Tichenor continued his maritime pursuits taking time off on occasions to serve in the legislature, round up stray Tututnis and promote Port Orford. During the Indian War of 1866, he served as a guide for Colonel Buchanen along the south coast and up the Rogue River. Although many historians credit him with building the first schooner along the south coast, the vessel *Alaska* was actually laid down on the Oregon River near Portland in 1863, although, according to a Bancroft narrative the small boat *Nellie* was probably built at Port Orford. He eventually retired from the sea, surviving marital and financial difficulty in his later years. In 1887, he died in San Francisco.

The narrative entitled *Life Among The Oregon Indians* along with several other variations of the same text is on file in the Port Orford Library, as well as letters and other related materials.

Captain William Tichenor and the Founding of Port Orford

The first documented landing at Port Orford occurred on June 9, 1851 when Captain Tichenor dispatched nine men from the 400 ton steam schooner *Seagull* to survey a Donation Land Claim. This expedition, the first attempt at establishing a settlement on the southern Oregon coast, was the first step in a plan originated by Tichenor after a reconnoiter the previous spring. At that time he was owner and master of the 160 ton schooner *Jacob M.Ryerson* which he purchased in San Francisco. On March 20, 1850, he sailed from San Francisco with 85 passengers bound for the Trinity River in northern California. A brisk gale forced him off the coast and on the 25th found him about 30 miles west of Cape Blanco. On the 27th he lowered the whale boat and proceeded to explore the coastline from the Cape to the roadstead at Port Orford. He later wrote, "Entered the roadstead now called Port Orford. I wished to land and examine the place but apprehending the difficulty with the numerous naked savages and their hostile appearance prevented me from landing as I was not prepared for a fight nor did I wish one." He continued on south and met the schooner off Crescent City and from there made a successful bar crossing into the Eel River on April 3, 1850. Upon returning to San Francisco, Tichenor sold the *Ryerson,* sailed through some exciting events on the brig *Emily Farnham,* and accepted the command of the *Seagull* March 6th. He made four trips on the Columbia River trade before outfitting the small party at Portland for the purpose of the Port Orford landing. The party consisted of J.M. Kirkpatrick (captain), J.H. Eagen, John T. Slater, George Ridoubts, T.D. Palmer, Joseph Hussey, James Corigan, Erastus Summers and Cyrus Hedden. They departed from Portland on June 3, 1851, and after securing additional arms and supplies at Astoria, arrived at Port Orford on June 9, landing just below what is now called Battle Rock. After setting up an old line gun on the rock, the party established camp behind it. Kirkpatrick feared that the intrusion would arouse the natives and he was right for immediately after the *Seagull* sailed south, the Indians "appeared very cross and ordered us away, making signs to us that they would kill us all if we did not go." The following morning the natives attacked and were repulsed by the fiery discharge of the old cannon which killed 17 braves who were bunched together on the narrow approach to the camp. After several more skirmishes the party eventually escaped under cover of darkness and made their way to Scottsburg on the Umpqua River. (See *Pioneer History of Coos-Curry,* Orville Dodge, pps. 33-50)

Thus the southern Oregon coast was opened for settlement and the next five years saw the decline of the ancient Indian occupation and the settlement by whites.

The preceding account was penned 46 years after the actual landing at Port Orford and is the most complete version of the event. It should be noted that several of the original party filed an affidavit several years later which attested to the fact that they were in the employ of Tichenor, Hubbard and Smith and had as of that time not been paid for their experience at Port Orford. Tichenor, in his unpublished statement, stated that he hesitated to make a landing at Port Orford the year before because of the apparent hostility shown by the Indians on the beach and yet he attempted to persuade the landing party that the Indians were peaceful and friendly.

Another interesting point to ponder is the actions of the stranded Russian sailor, (the one in the red shirt), who supposedly led the charge up the narrow trail on Battle Rock and in the direct line of fire of the small cannon. He surely would have been aware of the destructive capability of the cannon — any cannon. Perhaps Kirkpatrick had the piece hidden well enough that the Russian did not see it.

Captain Tichenor's biography relates in some detail the events of that historic landing: "When weather permitted, on every passage of the *Sea Gull* the coastline was carefully examined. Sunken rocks, reefs, shoals and currents and every peculiarity were noted for future reference. The last of May was chosen as a proper time to commence a settlement at the long determined point, Port Orford, named after the cape seven miles to the North of the roadstead. Nine men were engaged by Captain Tichenor, a good supply of arms, ammunition and provisions secured and upon the down passage of the *Sea Gull* on June ninth, a landing was made. All supplies, together with the ships gun (a line gun) and copper magazine was placed upon a rock, since named Battle Rock, the gun commanding the access. The men were to have their number augmented in 12 days on the return of the steamer. Upon arriving at San Francisco it was found necessary to repair and paint the ship. Captain Knight of the Pacific Mail Company ship *Columbia* kindly offered to take up the recruits and additional supplies, Captain Tichenor to accompany him — entered Port Orford in the morning and saw a number of canoes paddling for dear life to the southward. The ship fired her gun to let the men on the rock know of her approach. The moment the gun was fired every Indian in the canoes plunged overboard, giving evidence that something was wrong. Coming to anchor, a boat was lowered and then pulled ashore, and immediately at the base of the rock at the point of ascent lay a dead Indian. The indications were anything but flattering for the safety of the men left by the *Sea Gull*. A search was at once instituted, fragments of a diary were found scattered around embracing every circumstance of all the attacks up to the previous evening. The carriage of the gun was broken up, the magazine gone, the two tents, hardbread and port scattered around. Desertion presented itself everywhere. After diligent search with no clue to solve the disappearance of the men (we) returned to the ship and proceeded upon the voyage, returning to San Francisco on July 1, 1851."

Upon his return to San Francisco, Tichenor proceeded to promote the settlement at Port Orford. Handbills were printed extolling the ease of joining the company and getting rich from the fabulous gold mining prospects in the area — a ploy which fired the interests of the many men who had failed to "strike it rich" in the Mother Lode country of the Sierra Nevadas. Tichenor posted the bills near the most active and pretentious bistros around Portsmouth Square and signed up 67 adventurous men led by one James

S. Gamble. They landed at Port Orford July 15, 1851 and off-loaded three six-pound cannons and four months of provisions and supplies. "Fort Point (just west of Battle Rock) was picketed in immediately, two block houses erected inside of heavy logs and everything done for permanent settlement." Tichenor then proceeded to Portland where he filed his Notification of Settlers Oath at Oregon City. Six horses, some swine and other stores were purchased and the captain returned with Col. Wm. T. T'Vault to Port Orford. The Indians now had turned friendly and the fate of the original landing party was now learned and the prospects of a thriving community appeared likely. The roster of the men who landed on July 15 are as follows:

First Settlers to Land at Port Orford, Oregon Territory

Anderson, A. J.
Anderson, J. R.
Book, George
Brush, Gilbert
Buckley, John
Burns, E. W.
Caston, George R.
Corbilt, A. H.
Cornish, William
Costello, Thomas
Davenport, Thomas J.
Densen, Joseph
Doughty, A. S.
Dougherty, Cornelius
Farlee, John
Finerty, Thomas
Foster, Charles
Frasier, John
Frazer, William N.
Gilman, William

Grant, Charles
Holland, John P.
Holmes, James
Jefferson, Thomas
Keen, Andrew J.
Kelly, A. J.
Kennedy, William N.
Lake, Robert N.
Lewis, Henry I.
Lewis, Isiah
Locke, James
Lount, George
Lount, Seth N.
Lowered, William
Muffitt, Joseph
McKay, E.
McPherson, Charles J.
Melville, Thomas
Merrill, Rufus
Moucrieff, William J.
Munson, Lyman B.

Murphy, Patrick
Murray, Edward
Nickerson, A. J.
Nolan, William
Pepper, J. P.
Rattan, John
Robinson, Alex
Ryan, Jeremiah
See, George W.
Simens, A. R.
Sinclair, Arch
Stewart, George
Taff, John
Thompson, John
Tichenor, Randolf
Tyler, Rowland A.
Unican, Fred
Valleau, Charles S.
VanBussum, Joseph V.
Wackewreuter, Vitus
Wallace, William
Willett, John
Williams, Lorine S.

Led by James S. Gamble
Employed by Isaac W. Hubbard, Fredrick M. Smith and William Tichener

Tichenor, in the hopes of setting up a supply line to the miners at Jacksonville sent out two parties to locate a suitable route through the rugged Klamath Mountains. On August 24th, 23 men led by William T'Vault and William Nolan struck out to locate the trail east to the

Oregon California road believing that it could only be 50 or 60 miles from Port Orford. Tichenor advised them to stay on a southeast course, following the high ridges from Sugar Loaf (Humbug) Mountain which he believed to be the western terminus of the Siskiyou Mountains. His men reached Rogue River and for two weeks they struggled up the trailless north side of the river finally reaching Foster Creek on September 7th. Thirteen of the party had already turned back and disgustingly renamed Sugar Loaf Mountain "Tichenor's Humbug." T'Vault persuaded the remaining men to continue and after incredible hardships the group, fatigued, lost and subsisting on wild berries and horseflesh, wound up in the drainage of the Coquille River. As the weary explorers approached the large Indian village at the mouth of the river they were attacked by the men of the Coquilles (Kokwell*). Five men, Doughty, Murphy, Holland, Pepper and Ryan were killed while Williams and Bush received severe wounds. T'Vault and Bush made it back to Port Orford. Hedden, Williams and Davenport escaped to the more friendly environs of the settlement at Scottsburg on the Umpqua River.

Tichenor in the meantime pressed hard to convince the military at Fort Vancouver that a detachment of troops was sorely needed at Port Orford to protect the miners, settlers and merchants who, he was sure, would be attracted to the area. Yielding to the power of the press and perseverance of the politicians, (the four Ps) General Hitchcock sent a detachment of 20 men (Company I, First Artillery) under the command of Lt. P. T. Wyman to lay out and construct a post and conduct the affairs in keeping with the military obligations of territorial settlers and the Indian population. The T'Vault massacre bolstered the justification for this small fort and Wyman selected a site just west of the town on the bluff which commanded a view of the roadstead to the south. Although plagued with early winter storms the troops felled the nearby cedar trees and constructed several buildings.

Colonel Silas Casey led a punitive expedition against the Coquilles during October and November and at the same time Captain Andrew Jackson Smith and Lt. George Williamson led a party east attempting to locate a suitable route to the Oregon road. The first group succeeded, managing to rain terror on the main village on the Coquille with musketry fire and several rounds of cannon shells from a mountain howitzer. The second group wandered somewhat aimlessly in the back country but did acquire enough information to compile a fairly accurate map of the area. Casey and his men sailed south to San Francisco (Benecia) but 92 men under Lt. Horatio G. Gibson stayed on to assist with the completion of Fort Orford.

Following is information on Fort Orford from army records:
1. Records of the War Department, Office of the Quartermaster General, Record

Group 92. Consolidated correspondence file, Fort Orford, Oregon Territory.

2. Diagram of Fort Orford, Oregon Territory as of January 28, 1855. August V. Kautz, Second Lt., Fourth Infantry, A.A.G.M. A letter reporting upon the condition of public buildings. Received 2/1/55.

3. Port Orford, Oregon Territory, January 28, 1855.

Sirs:

In compliance with a circular from your office dated January 16th, 1855, I herewith enclose a diagram of this post, drawn to a scale of 50 feet to the inch, which illustrates the relative position and size of the buildings and outbuildings at the post. The dimensions of each building are indicated on the diagram. The following are the uses to which the various buildings are applies. viz:

Number 1 is occupied by the commanding officer and surgeon. It has three rooms with a porch running half round the building.

Number 13 is used as a kitchen and messroom for officers. These are the only buildings at present used by the officers.

Number 10 is occupied by a detachment of company M, Third Artillery; a small room is partitioned off for the non-commissioned officers of the detachment.

Number 9 is the cookhouse.

Number 5 is the guardhouse with two cells and a porch.

Numbers 7 and 8 are the commissary storehouses.

Numbers 3, 4 and 6 are quartermaster storehouses. A small addition to Number 4 has been used as an ordinance storeroom but becoming leaky, Number 2 is at present appropriated for that purpose, having been formerly used for officer's quarters.

Number 15 is a stable recently erected for public animals.

Number 12 is the post backhouse.

Number 11 quarters ordinance Sergeant Kelly. These buildings are all in good repair.

(s) Very Respectfully Your Humble Servant,

August V. Kautz

To: Major D. Cross, Chief Quartermaster, Department of the Pacific

The fort occupied an undefined area west of Oregon Street and south of Seventh Street on lands later used by the school district (the old high school) and the Neptune Motel. It appears that the basic structures were formed up with logs and eventually roofed and sided with sawed lumber shipped in from Benecia or perhaps Eureka. Doors, windows and flooring along with interior fixtures and furniture were also shipped up from Benecia. During the hostilities of Indian uprisings in the spring of 1856 a plank wall was raised which surrounded the principle buildings. A glacis (earthen slope designed to expose attackers to fire from the wall) was constructed around the perimeter of the wall and a blockhouse was erected.

The advent of the troops and the establishment of the fort enabled Tichenor and his partners to pursue their interests with confidence. Port Orford became a boom town populated by miners and entrepreneurs who were spurred on by "gold fever," a contagious malady brought on by "truth-like" rumors of rich strikes spread among the idle prospectors who roamed the streets of San Francisco and Portland. They scraped together enough money to buy passage on Captain Dall's ship *Columbia* and Tichenor's *Sea Gull* in the hopes of getting in on the ground floor of the rich diggings or at least becoming a part of the establishment of a new port city which would rival San Francisco and Portland in trade potential. For most, the escapade would prove to be a financial disaster but a few would make better than wages mining the "black sands" along the solitary beaches and the placers located on the south fork of the Sixes River.

The farthest west town in the territory was off to a rousing start. Titus Wackenreuter, Tichenor's surveyor, had platted a townsite and buildings sprang up in the area which is now the southwest section of town just north of Battle Rock. The structures faced east and west lining what is now Jefferson and Jackson streets. Herman Reinhart, who operated a small store and eatery near "The Sisters" (Frankport) describes Port Orford in 1854: " ... it was a lively town of about a thousand inhabitants. There was a garrison and fort and some troops stationed there, and many stores and hotels and saloons, and there was lots of business done by miners from Cape Blanco and the mouth of the Sixes River and Floras Creek had some very rich gold claims along the beach ..." Rodney Glisan, an army doctor, arrived at the fort in June, 1855 and reported in his diary, "Adjoining the Military Reservation of this fort, is a little village called Port Orford ... it still numbers about forty houses, and one-third of these are tenantless." And so it appeared, for Port Orford at least, the gold rush was over.

Tichenor was not about to give up on his dream of a prosperous town. Recognizing the need for lumber in the San Francisco area to replace buildings razed by frequent fires he and a man named Neefus purchased a steam powered sawmill which was delivered to Port Orford on the steamer San Diego in the spring of 1854. Eighteen days later the mill, located in the vicinity of the present site of Coos-Curry Electric's headquarters, began operation. Employing 25 men, the little mill turned out over 5,000 board feet per day, mostly cedar, which brought $125 per thousand in the bay area. William Winsor acted as millwright and is attributed with the coining of the name "Port Orford Cedar" to the tree that is now world famous but at present disappearing due to a virus that attacks the tap root and is 100 percent fatal to the majestic tree. This little mill also produced thousands of laths but the market soon dried up and Tichenor sold it to A. M. Simpson of North Bend.

A smaller mill, probably a "whipsaw" operation, was located earlier in an area near Nineteenth and Jackson Streets although most of the lumber for the first houses and business buildings was shipped from Portland.

Meanwhile, the troops stationed at Fort Orford busied themselves brushing out trails, cutting firewood, repairing leaky buildings, hunting and fishing to bolster the larder and visiting the "downtown" social facilities … namely one operated by Spanish Mary who it seems killed a man in San Francisco and was smuggled out by a man named Nollan. They were married in Empire City and according to Herman Reinhart, "she always done a big business in Port Orford." Herman discreetly remained silent as to the nature of her business.

The number of troops stationed at the fort varied from a low of nine during the winter and spring months of 1853, to a high of 244 men in June of 1856, the end of the Rogue River War. Desertions ran high among the bored enlisted men who were easily tempted to skip out to the gold fields and as a result the guard house, perched high on the hill overlooking the present day dock, was usually full. Confinement there during the stormy months was, to say the least, miserable.

2

Rogue River
Indian War

Activity along the south coast slowed considerably after the miners among the initial flurry had determined that the area was not rich in gold after all. Most had moved on to other areas and the few that remained worked the beaches with "long Toms" at Rogue River, Cape Blanco and north of the Coquille (Kokwell) River. Adverse weather had caused the loss of the *Captain Lincoln,* a three masted transport schooner, which carried 35 dragoons under the command of Lieut. Henry M. Stanton from Benecia to Fort Orford. She was "driven by" Port Orford in a fierce gale and eventually struck just north of the entrance to Coos Bay on January 3, 1852. A makeshift camp was set up on the beach and the weary troopers salvaged the equipment and stores which were protected from the incessant rains by a "sail cloth village." It was four months before the troops could make it back to Port Orford, a distance of 60 miles (see Dodge, History of Coos-Curry, pp. 114). Lieut. Stanton's fortunes turned sour several years later while he was serving in the southwest among the Apaches. His patrol was ambushed and annihilated. His bleached bones were returned to the fort ... tied in a bag and secured to his unbridled horse.

Disaster greeted Captain Tichenor in the same month as the old steam schooner *Seagull* lost a flue on the Humboldt bar and was wrecked. She was a total loss but the doughty skipper saved his passengers, crew and cargo. His charges, recognizing his able seamanship, presented him with a gold watch. Another vessel, the *Anita,* chartered by the army slipped her chains and grounded in one of the coves under the Heads ... she was a total loss. The schooners *Iowa* and *Francisco* met the same fate in May and June of 1856.

The pressure on the Tututnis was mounting as the miners began to prospect farther inland from the coast. The native Americans observed the invasion rather passively although minor differences cropped up. In February, 1854, Augustus Miller operated a ford on the north side of the Chetco River which was in competition with the one established much earlier by the Chetcos. In order to gain complete control of the crossing Miller and several other henchmen torched the ancient village, killing several inhabitants in the process. Miller was arrested, brought to Fort Orford, but later released for " … lack of evidence." The killings continued.

A council was held at Myrtle Grove (Huntly Park - ed.) on the lower Rogue River in August, 1855. At this time Joel Palmer, the general superintendent of Indians in Oregon, concluded a treaty with the bands of the Port Orford District which in return for blankets, calico, kettles, clothing, small hand tools, tobacco and (of course) beads the Tututnis would receive transportation to a distant and unfamiliar reserve far removed from the troublesome miners. This treaty, although never ratified by Congress, sufficed as the legal document empowering the federal and territorial governments to "clear the title" to lands of the Tututnis … ancient, sacred ancestral lands which had been occupied by the Tututnis and their predecessors for thousands of years. They had been in residence on the land before the giant redwoods were seedlings, before the limestone blocks of the pyramid Cheops were quarried at Tura and when the summit of Mount Mazama reached nearly 12,000 feet. Dr. Rodney Glisan describes the events including the Indians in his work, *Journal of Army Life:*

"Leaving Fort Orford on the 29th ultimo, we arrived on the "ground" the same evening, after a journey of 30 miles over the roughest road I have ever traveled. For two-thirds of the distance the rider is in constant peril of neck and limb. Woe to him if his animal makes a misstep; his journey to the bottom of some gorge would excel the velocity of the stream. At one place it is necessary to ride across a stream on a <u>log</u> — a short, broad one, it is true, but still a <u>log</u> — and should your horse make a careless step a heavy tumble would be the consequence at least. In traveling up one mountain gorge (Brush Creek - ed.) it is necessary to cross a creek 17 times in a distance of about four miles. The trail then turns abruptly westward, and the broad Pacific lies before, and 300 feet beneath us. Yes, literally beneath us; for its bank is perpendicular, and the trail within three feet of its brink. The view is grand. Niagara itself, of which the roaring breakers below remind us, is not more sublime.

"Again the road meanders through the mountains for a few miles, and then descends to the water's edge. It now continues for a few miles along a sand beach, which is admirable traveling at low tide."

Glisan enjoyed observing thousands of gulls, ducks and pelicans gormandizing on smelt and noted little mining activity except at the mouth of Rogue River.

"The gold is distributed in such minute particles through the sand that but little can be got out by the ordinary mining process. This whole coast for a hundred miles in extent will, however, be an immense field for mining some 20 years hence, when labor becomes cheaper, and machinery more perfect.

"The council ground was located in a beautiful myrtle grove on the south bank of Rogue River, three miles from its mouth. The object of the counsel was to form a treaty with the various bands of Indians belonging to the Port Orford district, with the view of settling them, together with all other bands and tribes living on the coast of Oregon, on an Indian reserve; that is, a tract of land set aside for them exclusively — on which the whites are not permitted to reside. This system of disposing of the Indians has been for many years adopted by our government. It is the only plan to prevent their entire extermination."

"That some system of this kind is requisite is but too painfully felt by every man of sensibility and intelligence, who has ever been in our new territories and seen how badly the Indians and whites get along together. This is more apparent on our Pacific coast than east of the Rocky Mountains. For the excitement of the gold mines has filled California and portions of Oregon more rapidly than any other parts of the United States Territory, and consequently, brought the whites and Indians in more frequent conflict."

Describing the effect of settlers adhering to the Donation Land Claim Act and taking up lands which have not been legally acquired from the Indians Glisan notes:

"And what makes matters worse, some of the rougher class of miners will submit to no control in their intercourse with the Indians."

"If an Indian steals anything from, or hurts one of these persons, his life is generally the forfeit. The Indians around here formerly acted upon the same principle, but their frequent conflicts with the whites have so intimidated them that they are now generally inclined to peace. They have sufficient bad and desperate fellows among them, however, to keep their bands in constant difficulty.

"An instance occurred during the session of the council of a most painful character — the more so as it terminated in the death of three American citizens, together with two Indians, and came within an ace of not only breaking up all further negotiations with the Indians, but of bringing on another Rogue River war. The circumstances were these:

"An Indian and a white man had a quarrel, which resulted in the latter being wounded in the shoulder by the former. The Indian fled. Captain Ben Wright, a sub-Indian agent, being on the treaty ground for the purpose of assembling the

Indians preparatory for the treaty, happening to hear of the difficulty, and wishing to prevent further bloodshed, went personally and arrested the Indian with the view of having him properly tried, and punishing him for his misdemeanor if found guilty. At night, whilst he, some others, and the prisoner, were lying asleep in a small shanty, a shot was fired by an unknown person, which shattered the prisoner's arm. Wright having dressed his wounds, placed him between himself and the wall; thus with his own person, afforded protection to the Indian. The night passed off quietly, but as it was evident that the populace intended getting forcible possession of him in the morning with the view of hanging him, the Agent rose early and took his prisoner to the treaty ground, and there placed him in a small hut. He had scarcely done so, when the mob assembled to the number of 60 persons, armed with Colt's revolvers, and demanded his prisoner. Wright stood in the door, and by his determined manner and strong arguments, managed to keep them at bay until the arrival of a detachment of 15 U.S. troops, who had opportunely reached the opposite side of the river; and for whom he secretly dispatched a messenger. The prisoner was then turned over to their protection. The crowd hung around for some time blackguarding the soldiers, but finally dispersed.

"On the following day, the 27th of August, a constable took the prisoner in charge with the intention of taking him before a magistrate some three miles down the river. At the solicitation of the constable, and request of General Palmer … who had arrived in the meantime, a corporal's guard of troops was furnished the prisoner. After the latter had been properly committed by the magistrate to stand his trial at the next term of court, he was remanded to the corporal for conveyance to prison. As the guard was ascending Rogue River late at night (moonlight) three men came alongside. The corporal ordered them to keep off, but instead of doing so they commenced firing into his boat, killing the prisoner, who was at the time between the corporal's knees, and another Indian rowing the boat.

"The corporal then commanded his men to return the fire. The three men were instantly killed, each receiving a ball through his chest. The (sic) five corpses were taken to camp. The Indians fled from the council ground in consternation. An attack was expected on the general's camp by the exasperated citizens. A gentleman was dispatched to the mouth of Rogue River to explain the matter to the Vigilance Committee. On arriving there he ascertained that the three men, who had met such an untimely fate by their rashness, were to have been supported by a strong party in another boat. But this party is said to have returned home and gone to bed, after hearing the fatal shots, without even ascertaining the fate of their companions. The miners composing the Vigilance Committee were, of course, much excited, but after understanding the matter thoroughly, came to the conclusion that the soldiers acted only in the discharge of their duty. This was also the verdict of the coroner's jury, held on the deceased the following day.

"The event is to be deplored. But it will probably prove a lesson to a large class of persons in this community who wish to take law into their own hands, and execute it in accordance to the dictates of interest or passion. It is probable that the Indian in this case was to blame; if so, he certainly would have met with proper punishment when tried by a jury of Americans. Why then attempt to frustrate the ends of justice by mob violence?

"The Indians returned to the ground again on the 30th to the number of 1,220 (This count corresponds with the 1854 enumeration made by Agent Parrish.), and after having signed the treaty, received from the agents various presents ... "

This event was somewhat remarkable considering the growing unrest of the Indian population on the upper Rogue River. The tragedy of the murders of the (sic) Indians and subsequent killing of the three miners by the troopers clearly indicated the attitudes of the three factions. First the Indian bands demonstrated a high degree of trust mixed in with, of course, fear and wariness. It appears by the number present that the greater share of the adults in the Port Orford District were in attendance. Secondly, the regular army went about the task of keeping order in a professional and businesslike manner and most importantly they were just in the treatment of both factions. Third, the miners for the most part were an unruly, unsympathetic mob bent on one plan ... extermination of the Tututnis.

During the next six months the hostilities erupted in the upper Rogue River valley. On October 7th, a group of men riddled the stick houses of "Jake" and "Sambo's" bands near Butte Creek in a "daring" night ambush. Twenty six elderly men, women and children were killed. The toll might have gone higher had not the officers at nearby Fort Lane warned the natives to be on the alert. Lt. August V. Kautz, leading an exploratory expedition to locate a road from the coast to the Oregon road, was attacked on October 25th between Cow and Grave Creeks. Privates David Adams and John Hill were killed, Kautz and several others were wounded. The war continued to spread and dozens of settlers, volunteers and Indians were killed until finally in January and February 1856 Palmer succeeded in herding nearly 1,000 surviving Umpquas, Mollala, Calapuya and Rogue River Indians to the reservation at Grand Ronde near Yamhill. The hostilities now shifted to the coast.

The general mood of the settlers along the coast was one of caution and fear. The Tututnis had been, save for a few isolated incidents, quiet and generally cooperative. But the truths and half-truths of the events of the upper Rogue motivated the pioneers to "fort-up." The volunteers erected Fort Lamerick above Mule Creek to serve as a winter head-quarters on Rogue River, while the settlers built Fort Johnson between the Chetco and Winchuck Rivers; Citizens Fort (Fort Miner) at the mouth of Rogue River was laid out and started but not finished; Tichenor's blockhouses at Port Orford were reinforced and a blockhouse was hastily constructed at Empire City. The Tututnis, huddled about their scattered camps found the winter of 1955-1956 a hardscrabble. Harassed by the volunteers bent on extermination, short on food and supplies and without adequate firepower to defend themselves, many sought the refuge of Fort Orford and the compassion of Major John Reynolds, the Commanding Officer of the post. The weather, meantime, was severe. Rain, hail, wind, lightning and snow persisted for six weeks. During the first three weeks of December over 19 inches of rain was recorded at Fort Orford … snow piled up in the upper reaches of Rogue River. The volunteer camps ran low on provisions and the holdouts of the Tututnis, joined now by several bands from the Applegate River country led by Te-cum-tom, (Old John) faced starvation. They scavenged for food in the abandoned mining camps and learned to melt down the lead tea containers discarded by the Chinese miners in order to fashion crude but deadly bullets and shot.

Captain Tichenor arrived back in Port Orford on the 19th of February and immediately recruited a small group of "volunteers" who were dispatched to the headquarters of the volunteers several miles up the Rogue River. The eventual objective of the "exterminators" was quite obvious to the settlers and, of course, frightening to the Tututnis, who decided to strike first. Egged on by Enos, a half-breed French Canadian, a vicious attack was launched on the night of February 22nd. While the miners and merchants gathered at the mouth of the Rogue River to celebrate Washington's birthday, the enraged Tututnis killed 23 men and torched every structure they could find. Among the dead were Ben Wright, the sub-agent, and the Captain of the volunteers, John Poland. John Geisel, who operated a store at Elizabethtown (near Nesika Beach) was murdered, together with his two teenage sons, by Hi-tul-ee. Eu-qua-chee, his wife and two daughters were captured and held prisoner at the camp on Rogue River. Charles Foster escaped the onslaught and eventually made it safely to Fort Orford while the remainder of the more fortunate holed up at the Miner's Fort on the north side of Rogue River. The situation was indeed desperate.

Captain Tichenor immediately sailed his vessel the *New York* to the mouth of the Rogue but dared not enter. Observing many Tututnis lying in ambush among the logs on the beach and seeing that the entire settlement had been torched, he proceeded to Crescent City to inform Lt.Delancy-Ford Jones of the regular army. At Fort Orford, Major Reynolds, with a mere handful of troops, dared not to initiate an offensive as he had no idea of the whereabouts of the insurgents and could not leave the settlement at Port Orford unprotected as its population was now swelled with native bands and settlers from miles around.

Citizens and soldiers alike immediately turned to the task of improving the defenses at Port Orford. The forest which surrounded half of the military post was cleared and the principal building enclosed with a double plank wall filled with earth. A glacis (sloping bank to ensure complete coverage of any approach to the walls by fire from the walls) was fashioned and sally-ports (opening in the walls to allow movement of troops and cannons) constructed. The Citizens Fort, located on Fort Point just west of Battle Rock was reinforced with a two-story blockhouse and a double walled passageway between it and the old single story fort. The bunkhouse at the mill was forted up. During the next few months all the residents of Port Orford were to use these facilities every night while military and civilian sentries were posted at strategic locations around the forts and the mill which was located north of the settlement out Jackson Street — then considered out "in the forest" (Elizabeth's letter).

It was over two weeks before any help came and finally on the ninth of March, the steamer *Columbia* brought down 41 recruits from Portland (Fort Vancouver). This detachment, although a welcome sight, lent little peace of mind to the frightened residents due to their inexperience. General Wool, the commander of the department of the district, was aboard the *Columbia* and advised Major Reynolds that a three-pronged attack was being prepared against the Tututnis. Captain Smith from Fort Lane (near Medford) was to proceed down river; Colonel Buchanen would bring over 100 regulars up from Crescent City and Captain Augur would lead 70 from Fort Orford. It was hoped that this show of force would convince the insurgents to surrender at Oak Flats (near Agness on the Illinois River).

On March 14th, 102 regulars of the Third Artillery and Fourth Infantry led by Captain Christopher C. Augur, Bvt. Major John Fulton Reynolds, Lts. Macfeely and Drysdale and Dr. Rodney Glisan, assisted by 15 guides and packers, set out from Fort Orford on their way over muddy, slippery trails to Rogue River. Most would not return until June after spending three miserable months in the wilds of the steep upper Rogue country attempting to put down the Tututnis uprising. A few would never return.

Buchanan's command eventually relieved the plight of the civilians at Fort Miner on the evening of March 20th, having taken five days to march from Crescent City. (Critics afterward accused him of being somewhat languorous.) During this advance, Buchanen was encumbered by a battle between volunteers and Chetl-essentans (Pistol River). The volunteers, in their haste to "get there first," ran afoul of one of the larger bands in the area who quickly surrounded them, scattered their mounts and forced them to take cover behind some beach logs. Buchanen, after unlimbering the howitzer at the mouth of Rogue River and touching off a round or two at the scattering Tututnis, crossed the river on rafts and made camp a short distance from Miner's Fort and awaited word from Captains Smith and Augur who had awaited his arrival near the junction of the Illinois River.

The following is a letter from Elizabeth Tichenor to her son, Jacob, penned during the uprising:

Port Orford, March 17, 1856

My dear Son:

I should have written to you immediately after your father's return from Salem, but owing to the great Indian excitement here and your father leaving home again in less than a week was why I did not write. Now, my son, I suppose you will be disappointed when I tell you that I cannot come this spring but do not be discouraged for I will come by Fall if the Lord wills. If your father cannot, he wishes me to remain until June so as to secure my claim of land and then he says it will be too late in the season. I received a letter from Anna and Mr. Dart by the last mail. They said they were going to send for you, I hope this will reach you first. Be a good boy and I hope we will all soon meet again. Now, my boy, I must tell you something about the Indian troubles here, about three weeks ago, the Rogue River Indians commenced their hostilities. They have joined the hostile tribe and have destroyed everything at T. River, killed a great many of your acquaintances. About one hundred men, nine women and several children saved themselves by getting into a fort which they had prepared which is the only thing standing. It is at Prattsville on the bluff. We have had no news from there for more than a week when two men ventured out at the risk of their lives by night and arrived here in safety. They say if they keep their position at the fort they are safe. The Indians have made several attempts but did not succeed and several were killed each time.

Troops were sent for immediately who arrived here by steamer. There were over a hundred started from here yesterday for that place. Ben Wright was killed at Tututni Village, where he had collected the Indians from the mouth of the river and all about to prevent all communication with the hostile Indians as he thought, most of the volunteers were killed who had been staying at Big Bend all winter but were with Ben Wright at the time. I cannot tell the number. Mr. Lawrence was killed at his house and the house burnt. Old Mr. Seamen was killed. He was there at the time hunting. Mr. Geisel and his two sons were killed, his wife and daughters were taken prisoners but they have succeeded in getting them. They are now at the fort. Mr. Landry came with the schooner immediately to save himself and it and brought the news. Your father returned with him the same night with a message from the Major to R. River if he could not go in the River to go to Crescent City. He could not go in the River on account of the many Indians at the mouth so he went to Crescent City and sent his schooner to San Francisco with a message. There were a hundred and fifty troops landed at Crescent City by the last steamer. Your Father is their guide through the mountains. Don't be uneasy about us for we have a good fort here up on the hill where the old fort was and we all go there every night. The Port Orford Indians appear friendly. They have collected them all together on the other side of the garrison from Coquille down and taken their arms. Your little sister often speaks of you and would like to see you and then she peeps at your (sic) garrutype. Your Father intended writing to you but was called away in such a hurry. I must stop and get ready to go to the fort for it is almost night. Tell Aunt Abby I intended writing to her by this mail but the steamer is due today and will not have time. Tell Aunt Lydia to write. I wish you to write too. Sis sends her love to you. Give my love to all. Get your uncle to please read this to you if he can make it out. Do not be uneasy about us, we will try and come soon for I cannot stop in Oregon.

Your affectionate,
Mother E. Tichenor

P.S. About two weeks ago, eight men started to go to Rogue River in a whale boat to learn the conditions of things there as there is no safety in traveling by land and in attempting to go ashore, the boat capsized in the surf and six of them drowned. One of the drowned was Mr. Gerow, Silverter Long, Old Dick, the boatman, and Little Billy, the others I did not learn their names.
(From the Orville Dodge Book, the names of the men drowned were: John O'Brien, William Thompson [Little Billy], Richard Gay [the boatman "Old Dick"] and Felix McCue.)

Several search and destroy expeditions were initiated by the regulars over the next several weeks, along with the constant extermination activities of the volunteers. The regulars found themselves having to protect the natives from the wanton attacks of the volunteer exterminators who were bent on killing men, women and children. By late May, most of the bands had assented to come in, lay down their arms and accept life on a reservation. Most that is, except Te-cum-tom or "Old John" as the troopers knew him. He led a small band of well-armed warriors whose bands lived along the Applegate River and vowed more than once to fight. Tagonicia, the Port Orford (Quo-to-mah) chief

(Tyee) was unable to convince him the hopelessness of the situation. Captain Smith had proceeded to Big Bend in order to assist Chiefs George and Limpy and their tattered bands down the river. George advised Smith of "Old John's" intention of over-running his camp and Smith immediately moved to higher ground above Foster Creek. Just as predicted, a group attempted to gain access to Smith's camp but were ordered out. The braves retreated a few short yards, armed themselves and commenced firing. Smith's command faced several hundred holdouts from various bands, including some who were already in custody. The Captain's position was, to say the least, precarious. The men spent the first night digging "foxholes" with their haversack spoons and piling up packsacks and blankets up around them for protection. Water was in short supply and the howitzer was of little use due to the slope of the ground. The unmounted dragoons were armed with musketoons and pistols which proved ineffective in brush warfare. The diminutive Charley Foster was able to slip by the attackers at night and get word to the commands of Christopher Auger and John Reynolds. Augur arrived first and in true Old West form relieved Smith in the nick of time. Losses to the troops included none on the field and several who died later. Nearly half of the command was wounded. John's casualties were never recorded.

Several days later, Augur and the volunteers routed the insurgents at So-ho-my Creek (Painted Rock) killing 14 by gunfire and capturing many women and children. Many were drowned while trying to escape in their canoes. Back at Port Orford, the citizens were deluged with wild rumors of imminent attack. They kept a watchful eye on the Tututnis that were camped near the fort — and the Tututnis undoubtedly kept a watchful eye on the whites for the same reason. By late June, several thousand Tututnis had gathered at Port Orford, awaiting shipment by steamer to their "new home." Old John surrendered to Captain E.O.C. Ord at Reinhart's old ranch south of Humbug on June 29th and reluctantly brought his band to Port Orford where he camped at the old village site near the outlet of Garrison Lake. John Reynolds was to march his band overland to the reservation for reasons of security — a distance of about one hundred miles. Before departing, fourteen Port Orford citizens presented him with a gold watch.

Old Book Linked to Early Southwest Oregon Coastal Exploration

An 1835, 6th edition of Nathaniel Bowditch's *Practical Navigator* has recently been linked to Captain William Tichenor (1813-1887), early day sea captain, explorer and settler of the Southern Oregon Coast, by its present owner, the author. A transcript of a narrative on the exploits of Captain Tichenor relates the purchase, by Tichenor, of the schooner, *Jacob M. Ryerson* at San Francisco in 1850. The name of that old vessel literally jumped off the page, for on page 608 of that old book are penciled the words "Friday, July 19, *Schooner J.M. Ryerson.*" There is no doubt that this old book, regarded as a bible for early day seamen, did in fact play a part in the early navigation, exploration and settlement of the Southern Oregon Coast. It, no doubt, was in the wheelhouses of the schooners *Ryerson, Seagull, Quickstep* and *Alaska,* all of which Tichenor captained.

The book is a treasury of nautical terms, navigation and land surveying instruction and accepted latitudinal and longitudinal positions of the capes, bays and prominent landmarks of the world of 1834. As of that date there were nine Cape Blancos, three Cape Orfords and three Cape Sebastians.

3

Aftermath Of
The Indian War

Within a few short years, the vestiges of the Tututnis would remain only in the minds of a few hardy pioneers. Some would speak of them with compassion and sorrow while others would (and still do) refer to them as murderous savages. The fact remains that this remarkable culture managed to survive for thousands of years, passing from generation to generation the skills required to harvest the fruits of the land and to respect of the wonders of nature. The onrushing "civilization" of the white man sacrificed these inhabitants for a few pounds of gold. One might ponder this when examining artifacts or old campsites.

Rogue River War ... Epilogue ... There have been several historical works dedicated to the Rogue River War or at least partly so. *Early Indian Wars of Oregon* was published in 1894. While the author, F.F. Victor, relied heavily on information derived from participants nearly forty years after the fact, her main thrust was to justify the actions by the Militia or "Volunteers." Glassley's work, *Pacific Northwest Indian Wars,* relies heavily on Victor's deductions. Stephan Dow Beckham's *Requiem For a People,* 1971, is a well-written work which is must reading for those interested in an objective treatment of the war. But what of the actors of the drama ... what became of the principal players? In retrospect one must examine the backgrounds of the men concerned and the stage of development of the country in order to appreciate the true legacy of the war.

While the British maintained good relations with the Native Americans of the Northwest and conducted their trading activities within the bounds of set policy, the Americans acted without either policy or understanding. Samuel Parker, a missionary in the west from 1835 to 1837 observed, "The American fur traders never had a system or policy of trade. The goodness of the captain of one sailing vessel was more than destroyed by the infernal murder, rapine, and firebrands by which the next sea captain killed, burnt and laid waste the coast. The fair dealing trader was the next year opinionated because of the hearty degrees of the year before heartless fellow's traffic." This observation explains the difference in attitudes between the Tututnis' spontaneous and friendly visit to Vancouver's ship in 1792 and the fright displayed by them during the visit of the *Columbia* 25 years later.

The attitudes the early settlers brought with them in regards to the Native Americans was, for the most part, unsympathetic and devoid of any preconceived understanding of the legal rights of the tribal boundaries. The miners consisted, in the main, of men who bent on the dreamy illusion of getting rich, swept aside any obstacle which got in the way whether it be the government, the Native Americans or their own ranks. Death and destruction were as commonplace as cheap whiskey and moldy jerky. Most of these exterminators left the Tututnis country shortly after the war save for a few who settled down here and raised families. Some would, in their waning years, write glowing testaments to the heroics of their kind … testaments which should be taken with a grain of salt.

The officers who led the regular army during the campaign here were to face a much larger challenge in a few short years as they had to choose between the Union and the Confederacy. Most chose the Union. Major John F. Reynolds would become General Reynolds and, after having refused the command of the Army of the Potomac, would become the first general killed at Gettysburg, July 2, 1863, while in command of over 50,000 troops of the I, III, and XI Corps of Meade's entire left flank. His troops and the people of Pennsylvania honored him with three large monuments at the scene of the battle and one in front of the city hall at Philadelphia. He was a son of Lancaster, Pennsylvania. Edward Othello Cresap Ord proved to be an able general but was better known for his close association with Mr. Lincoln as his advisor. Ord was present at Appomattox and was riding horseback near Mr. Lincoln at a troop review of the Army of the James when Mrs. Lincoln threw a tizzie and demanded to be brought up to Abe's side as she thought Ord was "trying to become President." (In that point in time, perhaps he was!) Lt. August V. Kautz, the young West Pointer who served the most time at Port Orford, ended up the Civil War as one of those commissioned to examine the evidence and try the conspirators in the assassination of Lincoln. The fiery Prussian also commanded the only all-Black regiment in the war. Captain C.C. Augur was in charge of security forces at Washington, D.C. at the time of the assassination. Captain Andrew Jackson Smith defeated Bedford Forrest at the Battle of Tupelo. Smith, you will remember, narrowly missed being the "Custer of Curry County" at the Battle of Big Bend. Lt.

Henry Stanton left the West Coast before the eruption here and was brutally killed in the Apache country of New Mexico in 1855. Lt. George Stoneman later became Governor of California while the founder of the little fort, Lt. Powell T. Wyman, was mortally wounded at Glendale, Virginia in June of 1862. All these former visitors at Port Orford attained the rank of general save for Wyman and Stanton. For most, their baptisms of fire occurred in the mountains of Curry County.

During the Fall and Winter of 1856-1857, Captain Tichenor, Elisha Meservey and Alexander Thrift contracted with the government to round up the Tututnis that had not yet surrendered. On the Chetco, the captain, assisted by Lt. Lorraine, flushed out 50 or more that were holed up in "stone houses" or caves, including the Ya-shute Tututnis' "Higtley" who was deeply involved with the murder of the Giesels. Tichenor eventually delivered 152 holdouts to the reservation (by his narrative) and was paid up to $150 per head for his efforts. He also made several trips by sea to the reservation delivering stores. The first trip ended with a shipwreck of beaching, and he claims to have been the first to cross the Siletz bar in the vessel *Calumet*.

Michael Riley, the first sheriff of Curry County, brought Enos Thomas the notorious promoter of the general uprising back to Port Orford in the Summer of 1857. A trial was scheduled but the chief witness, Mrs. Geisel, could not be located and Riley was obliged to free the prisoner. The citizens seized Enos, plied him with whiskey and obtained a confession of sorts … of sorts enough to doom him and he was promptly hanged on Battle Rock and buried there. A year before, a Coquille native suffered the same fate after he had brought his family down to Fort Orford seeking protection. It was during this event that the doomed man's mother sat on Fort Point, just west of Battle Rock, and wailed out a curse upon Port Orford and it's inhabitants. Just how many "moons" this curse was to be in effect is anybody's guess but some say it has a long way to go!

During the next several years, the residents of Port Orford busied themselves with forming the 33rd state. William Packwood, the notorious "exterminator" and soldier, was elected to serve Curry County as the representative or delegate to the Constitutional Convention and, as such, helped design the Great Seal of the State of Oregon in the home of Robert Smith, the town's first Postmaster. This seal depicts a British vessel leaving and an American ship arriving off the Oregon coast while Cape Blanco juts out on the left of the logo symbolizing the farthest west point in the United States. At least until 1889, when the state of Washington was admitted to the Union and Cape Alava gained that honor. Just below the Cape stands a magnificent bull elk. Packwood recognized the importance of the animal for the subsistence it provided the early settlers and soldiers. News of the admission to the Union arrived at Portland aboard the *Brother Jonathan* one month after the fact. When Oregon became a state, the county seat of Curry County was moved to a more centralized location at Ellensburg (Gold Beach), having been located at Port Orford during the territorial years. Chairs around a pot-bellied stove undoubtedly served as the first courthouse while contracts, deeds and other legal documents were probably stored in a strongbox under some merchant's counter.

The Tichenor mill continued to operate and provided the much desired grub stakes to many future Coos and Curry residents who made their first landing at Port Orford. The mill was relocated several times in order to reach into the standing timber north of town. The first mill in southwestern Oregon was located in the area between 18th and 21st Streets west of Jackson Street. A blank road served the mill down Jackson Street and the lumber was loaded on ships by the use of lighters. This first mill was built by Captain William Tichenor and his relatives, Neefus and H. B. Tichenor. The Captain later sold out to the two. In 1857, Neefus returned to New York. The H. B. Tichenor and Co. mill operated until about 1866, when it was purchased by Simpson of North Bend. William worked as the millwright for both Tichenor and Simpson.

Captain Tichenor and Simpson maintained a light feud for many years after Tichenor sold Simpson some operating mill equipment which Simpson deemed was "junk." Feuds were not uncommon for the doughty captain as more than once he found himself in hot water. In 1851, the army located Ford Orford on the southern portion of his Donation Land Claim and for many years he attempted to clear the title of the land even though the army had abandoned it. R.W. Dunbar attempted to gain the appointment of Collector of the Customs at Port Orford and at the same time occupy the remaining buildings of the old fort. This infuriated Tichenor who wrote a scathing letter to the then Secretary of War, Stanton. This letter aroused the ire of the Commandant of the Pacific Division, General McDowell, who immediately dispatched troops to capture and arrest Tichenor. The Captain and his young son Jacob were placed in irons and carted off to Alcatraz for " ... occupying public domain ... and being a desperate man ..." The issue was finally resolved and the two desperados were allowed to return to the sanctity of their home in Port Orford. The probable cause of this event was the attempt to disprove Tichenor's original Donation Land Claim which encompassed the potential wharf and dock areas needed for shipping by Nay, Dunbar, Simpson and others in the lumber business. The disqualification attempt was based on: one, that Tichenor had platted a townsite on the Donation Land Claim, and two, that he had not fulfilled the residency requirements. When the smoke cleared, Tichenor won out and he immediately replatted the townsite in 1865.

In September of 1868, a huge fire swept through large sections of the Oregon Coast. The Roseburg *Ensign* reported major fires at Yaquina, Coos Bay and Port Orford, blanketing these areas with so much smoke that ships could not see to enter the harbors.

Save for two houses, Port Orford underwent instant "urban renewal" and the few families in the area were fortunate to survive. The entire population saved themselves on the beaches while Fred Unican's family near Elk River huddled in a shallow well to come through unscathed. The mill was all but leveled.

The first permanent government facility in Curry County was constructed at Cape Blanco in 1870. Still functioning, the Cape Blanco Lighthouse has withstood 115 years of the severest weather on the Oregon Coast and is the oldest, highest and the farthest west. At an elevation of 245 feet, the light from its 320,000 candlepower Fresnel lens is visible for 22 miles at sea. While the Cape is not the farthest west point in the United States, the lighthouse is and the Cape is the farthest west that you can drive. (This was mentioned earlier with no reference to the lighthouse.) The structure and two keeper's houses were constructed of locally fired brick. Louis Knapp, Sr. took the contract to clear the point of old spruce trees which he drilled and burned, pushing the debris over the steep cliffs. Building materials unattainable locally were brought in by ship along with the $25,000 lens, cut and polished in France. During World War II, the coastal residents were required to undergo blackout conditions but the Blanco light beamed on … allowing the Japanese submarine *I-25* to maintain it's station with ease.

From the weathered bluffs of Blanco the western panorama encompasses Cape Argo to the north and Cape Sebastion to the south. The hoary sea stacks of the Orford and Blanco reefs, at times, are engulfed by the raging seas and at other times are teeming with nesting sea birds whose constant chatter is overwhelmed by the roars and barks of the sea lions whose beach-masters swagger and sway from side to side and, with head lifted high, announce to the world that they are the kings of their harems. During the migration months, hundreds of grey whales pass by and occasional sightings of humpbacks and Orcas occur. To the northwest, one overlooks the ancient village site of the Kaltserghea-tunne band of the Quo-to-mah people located on the north side near the mouth of the Sixes River. This village was appropriately named as it translates "… people who lived on a point of land extending far out into the ocean …" To the south, at the first break in the high bluffs, is the site of the old mine at "Sullivan's Gulch" which is an ancient river course. Farther south, the headlands at Port Orford and Humbug Mountain are seen, while to the east can be observed the meeting place of the Coast Range with the ancient Klamath Mountains, now penetrated by roads heading in all directions. Oregon history, as far as white settlement is concerned, begins here and sadly enough for the Tututnis, it ended here.

Near the mouth of Elk River (Tit-una), on the Donation Land Claim of George Duer, now a portion of the McKenzie Ranch, Minnie Myrtle Dyer (Theresa) met and married the famous or infamous "Poet of the Sierras," Joaquin (Cincinnatus) Miller. Miss Dyer had come west in 1859, and from the isolation of the Seaview Ranch, submitted poetry for publication in the various newspapers in the area. Joaquin, then editor of the Eugene City *Democratic Register* took interest in her poetry and began a friendly correspondence which blossomed in to a postal romance. In the summer of 1862, Joaquin rode into Port Orford astride a highly decorated mount whose Mexican saddle was adorned with silver coins. He must have looked like a Barnum and Bailey parade leader who had lost his way to the citizenry of these parts, with his long locks and buckskin attire, but no matter. He quickly won the heart of Minnie and in four short days after an outdoorsy courtship, their wedding ceremony took place at the Seaview Ranch on Elk River. A hurried up affair, Minnie borrowed much of the formal attire associated with such events, including a two-piece trimmed cotton negligee from a Sixes River neighbor, Jane Hughes. (This exciting item now hangs in the closet of one of Jane's descendants.)

They rode off and over the mountains ... back to Eugene City where Miller's support of the Confederacy stirred the fervor of the abolitionists and he was promptly "run out of town." They settled then in Canyon City in Umatilla county. (Not Grant county.) Minnie left him to return to Curry and Coos Counties where she taught school and continued her writing. She died in 1884.

The period from 1870 to 1900 was somewhat sporadic as far as economic development was concerned, and sparse as far as newspaper reports of the activities in and around Port Orford. The Homestead Act of 1862 enabled settlers to open up lands for agricultural purposes but most had to rely on employment at the small sawmills, limited fisheries, mining, logging or land clearing on the larger established ranches. Roads into the area were either nonexistent or impassable during the wet winter months. Only the hardy and persistent stayed on.

There were several methods of acquiring the government lands that were available under the Homestead Act. The Homestead Entry allowed the citizen 160 acres (320 after 1909 of non-timber, mineral or irrigable lands) of land to prove up on by residency and improvement within three years. When proven up, a patent was granted. After 1909, the filer could, after fourteen months, pay $1.25 per acre in order to obtain title and thereby commuting the three year requirement. Other methods of securing lands were cash entry, timber cash entry, soldier's warrants or script, Indian allotments and Donation Land Claims. Only two of the latter were filed and patented in the Port Orford area, that of Tichenor's at Port Orford and the Dyer's claim at the mouth of Elk River.

It was during this period that the larger ranches began to be blocked in and cleared. Although the great fire of 1868 cleared a great deal of brush and timber in the hills, most of the bottom lands along the Sixes and Elk Rivers were covered with large stands of spruce. As this wood had little marketable value, these great monarchs were drilled and burned, the stumps blown and rooted out with teams of horses. Brush was cleared, the labor for which was contracted by the acre. Several families of Sixes and Elk River Tututnis left the reservation, living unmolested along the rivers and working, from time to time, on the Joe Ney, McKenzie and Hughes ranches. Aside from meeting local beef requirements, stock was sometimes driven over the mountains to the railhead at Roseburg … a long and costly drive. Dairy operations blossomed in the eighties and nineties. The Zumwalt, Marsh, Forty, McKenzie and Hughes ranches began building fine dairy herds from which butter was produced and marketed in San Francisco in 25 pound boxes. It should be noted that the early trade developed between San Francisco and Port Orford rather than Portland.

Point Blacklock

According to a Port Orford writer, Neonta Hall, before the year 1900, a total of eighteen public buildings in San Francisco were faced with Blacklock Point Sandstone quarried from an ocean-front operation just north of Sixes River. The Hibernia Bank is the only one still standing today.

New Zealander, William John Blacklock arrived in San Francisco in 1872, followed by his brother James several years later. Plagued by ill health, James retired to Port Orford where he died in 1874. John and associates formed the Blacklock Sandstone Mining company, acquiring 1400 acres at the Point and 18 acres of tidelands from the State of Oregon. In 1886, several buildings were erected including a home, sawmill and machinery shops. A tramway was constructed which was used to carry the large rectangular blocks of quarried sandstone to a loading dock situated at the outer portion of the point. A townsite named Port Blacklock was platted and a post office established. The venture eventually failed owing to the costs and difficulty in moving the heavy stone blocks and the loss of markets.

Newburg State Park

The Oregon State Park Commission acquired the old Blacklock property in February, 1943, purchasing 1400 acres for $3,600. That same year the commission leased 700 acres of it to the county for the purpose of locating an emergency airstrip requested by the Navy through the Civil Aeronautics Administration. The field was designed to handle large transports in the eventuality of increased traffic created by the planned invasion of the mainland of Japan during World War II. Many locals were hired to construct the mile long strip which was contracted by Leonard and Slate Company. The remainder of the park, described by the late Sam Boardman of the Park Commission, as "one of the finest parks in Oregon," remains unmarked, inaccessible and undeveloped

45 years after the acquisition. Descendants of the Blacklocks, (John and Agnes) who include Edna (Richards) Jamieson, Zumwalts, Hawkins and Otts families, would undoubtedly like to see the name of the park expanded to Newburg-Blacklock to more accurately reflect this area's pioneer origins. (See OHS Quarterly, 9/54; CCHS Echos, 12/73, 7/78, 8/78)

The following appeared in the *Coos Bay News,* August 25, 1986: " ... The wharf is completed and ready for rails. It is what is termed a composite structure, being formed of wood iron and concrete, the latter material being used in filling cylinders, some of which are four feet in diameter and of various lengths, short ones answering for foundation purposes where rocks were in place suitable for the cylinders being put on them. All of the foundations are clamped to solid rock. The deck span of (the) landing platform is formed of four heavy Howe trusses and measures 50 x 40 feet and is covered with four-inch decking. From this platform and running shoreward is a Howe truss deck bridge 40 x 24 feet, to which is added an iron combination bridge 19 feet wide and 80 foot span, the shore being reached by a double track trestle about 200 feet in length and 18 feet wide, the whole said span being secured on rock and cylinder foundations. From where the wagon road from town forms a junction with the railroad track between this point and the quarry workings, is a distance of about 1200 feet formed by rock thrown from the cliff by blasts,thus making a substantial safe and ever enduring road bed not liable to be damaged by the ocean at it's base. The track is laid with heavy T-rails, and the company has a complement of cars made of rolled iron, capable of carrying upwards of ten tons each. We also saw some heavy castings belonging to the crane which is to be erected at the landing capable of lifting ten tons, as well as other large derrick iron for quarry purposes.

" ... The quarry, tapped by the above described, gives promise of a capacity to yield multiplied cargoes of the finest building stone known to masons, for generations indefinite in number. The face of the huge mass which lies exposed towards the ocean is 120 feet high, while it is known that the deposit extends inland to the eastward for a distance of nearly half a mile; and it may extend downward beneath the water level for a distance unfathomable."

4

The Quo-to-mahs Of Port Orford

The history of the Native Americans who occupied the land surrounding Port Orford and who clashed with the white settlers, and eventually were displaced by them, is an intriguing narrative that has taken a long time to unravel.

Anthropologists, archeologists and historians have pondered for many decades over the origins of the Native Americans and the land (or sea) routes used by them to migrate to the North American continent. Until recent years, serious research was conducted somewhat spasmodically over a large area and analysis of the accumulated data led the researchers to a variety of conclusions. The "jigsaw puzzle" of origins still defies solution as new and archeologically rich sites of prehistoric campsites and villages are excavated and evaluated scientifically — from Yakutia, Siberia and the far east of the Soviet Union across the Bering Strait into the ancient river banks of the Yukon.

Despite the diversity of geographic locations, researchers seem to agree that the preponderance of similarities pertaining to physical features, culture and language of Indian ancestors indicate that a west to east migration began about 25,000 years ago during the last Ice Age when the Bearing Strait was a land (or ice) bridge. Slowly these nomadic hunters fanned out to occupy North America. The Quo-to-mahs in the Port Orford area were of Athapascan (or Athabascan) linguistic stock of the Nadene type and specifically identified as the Chasta-Costa dialect. The term Tututni was a name applied by the white man to describe the Indian population from Floras Lake to Pistol River, but in reality the term referred to a bank that resided several miles up Rogue River. The approximate span of years that these people occupied the area keeps getting pushed back with each scientific excavation and has now reached nearly 6,000 years or about the time Mount Mazama erupted to form Crater Lake.

Occupational sites along the coast rarely exceed 1,500 to 2,000 years due to the changing of the water levels since the last retreating Ice Age and erosion. As the level has increased several hundred feet it is presumed that many very ancient sites have been inundated.

The Quo-to-mah band occupied an area from New River to Brush Creek living in three and perhaps four main villages or rancherias as the early settlers and soldiers named them. The northernmost site was between what is now the outlet of Floras Lake and where Floras Creek flows into New River. (The Indian name for Floras Creek was Quo-to-mah.) A large settlement was located on the north side of the mouth of Sixes River (Sa-qua-mi) whose Indian name was Kaltsergheat-tunne and a third village was situated at the mouth of Hubbards Creek. A possible fourth site was at the mouth of the Elk River (Ti-tu-na). If this area was not a village site it was a very important food gathering locality judging from the abundance of artifacts unearthed there. The census taken in 1854 by Agent Parrish indicated 144 adults and adolescents, but infants went untallied. The terrible epidemics of diseases brought on the Indians by contact with the whites in the 1830s may have decimated their ranks considerably but hard evidence of that is impossible to document. Tribes and bands of the Willamette and Columbia Rivers were all but wiped out by terrible outbreaks of smallpox and other communicable diseases for which the Native Americans had no immunity.

The dwellings of these people were constructed of split cedar planks placed over rectangular pits dug from three to four feet deep. The framing was made of poles and the roof boards were secured by the use of poles placed outside and parallel to the interior support poles which were then lashed together. One board was purposely left loose to allow smoke to escape. The entrance was a circular hole large enough for a human but small enough to prevent marauding bears from raiding the smoked jerked fish and game stored inside. An earthen bench was formed around the inside perimeter which served as sleeping areas and storage shelves. The fire pit was located in the center of the dwelling while baskets were used to store necessary food items for survival through the stormy winter months. Woven fibre mats provided sleeping pads and elk and deer hides provided warmth as blankets. Ten to fifteen persons occupied each dwelling or "wickiup."

Sweat houses were much on the same order although the pit was usually deeper and the roof was covered over with bark and dirt to provide more insulation. These were used for purification rites, medical treatment and often times sleeping quarters for the men. The latter utilization ensured birth control. By separating the men from the women in this manner, effective control could be exercised over the timing of births. Babies born in the spring had a much greater chance for survival than those born in the winter months.

Another type of shelter used at food gathering sites were conical "stick houses" made up of small branches and limbs. These shelters were found near all the good fishing holes on the Sixes and Elk Rivers or near the elk grounds or other resource gathering locations.

Much of the information used by authors and scholars when addressing the lifestyles, customs and mores of the South Coast Native Americans are mirror images of bands and tribes to the east (Takelmas) and south (Yuroks) whose lifestyle was not shattered by relocation, and documentation in the mid to latter 1800s was accomplished. Although the Quo-to-mah may have been similar to the Yurok there were many differences as noted by Dr. Berriman in his research and excavations in the late 1930s.

Aside from the census taken by the Indian Agent Parrish in 1854, the first scientific expedition to focus on village sites and graves was undertaken in the early 1870s by the Smithsonian Institution. (See Curry County Echos, 8-75.) Landing at Port Orford in early spring the large contingent of anthropologists with pack mules made a cursory study of sites from Cape Blanco to the Chetco. The mission was hampered by three obstacles: incessant rain, settler's fences and gardens (usually planted atop the old village sites) and surly remnants of the old tribes and bands who thought unkindly about strangers who would desecrate the sacred burial sites. The results of the Smithsonian endeavor did little to broaden the knowledge of the banished Tututnis other than mapping village sites and excavation of a few graves.

Doctor Rodney Gilsan and Captain E. O. C. Ord provided bits and pieces of information in diaries kept by them during the war of 1855-56, and later anthropologist Dorsey conducted interviews with Tututnis residing on the reservation at Grand Ronde (Siletz) in 1858. Captain George Vancouver's log (1792) describes in some detail the conduct and dress of the Indians at Port Orford and correspondents to Harpers in the 1850s provided some insight into life along the South Coast.

The main village sites have been identified for many years although the effects of time, construction and development and amateur archeologists and collectors have taken their toll and no site can be readily recognized today and none are marked. The village site at New River just north of Floras Lake has been leveled by "cat work;" the site at the mouth of Sixes River has been about 50 percent cleaned out by amateur diggers and collectors; the Hubbard Creek village was obliterated by the Port Orford Cedar Lumber Company mill in the 1870s. Five thousand years of activity is difficult to cover up however, and there are many areas that await scientific exploration, several of which are within the city limits of Port Orford.

The Quo-to-mahs depended heavily on salmon runs in the Sixes and Elk Rivers for subsistence, while acorns, berries, shellfish and elk meat complimented their diets. Each family had their favorite fishing hole which was considered as personal property handed down from generation to generation. The most common cause of feuds was the possession of this right. Weirs were constructed along the river to enable efficient harvesting of the salmon. Spear fishing from canoes at night with torches was well documented on the Chetco and Coos Bay and was probably done on the lower Sixes while ocean fishing was done with primitive but effective hook and lines. Whales and sea lions cast up on the beaches were carved up and shared by the whole village.

Elk were captured in a deep pit covered over with limbs and leaves. At the bottom of the pit crossed logs were placed heavy enough to hold the animal in a cradle preventing its hooves from reaching the ground. These pits were quite efficient when placed in the main trails frequented by the vast herds of elk in the area. They also worked on the settlers' cows, as Herman Reinhart described in his diary (Golden Frontier, pp. 84). Small game was gathered by snares and bows and arrows, undoubtedly a favorite pastime of the young boys of the bands.

The salmon was split and placed on racks to dry while the elk meat was cut into strips and jerked (smoked). The food was then stored in woven baskets inside the wickiups. Acorns were stored until needed when they were boiled, crushed and leached yielding a paste which was cooked in the open fire or over the coals and consumed as bread. Camas (wild onion) was also a favorite food and the coastal bands would travel many miles to trade for this native delicacy.

While the Yuroks to the south were skilled basket weavers it is not known if the Quo-to-mahs had mastered this art or if they had access to the necessary materials to develop it. They were excellent tool makers as evidenced by the fine arrow and spear points, ivory harpoons, fish hooks and pestles found in the area. Usually one person in the band made the points for the whole band. The largest site known for this activity is located in the sand dunes south of the Sixes River where a large flint rock near the beach provided the artisan abundant raw material.

The Quo-to-mahs practiced Shamanism and the Shaman was a very powerful individual. It was he who talked to the spirits of the animals, healed the sick, performed the rites associated with the taking of the first fish of the season and performed other necessary tasks. His position was precarious however, for if his remedies failed to save a life his life would, or could, be forfeit. The Headman, or Tyee, as the white settlers and soldiers called them, were the men of the villages who possessed the most wealth measured in bows, spears, fine headdresses pleated with red woodpecker scalps, dentalia (medium of exchange made from a particular sea shell), canoes and slaves. The latter asset is a conclusion reached by many scholars using the mirror image but not documented as to the Quo-to-mahs. It is interesting to note that the practice of Shamanism differs very little in western North American from that of the rituals and beliefs of the natives in Siberia and close linguistic similarities between the two groups have been recently documented.

The Quo-to-mahs held in reverence all of their surroundings believing that everything, animate or inanimate, had a spirit, and in the case of elk, deer, salmon or other game, the spirit must be appeased before taking them for use and once taken no part of it was to be wasted. Offerings were made to the spirits in the form of food or other valuables in caches strategically placed in the hunting areas. Prior to the seasonal salmon runs huge bonfires were lit at the mouths of the rivers so as to attract the fish. All of the harvest was shared equally among the bands, the distribution of which was performed by the Headman. While many accounts have been written describing the easy life of the Indian people such as, "when the tide went out the table was set ..." just the opposite was true. Extremes of weather, the effects of the occasional "El Nino," raging forest fires and other adversities took a heavy toll and the average life expectancy was less than thirty years. Today's residents of the area should reflect in wonderment the plight of the Quo-to-mahs during the 100 mile an hour winter gales and driving rains that are commonplace here. (One expert maintains the the Sixes River band had permanent houses constructed on Cape Blanco! I would give the Natives a little more credit than that and if any structures were built there I'm sure they didn't last long.)

Compilation of Various Bands of Tututni (Indians of North America)

Parrish, 1854:
1. Nasohmah (Nasumi) – Coquille. Kusan (lake) village Bandon.
2. Chocreletan (Chocrelatan) – "People away from the forks." Coquille River.
3. Quahtomah (Kwatami) – "People on the gulf (bay)." Port Orford.
4. Cosutthentun (Kwusatthlkhuntunne) – "People who eat mussels." Arizona Beach.
5. Euquachee (Yukichetenne) – "People by the mossy creek." Ophir.
6. Yashute (Chemetenne) – "People on the ocean coast." Mouth of the Rogue River.
7. Chetlessenttum (Chetlesiyetunne) – "People of the bursted rock." Pistol River.
8. Wishtenatin (Khwaishtunnetenne) – "People among the gravel (springs)."
9. Cheatte (Chetco) – "People by the mouth of the river (stream)." Chetco.
10. Tototin (Tututunne) – "Northern Language," "All the people." Bagnell.
11. Mackanotin (Mikonotunne) – "People among the white clover roots," "People by the land along the river." Quosatana Creek.
12. Shistakoostee (Chasta Costa) – "People by the hills." Agnes.

Dorsey, 1858:
1. Chemetunne – "People on the ocean coast." Yashutes.

2. Kaltsergheatunne – "People on a point of land extending far out into the ocean." Sixes, Cape Blanco.
3. Kosotshe – No translation available.
4. Kwatame – (same as Quo-to-mah) French interp. "Goddamn" 1835.
5. Kthukhwottunne – "Good grass people." Coquille area.
6. Kwusathlkhuntunne – "People who eat mussels." Arizona Beach.
7. Natutshltunne – Bradley Lake.
8. Nilestunne – "People at the small dam in river." South of Bandon.
9. Yukichetunne – "People by the mossy creek." Ophir.
10. Chetlesiyettune – "People by the bursted rock." Pistol River.
11. Etaatthatunne – "People at the cover."
12 Kunechuta – No translation available.
13. Kushetunne – A village at the north side of the river.
14. Mikonotunne – "Clover," both sides of the river.
15. Targheliichetunne – "People at the mouth of a small stream."
16. Targhutthotunne – "People on a prairie sloping gently to the river."
17. Testthitun – "Where the bear reclined."
18. Thethlkhuttenne – "People at the smooth rock."
19. Thechuntunne – "People at the foot of the large rock," or "People by the rock land."
20. Aantun – An extinct village on Rogue River.
21. Chetleschantunne – Pistol River.
22. Enitunne – "People at the base of a plateau." (near mouth of river).
23. Khainanaitetunne – An exterminated village, two boys survived.
24. Kherghia – A village south of Pistol River.
25. Khwaishtunnetunne – "Gravel."
26. Nakatkhaitunne – No translation available.
27. Natthutunne – "People of the level prairie south of the river."
28. Nuchamatuntunne – No translation available.
29. Sentethltun – Former village at mouth, south side Rogue River.
30. Skumeme – former village at mouth, south side Rogue River.
31. Tsetintunne – Former village, highest of four on a tributary, Rogue River.
32. Tsetuttunne – "People where road (trail) is at the beach." Hubbards Creek.
33. Kthutetmetseetuttun – "People in a land full of timber, North."
34. Chockrelatan – "People way from the forks." Coquille River.
35. Kthukhwuttunne – "People where the good grass is."
36. Natthutunne – "People on the level prairie."

Chetco Villages:

Chettanne, Chettannene, Khuniliikhwut, Kakwutthume, Muchwuchutun, Settatun, Siskhaslitun, Tachukhaslitun, Thlcharghilitun, (Hedge, pp. 249).

Other Spellings of Bands:

Chemetunne, Chetleschantunne, Chasta Costa, Chetuttunne, Chunarghuttunne, Chunsetunneta, Chunsetunnetun, Chushtarghasuttlen, Chusterghutmunneten, Chuttushshunche, Chloshlekhwuche, Chotltacheche, Choalututunne, Ktheelutlitunne, Kushletata, Mekichuntun, Musme, Natkhwunche, Nishtuwekulsushten, Sechukhhtun, Sethltunne, Senestun, Setaame, Setaamye, Setsurgheake, Silkhkemechetatem, Sinarghutlitim, Skurghet, Sukechunetunne, Surghustesthitin, Tachikhwutme, Takasichekhwet, Talsunne, Tatsunye, Thethlkhutunne, Tsalatunne, Kushetenne, Sekhatsatenne, Kwatamitene. Kwatumati-tenne – "People by the little creek," Hubbards Creek. Siksestene – "People by the far north country," possible derivation source of Sixes River.

~ ~ ~

The following poem which was written by a person whose only identification was the letter "H" is worthwhile including in the history of Port Orford because it may have reflected the common feeling in the 1850s toward the "Red Man."

The Indian Chief

A warrior from a mountain crest
    looks down upon the vale.
For many moons his feet had pressed
    a long and weary trail.

He came from towards the setting sun
    where now his kindred roam,
Once more to fondly gaze upon
    his childhood's early home.

Before the pale faced hoards of men
    his race had passed away.
Nor ever might return again
    to claim their ancient sway.

Their hunting grounds and sylvan streams
    the haunts they loved of yore
Had vanished like a pleasant dream
    to be recalled no more.

Beside the stream a noisy mill
    sent up it's clattering sound,
And stretching from the rising hill
    were leagues of cultivated ground.

The foreman with ensanguined hand
    had slain his nation's "braves,"
And reared a crowded busy mart
    upon his fathers' graves.

He gazed in silence for a while
    upon the scene below.
Upon his lips a scornful smile
    a cloud upon his brow.

Where is the Maniton that speaks
    in thunder from the cloud,
And rears aloft the mount peaks
    to pierce it's misty shroud?

Has he decreed the "red man's" home
    to strangers shall be given,
And that as an outcast he shall roam
    beneath the face of heaven?

His hand was raised above his head;
    despair was in his eye;
With bitterness and gloom he said,
    "Our very race must die."

He turned his steps to seek again
    the remnant of his race;
A fiery hate was in his brain,
    and written on his face.

With savage eloquence he stirred
    his feeble band to strife,
And bade them by their sides to gird
    the tomahawk and knife.

Where thickest carnage strewed the ground
    arose the little band,
And pierced with many bleeding wound
    the savage hero fell.

And there he slept in death's embrace
    the bravest of his band.
A growl of hatred on his face
    his weapon in his hand.

This work appeared in the *Crescent City Herald* on July 8, 1854 and bore the signature "H".

The "Tu-Tu-Tenez"

Among the Indians who lived along the Rogue River were the Tu-tu-tenez. Following is information on tribal names and locations:

Rogue River – Heads at Boundary Springs in Klamath County at an elevation of 5,000 feet. It is 241 miles in length and drops an average of 20.8 feet per mile. The Indian name was "Too-too-tinez" meaning "the great river."

Map study – north to south:

Band Name	Population	Tyees	Village Sites	
Quo-to-mah	144	Hap-hult-a-lan		Flores Creek
				Sixes River
		Tag-o-necia		Hubbards Creek
Cosutt-hen-tens	27	Chac-tal		Mussel Creek
Euqua-chees	102	Ah-chees-see		Euchre Creek
Ya-shutes	130	Ene-wah-we-sit (Joshua)		Rogue River
Chetl-essen-tans	45	En-e-tuse		Pistol River
Wish-ten-e-tans	66	Nel-yet-ah-weshu		Whaleshead
Chet-coes	245	Cha-hus-sag		Chetco River
Has-on-tas	50	Ne-et-cas		Winchuck River
To-to-tins	123	One-an-ta		Rogue River (Upper)
Mac-an-o-tin	145	Yah-see-o-we-lee		Lobster Creek
Shas-te-koos-tees	146	Yah-chum-see		Agness (Rogue River)

Literal translations of main village sites:
Quo-to-mah – People who live on the gulf (bay).
Co-sutt-hen-tens – People who eat mussels.
Eu-qua-chees – People who live by the mossy creek.
Ya-shutes – People who live on the ocean coast.
Chetl-essen-tens – People who live by the bursted rocks.
Wish-ten-a-tans – People who live by the springs (gravel).
Chet-coe – People who live by the mouth of the stream.
To-to-tins – All the people.
Mac-an-o-tins – People who live among the white clover roots. Also, people who live on the lands by the river.
Shasta-koos-tee – People who live on the sloping hills by the river.

5

Early
Explorations

The fascinating West where the sun set in streaming gold was the object of early explorations, and inevitably the Port Orford area came under scrutiny when adventurers along the Pacific Coast made sightings and landings from their ships.

For convenience's sake a list by dates of early maritime exploration events for easy reference are included at the conclusion of this chapter.

The Strait of Anian was a geographic certainty or so thought the cartographers who sorted through the sketchy information brought back to Europe by the explorers of the 15th and 16th Centuries. This passage, when found, would allow ships to pass through the landmass of North America from the Atlantic to the Pacific and the monarchy that claimed this prize would have nearly complete control over the lucrative trade route to India and the Orient. The search began with Columbus' first voyage in 1492, and continued in earnest for three hundred years by brave and hardy explorers serving many flags and covering an area from Hudson Bay to Mexico on land and sea.

The land expeditions of deSoto, Coronado, Vaca and others which traversed the south, midwest and southwest of the present United States from 1528 to 1542 failed to return to base with any substantial treasures but they uncovered and investigated some imaginative rumors of fabled cities of gold and the elusive "passage." A plains Indian named Turk related to Coronado that in Quivira to the north there was a river six miles wide with fishes as big as horses. The people had canoes with sails that carried forty rowers and the Lords sat on poop decks sheltered by awnings while the prow was decorated with a figurehead of a golden eagle. He told of gold bells hanging in the tree under which the Lord took his afternoon nap and the everyday dishes of the people were of gold plate while bowls and jugs were pure gold. A wonderful place this Quivira. Needless to say, Turk was forced to admit the truth of the ruse and immediately garroted ... after Coronado had wandered for a year looking for it.

DeSoto, meantime, was obsessed with the myth of the Seven Cities of Gold. Vaca had hinted that he had been near them and deSoto had visions of discovering them on the shores of the Strait of Anian. His explorations of 1539 to 1542 covered an area from Florida to the Mississippi with little result other than seeing some new country. He died on the Ouachita River in May, 1542.

Although the expeditions were fruitless, the notion persisted that somewhere, within the vastness of North America there was a great Mediterranean Sea, and from it flowed rivers that would connect the Atlantic and the Pacific. This set the stage for the first attempts to explore the Pacific Coast. Hernando Cortez, the great conquistador of Mexico, constructed a shipyard on the west coast of Mexico on the Rio Balsas at Zacatula (170 miles north of Acapulco) in 1530. It was here that the first expeditions up the coast would originate. In 1542, Don Mendoza, the able Viceroy of New Spain, sent an expedition to the Philippines and a small two-ship probe up the Pacific Coast. The latter was under the command of Juan Cabrillo with Bartolome Ferrelo acting as navigator. They swung west of the tip of Baja California and sailed above San Francisco where a violent storm forced them back to the Channel Islands. Cabrillo died there in January, 1543, at Port Possession, an insular shelter off the coast of California, on San Miguel, the northernmost of the Santa Barbara Islands. The indefatigable Ferrelo pushed on and by March 1 had reached a point at 42 degrees latitude. Plagued by scurvy, bad weather, and an unforgiving coastline, Ferrelo, after sighting and naming Cape Blanco, turned south. (Davidson maintained his farthest northern point reached was Cape Sebastian and Rogue River.) Author J. B. Brebner noted, "It had been an extraordinary feat of navigation for two jerry-built vessels with inept crews on an unknown coast, but it settled for 60 years Spain's hopes for that elusive waterway which geographers felt sure would unite the Atlantic and Pacific." (The vessels, it should be noted, were 30 to 40 feeT long with a beam of 15 feet.)

Sixty years later the rumor of the Strait of Anian persisted. The strait and the lost kingdom of Quivira were a must for the early cartographers including the renowned mapmaker Mercator who placed Quivira on his 1569 edition of *The New World*. It appeared on ten different maps up until 1750. During this period the Viceroys of New Spain (Mexico) had developed a thriving trade with the Philippines which required transhipment of goods across New Spain from Acapulco to Vera Cruz. The routes of the Manila galleons were a closely guarded secret and after the capture of the *Santa Ana* in 1587 the ships were heavily armed. *(Oregon Shipwrecks,* Don Marshall, Binford and Mort, 1984.)

The adventurous freebooter Drake set sail from England in 1577, with the 100 ton

Pelican (Golden Hinde) and four other support vessels bound for the Pacific on a voyage of raiding and exploring for the Strait of Anian. While his ship was no match for the huge galleons which carried up to 600 well armed passengers and crew and rated up to 2,000 tons, he was successful in raiding small ports where the floating treasure chests were lying at anchor (namely the *Cacafuego).* (He hinted to the captain of this galleon that the English knew the secret of the Strait of Anian. This well placed rumor sent nervous ripples back to the Viceroy.) Drake purportedly sailed along the Oregon Coast and as far north as Vancouver Island, although the likelihood of this is improbable. He returned south and refitted and repaired near San Francisco, then sailed west to immortality.

Pressure by the entry of the English and Dutch in the Pacific concerned the Spaniards as they needed to locate harbors of refuge along the Pacific Coast for their huge galleons. In 1602 Sebastian Viscaino and Martin Aguilar set sail north from Acapulco to find the Straits of Anian and the site of Quivara. Father Antonio de la Ascension, the recorder of the expedition, was convinced that the peninsula of Baja joined together with a large part of what is now California to form the largest island in the world. He held also that the true location of the entrance to the Strait of Anian and Quivira would be found in the Mare Vermejo (Gulf of California). When Viscaino's expedition sailed west of the tip of Baja the Father knew the expedition would fail.

The ships, the *Tres Reyes* and *San Diego,* were separated in a severe southerly gale January 7, 1603, and on January 19th Aguilar, aboard the *Tres Reyes,* noted in his log … "When the wind became less violent they continued their voyage close along shore, and on January 19th the pilot, Antonio Flores, found they were in latitude 43 degrees where they found a cape or point which they named Cape Blanco. From that point the coast began to turn northeast and near it was discovered a rapid and abundant river with ash trees, willows and brambles, and other trees of Castile on its banks which they endeavored to enter, but could not from the force of its current." Viscaino reached Cape Blanco during this same trip. Thusly, Cape Blanco was named and yet another enigma entered the mapmakers minds … the River of Aguilar, which the imaginative cartographers noted, led to the "Land of Bright Stones."

The threat of piracy from English and Dutch mariners failed to materialize and only four vessels were lost in that manner over a span of 265 years. Storms and accidents accounted for 29 more, ten of which were never located. Landfall for the returning galleons was near Cape Mendocino and the need for refitting facilities was satisfied at Monterey, San Blas, Navidad, and later San Francisco, although that facility was never developed. The exigency then for any further Spanish exploration did not arise. The rugged, isolated coast of Oregon was ignored for well over 180 years save for isolated maroonings and accidents like the galleon *San Francisco Xavier* which was lost near Nehalem in 1705.

Activity began to pick up in 1774. Juan Perez departed San Blas, Mexico aboard a sloop of war *(Santiago)* with instruction to sail north as far as 60 degrees, return south and "… survey the coast southward to Monterey (California), landing at convenient places to take possession in the name of the King of Spain." (Joseph Gaston, *Centennial History of Oregon,* pp. 208, V-I.)

Another expedition followed in 1775 commanded by Bruno Heceta in the ship Santiago. He landed at Trinidad and claimed the lands for Spain then continued on north. Cape Blanco and the roadstead at Port Orford were bypassed. The first accurate description of Port Orford was made by Captain Robert Gray in August, 1788, aboard the consort sloop *Lady Washington.*

Gray's description was colorful. Wednesday, August 6, 1788. "On the six favorable breezes and pleasant in the morning, about eight o'clock we were abreast a cove where tolerable good shelter from a northwardly wind may be had. It is formed by a small bay to the northward and a little island to the southward. Here wood and water may be procured but what sort of anchorage remains unknown. (In all probability the *Lady Washington* was abreast of Hunter's Cove near them out of Pistol River and just south of Cape Sebastian.) The people were very anxious to come on board. They paddled after us an amazing distance with great alacrity (speed), waving something, I suppose skins, but we had at this time a good wind and pleasant weather and it was judged best to seek a harbor. While they continued we ran along shore with a cloud of sail, passing within a quarter of a mile of a bold, sandy shore in five or six fathoms of water. Above the beach appeared a delightful country thickly inhabited and clothed with woods and verdure with many charming streams of water gushing from the valleys. Most of the inhabitants, as we passed their scattered houses, fled into the woods while others ran along shore with great swiftness keeping abreast of us many miles. Cape (Blanco) bore distant about five leagues (15 miles)."

"Thursday, 7th. We now ran for a place that looked like an inlet. This place was in a large deep bay to the southward and eastward of Cape (Blanco). Having run in within about a mile of a small island we hove the jolley boat out and sent her to sound the channel between the Island (and) the Main and explore the harbor if any. She soon made a signal that there was plenty of water within the Island. (Island Rock) We then followed her but soon discovered what we supposed to be an inlet to be no other than two hills separated by a deep valley. We wore ship within one half mile of the land and found no bottom with a long scope of line. We now took the boat in and stood off on the other side of the Island which could be compared to nothing else but a hive with bees swarming, the birds were so numerous. They were of many species but most of them were pelicans. At four p.m. foggy. At 6 Cape (Blanco) bore N.N.E. distant about six or seven leagues. A long and very dangerous reef of rock ran out westward of this promontory. We stood off a proper distance to give this ledge a proper berth, and then stood to the northward of the land observed in latitude 43-20N." (This log entry has been edited slightly with punctuation and corrected spelling where appropriate.) The original log refers to Cape Mendocino rather than Blanco. The fact that the Indians indicated a desire to trade "skins" by waving them as they ran on the beach certainly suggests that prior contact had been made with them. Unfortunately, this intercourse was not recorded. When the writer (Robert Haswell) noted that they "took the boat in" he meant not that they ran the jolley boat to shore but rather that they hoisted and stowed it and when they "... stood off ..." meant that they continued on course. A recorded landing at Port Orford was yet to be made.

Any voyage along the coast of California and Oregon in cumbersome sailing vessels that was completed without serious mishap was indeed rather remarkable. And the one accomplished by a small group of traders from Bodega to Clayoquot in 1790 in a long boat must take first prize, however, as the most daring (or foolhardy) of all. Dispatched by Captain Colnett, this group rowed, sailed and drifted up the coast trading with the Indians most or all the way. Their map indicated that they obtained only three skins at Rogue River but they very accurately depicted the roadstead at Port Orford and the reef at Cape Blanco. The only entry on the map for this area was " ... much smoke ..."

Captain George Vancouver, in command of the 340 ton ship *Discovery* and the 135 ton brig *Chatham,* arrived on the west coast in April 1792 on an expedition designed to assert British rights against those of Spain on the northwest coast. He recorded in his log the following observations:

"April 24, Tuesday. The next morning the north point of Saint George Bay (Crescent City) bore, by compass, east two leagues distant. With a favorable breeze at S.E., and less hazy weather, our survey was continued to the northward along the shores, which were composed of high, steep precipices and deep chasms. Falling very abruptly into the sea. The inland mountains were much elevated, and appeared, by the help of our glasses, to be tolerably well clothed with a variety of trees, the generality of which were of the pine tribe; yet among then were observed some spreading trees of considerable magnitude. Although some of these mountains appeared quite barren, they were destitute of snow; but those at the back of Cape Mendocino, which were further to the south and apparently inferior in point of height, some small patches of snow were noticed. The shores were still bounded by innumerable rocky inlets, and in the course of the forenoon we passed a cluster of them. With several sunken rocks in their vicinity lying a league from the land; (Rogue River Reef and Redfish Rocks) which, by falling a little back to the eastward forms a shallow bay into which we steered. As the breeze that had been so favorable to our pursuit since the preceding Sunday died away, and as a tide or current set us fast inshore, we were under the necessity of coming to an anchor in 39 fathoms water, black sand and mud. The latitude of this station was found to be 42 degrees 38', longitude 235 degrees 44'. In this situation, the outermost rock of the cluster before mentioned bore, by compass, South 16 East, six miles distant; a remarkable black rock, the nearest shore being North 64 East, 3-1/2 miles: a remarkable high black cliff resembling the gable end of a house, North 1 East; the northernmost extremity of the main land, which is formed by low land projecting from the high rocky coast a considerable way in to the sea, and terminating in a wedge-like low perpendicular cliff, North 27 West. This I distinguished by the name of Cape Orford, in honor of my much respected friend the noble Earl (George) of that title; off it lie several rocky islets, the outwardmost of which bore North 38 West.

"Soon after we had anchored, a canoe was seen paddling toward the ship; and with the greatest confidence, and without any sort of invitation, came immediately alongside. During the afternoon two others visited the *Discovery,* and some repaired to the *Chatham,* from different parts of the coast in sight; by which it appeared, that the inhabitants who are settled along the shores of this country, may, probably, have their residence in the small nooks that are protected from the violence of the westwardly swell by some of the larger rocky islets, so abundantly scattered along the coast.

"A pleasing and courteous deportment distinguished these people. Their countenances indicated nothing ferocious; their features partook rather of the general European character; their color a light olive; and besides being punctuated in the fashion of the south-sea islanders, their skin had many other marks, apparently from injuries in their excursions through the forest, possibly, with little or no clothing that would protect them; though some of us were of the opinion these marks were purely ornamental, as is the fashion with the inhabitants of Van Dieman's land (Tasmania). Their stature was under the middle size; none that we saw exceeding five feet six inches in height. They were tolerably well limbered, though slender in their persons; bore little or no resemblance to the people of Nootka; nor did they seem to have the least knowledge of that language. They seemed to prefer the comforts of cleanliness to the painting of their bodies; in their ears and noses they had small ornaments of bone; their hair, which was long and black, was clean and neatly combed, and generally tied in a club behind; though some amongst them had their hair in a club in front also. They were dressed in garments that nearly covered them, made principally of the skins of deer, bear, fox, and river otter; one or two cub skins of the sea otter were also observed among them. Their canoes, calculated to carry about eight people, were rudely wrought out of a single tree; their shape much resembled that of a butcher's tray, and seemed very unfit for a sea voyage or any distant expedition. They brought but a few trifling articles to barter, and they anxiously solicited in exchange iron and beads. In this traffic they were scrupulously honest, particularly in fixing their bargain with the first bidder; for, if a second offered a more valuable commodity for what they had to sell, they would not consent, but made signs (which could not be mistaken) that the first should not pay the price offered by the second, on which the bargain would be closed. They did not entertain the least idea of accepting presents; for on my giving them some beads, medals, iron, etc., they instantly offered their garments in return, and seemed much astonished, and I believe not less pleased, that I chose to decline them. The first man, in particular, gave me some trouble to persuade him that he was to retain both the trinkets and his garment.

"We remained in this situation until near midnight, when a light breeze springing up from the S.S.E., attended with some rain and dark gloomy weather, we weighed and stood to and fro until daylight, April 25, 1792. Wednesday; when we directed our course round the group of rocks lying off Cape Orford, comprehending four detached rocky islets, with several dangerous sunken rocks about them, on which the sea broke with great violence; the outermost of these lies from the cape S. 38 W. distant about four miles; we passed close to the breakers in soundings of 45 fathoms (near Fox Rock) black sandy bottom. Cape Orford, which is situated in latitude 42 degrees 52 minutes, longitude 235 degrees 25 minutes, at the extremity of a low projecting tract of land, forms a very conspicuous point, and bears the same appearance whether approached from the north of the south. It is covered with wood as low down as the surf will permit it to grow. The space between the woods and the wash of the sea seemed composed of black craggy rocks, and may, from the masthead, be seen at the distance of seven or eight leagues; but I should suppose not much farther. Some of us were of opinion that this was the Cape Blanco of Martin d'Aguilar; its latitude, however, differed greatly from that in which Cape Blanco is placed by that navigator; and its dark appearance, which might probably be occasioned by the haziness of weather, did not seem to entitle it to the appellation of Cape Blanco. North of this cape, the coast takes a direction about N. 13 E; and south of it toward Point Saint George, S 18 E.

"The rocky islets, which we had seen in such numbers along the shore, ceased to exist about a league to the north of Cape Orford; and in their stead, an almost straight sandy beach presented itself, with land behind gradually rising to a moderate height near the coast; but the interior was considerably elevated, and much diversified both by its eminences and productions, being generally well wooded, though frequently interrupted with intervals of clear spots, which gave it some resemblance to a country in an advanced state of cultivation.

"The weather having become more clear and pleasant at noon, Cape Orford was visible astern nearly in the horizon, bearing by compass S. 11 E., five leagues distant; the nearest shore about a league distant east; a small projecting point, forming the north part of a small cove, off which lie five detached rocks, N. 23 E., distance seven miles; and the northernmost land in sight, which I consider to be Cape Blanco, N. 2 E.; the observed latitude was 43 degrees 6 minutes, longitude 235 degrees 42 minutes; and the variation 16 degrees eastwardly.

"Having now a fine gale from the S.S.W., with serene and pleasant weather we ranged along the coast at a distance of about a league, in hopes of determining the existence or nonexistence of the extensive river or straits, asserted to have been discovered by Martin D'Aguilar. About three o'clock in the afternoon we passed within a league of the cape above mentioned; and at about half that distance from some breakers that lie to the westward of it. This cape though not so projecting a point as Cape Orford, is nevertheless a conspicuous one, particularly when seen from the north, being formed by a round hill on high perpendicular cliffs, some of which are white, a considerable height from the level of the sea. Above these cliffs it is tolerably well wooded, and is connected to the mainland by land considerably lower. In this respect it seemed exactly to answer Captain Cook's description of Cape Gregory; though its situation did not appear to correspond with that assigned to Cape Gregory by Captain Cook; our observations placing it in a latitude of 43 degrees 23 minutes; longitude 234 degrees 50 minutes; whence the coast tends N. 21 E. About a league north of the pitch of the cape, the rocky cliffs composing it terminate, and a compact white, sandy beach commences which extends along the coast eight leagues, without forming any visible projecting point or headland. We sailed along this beach at a distance of from three to five miles, and had there been any projecting point or inlet in it, neither could have escaped our observation. This induced me to consider the above point as the Cape Gregory of Captain Cook with a probability of its being the Cape Blanco of D'Aguilar, if land hereabouts the latter ever saw. The difference in latitude between our computation and that of Captain Cook was seven minutes; our observations placing the cape that distance farther south. This might possibly have been occasioned by the tempestuous weather with which the *Resolution* and *Discovery* contended when off this coast, preventing the position of the several headlands being then ascertained with that accuracy, which the fair winds and pleasant weather have enabled us to assign to them. The land seen to the south of Cape Gregory by Captain Cook, and by him considered as answering nearly to the situation of Cape Blanco, must have been some of the inland mountains which to the south of Cape Gregory rise to a great height; whilst the land near the seashore, particularly in the neighborhood of Cape Orford, was much too low to have been seen at the distance which Captain Cook was at the time from it; and it is fair to presume, that the extremely bad weather led Captain Cook and his officers to consider the extremely white sand on the sea shore and on the hills to be snow. With us it put on the same appearance, except where it was interrupted by the clumps of trees, and until it was entirely lost in the forest. There could be no doubt of its being mistaken in the winter for snow; but as the general temperature of the thermometer since our arrival on the coast has been a 59 and 60, the error of such conclusion was sufficiently manifested."

The preceding excerpts were taken from Vancouver's narrative originally published in 1789. T. C. Elliot's pamphlet entitled, *Oregon Coast As Seen By Vancouver in 1792*, is available from the Oregon Historical Society.

Vancouver's observations while along this coast are particularly interesting for several reasons. He gave the first accurate description of the Quo-to-mah people; he put to rest the myth of the River of Aguilar; he described in detail the roadstead at Port Orford and the reef at Cape Blanco and his conclusions as to the location of Martin Aguilar's Cape Blanco are probably correct. In stormy or hazy conditions, Cape Blanco is difficult if not impossible to make out and as the early Spaniards were passing in the dead of winter they undoubtedly gave the Rogue River, Orford and Blanco reefs a wide berth. Many historians have attributed the shell deposits located on the south bluffs of the cape to the origin of Aguilar's designation but the stratum of shells deposited by an ancient sea floor is rather minute and certainly could not be discerned from a ship located west of the reefs. Aguilar's Cape Blanco was in all probability Cape Arago and the river by which he tried unsuccessfully to enter Coos Bay.

The Earl of Orford that Vancouver refers to in the naming of the cape (Blanco) was probably the third earl, George Walpole, who held that title when this expedition left England in 1791. "Britannica" refers to him as "reckless" with no further explanation. He died in December of that year being succeeded in the title by Horatio Walpole, a distinguished man of letters.

Orford and Orford Ness in England lie on the east coast just above the 52nd parallel. An important trading port in medieval times, the river Alde's channel underwent natural relocation to the south leaving Orford sanded in. (Does that ring a bell?) Vancouver's birthplace was Kings Lynn about 60 miles northwest of Orford in the same area as the Walpole family's birthright.

George Vancouver was indeed a remarkable seaman and navigator. At age 13 he entered naval service and at age 15 served with Captain Cook on his second voyage of discovery. He also sailed on Cook's third voyage and logged a total of eight years with Cook and from him learned the necessary lessons of accurate navigation and stern discipline. On a voyage of four and one half years, Vancouver lost but one man to disease — an unheard of accomplishment in those days!

The Russians visited the Port Orford roadstead in the early 1800s mapping the coast and sounding the bay. Their early maps are by far the most accurate and complete.

They designated the anchorage as "Indian Bay" and the reefs as the "Isles of Longnecker." A profile of Cape Orford is included although it is difficult to reconcile the outline on the map to its actual profile. It is purported that a Russian whaler wrecked here in the early 1800s and perhaps the soundings on the map were a result of a salvage expedition to that event.

In 1817 the British ship *Columbia* approached Cape Blanco but the Indians scattered "pell-mell in all directions ...," a sharp contrast to the friendly gestures made by them to Vancouver 25 years earlier. The Quo-to-mah were learning!

Land explorations to the area around Port Orford were very limited due to the isolation, ruggedness of the country and the lack of commercial interest. In 1827 a party of Hudson Bay Company trappers and buyers made their way as far south as the Rogue River looking for beaver skins that the Umpqua Indians had told them were abundant on the south coast. This proved incorrect and the party returned to Fort Umpqua nearly empty handed. Several other trips were made along the coast during the next eight years but no descriptions or narratives were left by the trappers.

Jededia Smith passed by Port Orford in late June, 1828, with a party of 18 men and 300 horses and mules. Traveling north, Smith's party had groped through the Trinity Alps of Northern California and were hacking and struggling their way to Fort Vancouver. Trapping as they went, the party was tired and hungry as they entered what is now Curry County. Harassed by the natives who were enthralled with the sight of the horses, the party pressed on and after contending with sporadic arrows directed their way and elk pits which plagued the horses and riders, the entourage finally made it to Rogue River on June 27th. Smith briefly described the Indian villages on both sides of the "bay" and related that he built rafts on which he would effect a crossing the following morning. This activity sounded peaceful enough but in fact he and his men proceeded to tear down several Indian wickiups (houses) to procure the timber. This callous act of depredation was to catch up to the party near the Umpqua River where the Indians attacked and killed 14 men.

Smith arrived at the roadstead of Port Orford on July 1st, crossed over the heads and proceeded up the beach to Cape Blanco where he crossed the neck and camped on the south side of Sixes River. (See *Century of Coos and Curry,* Peterson-Powers, page 14.) His trip through Curry County had cost 24 horses and mules and eventually the lives of most of his party.

Early Maritime Exploration Dates

1492   (Legend) Chinese pirates, see Peterson-Powers, Century of Coos-Curry.
"From broad Columbia down to Coos
They fiercely swooped in great canoes
To Orford, Coos and far Coquille,
They hewed a way with gleaming steel."

1499   Straits of Anian predicted by Gaspar Cortereal and/or Sebastion Cabot
and it was presumed that a navigable waterway existed which connected
Hudson Bay with the Pacific.

1519   Magellan, sailing through the straits mistook Tierra Del Fuego as the
northern extremity of another continent, thus Spain thought she controlled
the gateway to the Pacific on the basis of his incorrect discovery.

1542   Don Antonio Mendoza established New Spain in Central America. He
built the ships *San Salvador* and *Victoria*, sending them north under the
command of Juan Rodriguiz Cabrillo and although he died in January of
1543, his pilot Bartolome Ferell(o) continued on north and is credited
with reaching the 44th parallel and sighting Cape Blanco before severe
storms and diminishing provisions forced him to turn south.

1578   Sir Francis Drake, sailed up the south and central American coast plun-
dering Spanish vessels and ports supposedly reached Cape Arago where
some historians believe the cover there is the "bad bay" described in the
log of the *Golden Hinde*. (Possibility very unlikely). He did spend five
months in what is now Drake's Bay near San Francisco Bay repairing the
ship.

1603   Martin Aguilar and Antonio Flores sailing the *Tres Reyes* and Sebastion
Vizcaino on the *San Diego* while beating their ways north became separated in a fierce gale. Aguilar continued north to 44 degrees where he
described and named Cape Blanco. North of the cape he reported an
"abundant river, which he could not enter due to the strong current." Thus
the myth of Rio D'Aguilar which early cartographers concluded was the
proof of the fabled Straits of Anian. Vancouver concluded in 1792 that

Aguilar was at the entrance of Coos Bay while many modern historians believe that he sighted the mouth of the Umpqua River.

Vizcaino reached Cape Sebastion (Cape Blanco De San Sebastion) as shown on the De L'Isle map of 1752, Jeffery's map, 1768 (Cape Blanquial). All these maps label the general area as "Nova Albion" as named by Drake, and several show rivers on each side of the cape flowing west from the "Mountains of Bright Stones."

Between 1539 and 1542, a plains Indian nicknamed "Turk" related to Coronado the existence of "Quivira" to the north where there was a river "six miles wide with fishes as big as horses." The people there were purported to have canoes with sails that carried forty rowers and the lords sat on poopdecks sheltered by awnings while the prow was decorated with a figurehead of a golden eagle. He described gold bells hanging in the tree under which the Lord took his afternoon nap … everyday dishes were gold plate while bowls and jugs were pure gold! After wandering a year in search of the place Coronado had the Turk garroted.

1788   Captain Robert Gray on the ship *Columbia* with the tender *Lady Washington* sailed along the southern Oregon coast. On August 6th he found shelter in what was probably Hunter's Cove near the mouth of Pistol River. He reported that the natives were anxious to make contact and appeared friendly. On the seventh he sounded the outer reaches of the roadstead at Port Orford but made no landing.

1792   Captain George Vancouver anchored and contacted the natives. (Read from his log.)
Note the Russian sounding of Indian Bay and the wrecked whaler.

1817   Hudson Bay Company. Alexander Roderick McLeod, Thomas McKay (Mcgloughlin's step son) and Michael LaFramboise led an expedition to the Rogue River from Fort Vancouver in search of beaver pelts. Early English maps designate the Rogue River as McLeod's River.

1828   Jededia Smith traversed the length of Curry County with 18 men herding 300 horses.

1836   Hudson Bay Company's schooner *Cadboro* enters Rogue River.

1849   The ship *William G. Hagstaff*, a 90 ton schooner with a crew of seven and 24 passengers, had wandered lost for two weeks out of San Francisco searching for the Klamath River; it crossed the Rogue River bar and ran aground. The crew and passengers abandoned the vessel and struck out north eventually arriving at Fort Umpqua. The Indians stripped the ship of all metals and usable items.

1850   Captain Albert Lyman in command of the schooner *Samuel Roberts* mistook the Rogue for the Klamath on an expedition to search for tillable land on which to stake Donation Land Claims. He sailed to Cape Blanco then returned and entered Rogue River after launching a long boat which capsized with loss of two men.

1851   Captain William Tichenor landed a party of surveyors near "Battle Rock" on June 9th from the steamer *Seagull* after reconnoitering the area the previous year with the ship *Jacob D. Ryerson*. Thus the first formal and serious attempt at settlement on the Oregon Coast.

6

The Hero
of Battle Rock

From the book *Pioneer History of Coos and Curry Counties,* Orville Dodge 1898

The Proposed Settlement – Fire Arms – The Rock – Incidents of Fight –
The White Indian – The 15th Day – Diary – Flight – Lost In A Swamp –
Camp On Mountain – Mussels – The White Pole – Sand Hills – Fish –
White Men's Quarters – Jesse Applegate – Finding Of Diary –
The White Indian Again – A Place In History.

No history of Port Orford would be complete without presenting a narrative written by Capt. J. M. Kirkpatrick who was one of the nine heroes of a siege of fourteen days under as trying circumstances as men were ever placed. The account gives readers an exciting, and probably accurate, view of how white men considered the raw land of Oregon's Pacific Northwest as a great area of unbridled opportunity for which only the advanced westerners with lighter skin, blessed by God, were entitled to explore and conquer, subjugating the ignorant natives who were residents.

"I was working in Portland, Oregon, at the carpenter trade along in the latter part of May, 1851, when a friend of mine, by the name of Palmer; introduced me to Capt. Wm. Tichenor, who was at that time running an old steam propeller called the *Sea Gull,* between Portland, Oregon and San Francisco, California. Before introducing me to Capt. Tichenor, my friend told me that the Captain wanted eight or ten men to go down on the steamer with him to a place called Port Orford on the southwest coast of Oregon. There he intended to make a settlement, lay out a town and build a road into the gold diggings in Southern Oregon and that all who went down with him should have a share in the town he and his partners were going to build. His partners were Mr. Hubboard, purser on the *Sea Gull,* and the Hon. Butler King, then chief in the Custom House in San Francisco. After I made the acquaintance of Capt. Tichenor he painted the whole enterprise in such glowing colors that I was really infatuated with the prospect. He told me that there was not a particle of danger from the Indians, that he had been ashore among them many times and they were perfectly friendly, so I went to work to hunt up a party to go down with us on the *Sea Gull.*

I gathered together eight young men who were willing to go down on the trip. Their names were J. H. Eagan, John T. Slater, George Ridoubt, T. D. Palmer, Joseph Hussey, Cyrus W. Hedden, James Carigan, Erastus Summers and myself, making nine in all. Capt. Tichenor agreed to furnish us arms, ammunition and supplies, and take us down on his steamer. He told us all to get ready to go as he would sail from Portland on the fourth of June, 1851.

We were ready and sailed from Portland on time. On the fifth we arrived in Astoria. I had been selected by the party as the captain of the expedition so I went to Capt. Tichenor and told him I wanted to see the arms he was going to furnish us to defend ourselves with in case we had to fight. "Oh," he said, "there is no danger from the Indians." We then told him that we would go no further unless he furnished us with arms to defend ourselves. He then went ashore and bought at a junk shop, three old flintlock muskets, one old sword that was half eaten with rust and a few pounds of lead and three or four pounds of powder. We told him that he had certainly brought us a hard looking outfit of arms to fight Indians with. "You will never need them," said he, "but having them will make you look dangerous anyway." Just then a young officer from Fort George stepped up to me and told me he had a very good United States rifle he would let me have at cost, viz: $20. I went ashore with him and bought the rifle and also some ammunition. It proved to be a magnificent shooting gun. Our entire armament consisted now of one U.S. rifle, belonging to myself, one six shooting rifle belonging to Carigan, three old flintlock muskets, one old sword, one fine shooting revolver 38 caliber, one pair of derringers loaned to me by a friend in Portland for the trip, about five pounds of rifle powder and ten pounds of bar lead. This constituted our entire outfit to defend ourselves with when we left Astoria on the evening of the sixth of June, 1851.

On the morning of the ninth we were landed on the beach just below Battle Rock. There were a few Indians in sight who appeared friendly, but I could see that they did not like to have us there. I told Capt. Tichenor that I did not like the looks of things at all and those Indians meant mischief. There was one thing more that we wanted and that was the old cannon Capt. Tichenor had on board the *Sea Gull.* He laughed at us at first for wanting it, but when we told him we would not stay without it he studied a little bit and then said all right he would send it ashore. He sent his mate with one of my men, Eagan, who was an old man-of-wars man, back to the steamer for the gun. They soon returned bringing the cannon and copper magazine that contained three or four cartridges each holding two pounds of powder. As soon as the cannon arrived the Captain bid us goodbye and left for San Francisco, saying he would return in 14 days and bring a better supply of arms and more men to aid him in his enterprise. After he left we lost no time in making our camp on what was to be called Battle Rock as long as Oregon has a history. We hauled the old cannon to the top of the rock and placed it so as to command the narrow ridge where the Indians would have to crowd together before they could get to the top of the ridge where we were camped.

About half way up to the top of the ridge there was a bench of nearly level ground about 30 feet wide, from that to the top of the rock the ridge was quite narrow. After getting the gun in place Eagan and I went to work to load it and get ready for the fight that I felt was coming. We put in a two pound sack of powder and on top of that about half of an old cotton shirt and then on top of that as much bar lead cut up in pieces from one to two inches in length as I could hold in my two hands, then a couple of old newspapers on top. We then primed the gun with some fine rifle powder and trained it so as to rake the narrow ridge in front of the muzzle and the gun was ready for business. We cleaned up all our other arms and loaded them ready for use.

Just as soon as the Indians saw the steamer going away without us they appeared very cross and ordered us away making signs to us that they would kill us all if we did not go. Then they left us for their camps down the beach. On the morning of the tenth they were back again in larger numbers and shooting arrows at us from too great a distance to do us any damage. About nine o'clock a large canoe, containing 12 warriors, came up the coast from the direction of the mouth of Rogue River. Among them was one tall fellow wearing a red shirt who seemed to be their leader. As soon as the canoe touched the sand they all jumped out and carried it out on the beach. The fellow in the red shirt drew a long knife, waved it over his head, gave a terrible yell and, with at least 100 of his braves, started for us with a rush. I stood by the gun holding a piece of tarred rope with one end in the fire, the Indians crowded on the narrow ridge in front of the cannon, to let them have the contents when it would do the most execution.

The air was full of arrows coming from at least 100 bows. James Carigan had picked up a pine board about 15 inches wide, eight feet long and 1.3 inches in thickness. He stood right behind me and held the board in front of us both. Thirty-seven arrows hit the board and at least half of them showed the points through it. Two of my men were disabled. Palmer was shot through the neck and was bleeding badly; Ridoubt was shot in the breast, the arrow sticking into the breast bone making a painful wound, and Slater ran and laid down in a hole behind the tent. This left six of us to fight it out with the Indians who still kept coming. When they were crowded on the narrow ridge, the red shirted fellow in the lead and not more than eight feet from the muzzle of the gun, I applied the fiery end of the rope to the priming. The execution was fearful, at least 12 or 13 men were killed outright and such a tumbling of scared Indians I never saw before or since. The gun was upset by the recoil; but we never stopped for that, but rushed out to them and soon cleared the rock of all the live warriors. We counted 17 dead Indians on the rock and this was the bloody baptism that gave the name of Battle Rock to our old camp at Port Orford on the tenth day of June, 1851.

Some incidents that occurred during the battle are worth relating. There were two warriors who passed the crowd and were not hit by any of the slugs of lead fired from the cannon. One of these, a big strong looking Indian, made up his mind that he wanted my scalp; as soon as the cannon was fired he rushed to me with a big knife. Carigan shot him in the shoulder and Summers shot him through the bowels and still he came on. He made a lick at me with his knife which I knocked out of his hand with my left, when he grabbed for his knife I pulled one of the derringers from my pocket and shot him in the head, the ball going in at one temple and out at the other. He turned then and ran 20 feet and fell dead among the Indians that were killed by the cannon. The other Indian went for Eagan whose musket missed fire, as the Indian was in the act of fixing an arrow in his bow, when Eagan hit him over the head with the barrel of his musket bending it more than six inches. The blow stunned the Indian and as quick as lightning Eagan jumped at him and took his bow away, he then jumped back and turned his musket and gave him three or four blows with the butt knocking him entirely off the rock into the ocean.

After the fight was all over, probably an hour, an Indian chief came up the beach within hailing distance and laid down his bow, quiver of arrows and knife and then stepped forward and made signs that he wanted to come to our camp. I went down to the beach, met him and brought him up to the camp. He was by all odds the finest specimen of physical manhood that I ever looked at. He made signs to us that he wanted to carry away the dead Indians. I made him understand that he could bring another Indian to help him. He called out for one more to come up to the camp. They would take the dead ones on their back, pack them down from where they lay, across the narrow sandy beach and up a steep trail towards the north and over a ridge and out of sight. They did this eight times, and where they laid the dead was over 300 yards from our camp. Some of the Indians were quite large, several of them weighing over 200 pounds. As a feat of strength and endurance it was simply wonderful. They carried away all the dead except the fellow who wore the red shirt. I tried to get the big chief to carry him off but he shook his head and stooped down and tore his shirt in two and then gave him a kick with his foot and turned and walked away. We had to drag the fellow afterwards and bury him in the sand.

We all remarked that he was very white for an Indian, he had yellow hair and a freckled face. I pronounced him to be a white man. He turned out to be a white man who had been among the Indians for many years, they having saved him from the wreck of a Russian ship that was lost on the Oregon Coast many years ago.

Another incident of our day's battle was this: After the Indian chief and his man had carried away all of the dead warriors we went to work to make a breastwork on each side of our gun, this was to make it a little more difficult for the Indians to get into our camp. I was standing outside on the narrow ridge in front of our gun, watching some Indians who were about 300 yards away. I was leaning on my rifle when Joe Hussey came out of the camp and laid his right hand on my left shoulder, I turned my head to see what he wanted when spat, a bullet hit his thumb cutting it about half off. This was the first rifle shot that we had heard from the Indians since the fight began. The Indian with the gun had crawled down unnoticed by us, into a large pile of rocks about 60 yards away from where I stood when he shot. He was so sure that he had hit me that he jumped out from the rocks and showed himself; then it was my turn. I had a slug ball and five buck-shot in my rifle and in an instant I drew a bead on him and when my gun cracked he jumped three feet into the air and fell dead. Eagan said, "I am going after his gun." I told him to hold on until I had loaded my rifle for, says I, "There may be other Indians in the rocks and I want to be ready." As soon as my gun was loaded he ran down and picked up the gun and seeing it was of no account he broke the stock and came back bringing the Indian's head dress with him. It was made of sea shells of different colors and was quite pretty. He said the bullet from my rifle had broken his right arm and passed through his body and cut his left hand entirely off. He never knew what hurt him. This was the last Indian killed by us in our first day's battle. We could only count 20 Indians that we had killed, but years afterwards we learned from the Indians that there were 23 killed.

In our talk with the big chief we made him understand that in 14 days more the steamer would return and take us away and for 14 days we were not molested by them, in fact we never saw an Indian; but on the morning of the 15th they were there in force, some 300 or 400 of them in their war paint. They evidently meant business; now as we had lied to them, the steamer did not arrive as we had promised them and we could not make them understand why the vessel did not come. Two or three hundred warriors were going through with a regular war dance on the beach and every time they would turn around so as to face us they would snap their bow-strings at us and make signs that they would soon have our scalps.

The big chief was now their leader. He had his warriors all drawn up around him about 250 yards from us. He made a speech to them so loud that we could hear every word he said above the roar of the surf and he did some of the finest acting that I ever saw before or since. When he stopped talking he drew a long knife and waved it around his head, gave a terrible yell and started for us followed by not less than 300 warriors. I had called to my side James Carigan who was the best rifle shot of any of my men. I told him to take a good rest, draw his lungs full of air, keep cool and wait until they came near enough so as to be sure to kill the leader, for it was either the big chief or us who must go. When he got within about 100 yards of us I raised my rifle to my shoulder and said, "Fire!" We both fired at the same time and down he dropped, we had both hit him in the breast and one of our bullets had gone through his heart, killing him instantly. Had a hundred thunder bolts dropped among his warriors they could not have stopped them as suddenly as the killing of their big chief. They gathered around his body and with a groan that was terrible, picked him up and carried him away to the north out of sight.

In about an hour another great tall fellow, wearing an old red shirt, came up the beach and commenced calling the Indians around him. He soon collected a couple of hundred warriors about him and made a speech to them about five minutes in length. We could see by his frantic gestures and talk that he was urging the Indians to rush on us and wipe us out. When he stopped talking he waved his big knife over his head and started for us, pointing his knife at us and motioning that our heads must be cut off. We were ready for him and when he came close to where the other chief was killed, we fired and he dropped dead. This ended all efforts on the part of their chiefs to induce the Indians to rush on us. They had had enough of that kind of business.

They drew back to the edge of the woods, about 300 yards away from our camp, and had a big talk, after which they commenced going down the beach to a place a little over a mile from our camp, where there were a number of fires burning. We could see a number of canoes loaded with Indians coming up from the direction of the mouth of Rogue River and landing near these fires. They were evidently concentrating their forces for a night attack on us.

We had now taken note of our situation. We were surrounded on one side with thousands of miles of water and on the other side by at least 400 or 500 hostile Indians and 150 miles or more from any settlement of white men. We had also taken stock of our ammunition and had little left. About six loads apiece for our rifles. Something had to be done about that before night, for if they made a night attack on us we could not possibly stand them off, so I told the boys that if we could gain the woods and they would stand by me I would take them all through to the settlements. We made up our minds that it was the only chance to save our scalps.

We were still watched by 10 or 12 Indians not more than 200 yards away. To get rid of those fellows so that we could gain the woods was the next question we had to solve. "Now," said I, "If they contemplate a night attack on us we must convince those fellows on watch that we have no notion of going away." We all went to work as hard as we could to strengthen our breastwork. We cut down one of the pine trees that grew on Battle Rock, cut off the limbs and piled them on top of our breastworks. As soon as the Indians, who were on watch, saw what we were doing they were sure we were determined to stay. They then started down the beach to join the others. We counted them as they got up out of the grass, and there were 114. I will say that never, in all my experience with Indians before or since saw as fine a body of warriors as those. We were now pretty sure that they had all left, but Eagan climbed up to the top of one of the trees and looked in every direction but could see no sign of any Indians except down the beach where they were having a grand war dance.

Now was our chance. We left everything we had in camp; our two tents, our blankets and what little provision we had, and with nothing but our guns and an ax and all the small ropes we had, with two or three sea biscuits apiece, we bid farewell to our old camp on Battle Rock, and started on our fearful retreat through an unknown country. It was now about four o'clock in the afternoon. We had determined to keep as near the beach as possible. We travelled with all our might to get as far as we could before night overtook us. When we were about three miles from Port Orford just as we were going around a point of rocks on an old trail, we met about 30 Indian warriors fully armed, going down to join the others. We raised a yell and charged right at them. We never fired a shot, but they ran like scared wolves.

We kept right on and just between sunset and dark we came to quite a river and, as good luck would have it, we struck this stream just at the turn of the tide so that by wading out on the bar a little way we were able to get across without any trouble. Fifteen minutes later we would have had to build a raft to cross on. This stream was not down on any map that I had ever seen at that time. I think it is now called Elk River. After crossing this stream we struck into the woods and traveled all night, guiding our steps by the roar of the surf breaking on the rocks. There was no time to lose. We knew that the Indians would follow us so we traveled on as hard as we could, wading streams of water, some of considerable size, and making our way through a dense growth of timber and brush. About three o'clock the next day we came to the edge of what seemed to us a large plain. It looked to be miles in extent and was covered with a heavy growth of high grass and proved to be in immense swamp.

We now determined to try and cross this swamp and reach the sea after dark and travel all night. We floundered around in this swamp all night, sometimes in water up to our armpits, until after dark when we found a little island of about an acre of dry land and covered with a thick growth of small fir bushes. Here we laid down and tried to rest and sleep but encountered a new enemy in the shape of clouds of mosquitoes. There was no escape from them and they were the hungriest lot that that I had ever seen.

In the morning, as soon as it was light enough for us to see our way out, we struck for the beach again and in about an hour we reached an Indian trail fully 20 feet wide where hundreds of Indians had gone. They were now ahead of us. We followed on their trail a few miles when we came to a stream of water about four rods wide and two feet deep. Here the trail turned up this stream and left the beach. We at once came to the conclusion that the Indians had followed us that far the first night and when daylight came they found that we had not traveled on the beach, so they struck up this stream, thinking to intercept us when we reached this stream on our way. We crossed on the beach and were now ahead of the Indians. We now put in our best time traveling as hard as we could. About five o'clock we reached the mouth of the Coquille River where we were confronted by a large stream of water and on the opposite side of the river were 300 or 400 Indians all drawn up in line of battle reach to prevent our crossing. They were making signs that they would kill us if we attempted to cross, so there was now no alternative but to keep up on the south side of the river and do our best to prevent coming into collision with these Indians that were so numerous and hostile.

We now came to the conclusion that we had better try and cross the mountains and strike the wagon road that led from the settlements in Oregon down to California. About three or four miles from the mouth of the Coquille River, on the south side, rises quite a high mountain, so we determined to go to the top of this mountain in order to study the surrounding country. Three or four hundred Indians kept right opposite watching us with nothing but the river between them and us. Just as we reached the foot of this mountain the Indians stopped a few minutes and divided their forces. One part of over 100 turned off to the left and ran up a short ravine toward the north. They soon disappeared over a low pass to the left and went back towards their village at the mouth of the river. Their object was to get their canoes, cross the river, overtake us and kill or capture us. When we had ascended this mountain some distance we could see the Indians crossing the river in their canoes. We hurried on as fast as we would travel and between sun down and dark we reached the top of the mountain, tired, hungry and nearly worn out. Here we determined to rest and get some sleep. We worked our way into the thicket of brush where we found a kind of sink hole, about 20 feet in diameter and about three feet deep, covered on the bottom with a rank growth of grass with thick brush all around it. Here we all laid down and were soon fast asleep.

Just as soon as it began to be light in the morning, notwithstanding there was a thick fog, we were up and off, traveling in a northeasterly direction as hard as we could. In about an hour we struck the river again at a point where the timber came down close to the water. We found a lot of dry drift wood and soon made a raft large enough to carry the three men who could not swim and our guns and the balance of us swimming and pushing the raft ahead of us. The river at this point was about two hundred yards wide.

When we reached the opposite bank and landed we supposed that we had crossed the river but we had only landed on an island and did not know it until we had taken all our ropes off of the raft and let the logs go. We had not gone more than 300 yards when to our consternation, we discovered that we had another branch of the river to cross nearly as wide as the one we had crossed. There was not a stick of timber on the island to make a raft out of and as the fog was beginning to break away, there was no time to lose, so one of the men, George Ridoubt, volunteered to swim across with the ax and cut off a dry pine tree that projected out over the water toward us. Our intention was to get the three men, who could not swim, onto the tree, let them hold our guns and the balance of us swim along and guide the tree. Just as the tree fell into the water three Indians came around the bend in a canoe. They were busy watching the man that was chopping and did not see us until they were close to us. We hailed them and made signs that we wanted them to land and take us over the river to where Ridoubt was.

This they refused to do, but when they saw three or four rifles leveled on them they concluded to come to where we were. We all piled into the canoe and they landed us on the main land just as the sun broke through the fog. We did not tarry long till we were on our weary tramp again. We were now very weak, not having eaten anything for three nights and four days. We saw plenty of game, but did not dare to fire a shot, for it would have brought at least 300 Indians on to us in ten minutes, and they would have made short work of us. The men who were with me had no knowledge of woodcraft and but little of Indian warfare. They were on an average as brave a company of men as the same number that could be found. There was not one among them who could have taken the lead and kept a course without running around in a circle. When I found this out I saw that their lives as well as my own depended on my keeping in the lead. I had a good knowledge of woodcraft and could take a course and keep it as long as it was necessary. I had also some little knowledge of the cunning and trickery of the Indians, having crossed the Rocky Mountains in company with Kit Carson; and I will here say that of all the men that I ever came in contact with or association with Christopher Carson knew all the tricks and cunning of the Indians better than any man I ever saw. I hope you will not think me egotistical when I say that I felt equal to the task of leading my party through to a place of safety.

After crossing this branch of the river we struck out in a northwesterly direction, through the timber, intending, if we could, to reach the beach by night and then travel as hard as we could all night if necessary. We traveled on through the thick heavy timber until it got so dark that we could not get along, so we all laid down by the side of a big log and slept until daylight. We then jumped up and were off in the same direction we had been traveling the day before. In about an hour we emerged from the timber and soon got down to the beach. We struck the sea at a point where a long reef of rocks extended quite a ways out into the ocean. These rocks, near the shore, were covered with mussels which we broke from the rocks and commenced eating them raw. They soon made us sick, so we built up a fire and began roasting them and that made them much better. We were eating our first lot of roasted mussels when one of the Indians, who had crossed us over the north branch of the Coquille River the day before, came down to us. As soon as he got near to us, he commenced talking Jargon. He said he had seen me in Portland, that he had kept right behind us in the woods after we left the river, and that he was afraid to come to us in the woods believing we would kill him. He said that the Indians were coming up on the beach from the mouth of the Coquille, and we must hurry as fast as we could. Each one of us took all the live mussels we could carry, but did not stop to cook them as we intended to roast them when we got to a place of safety. We now struck up the beach as fast as we could go, the Indian in the lead.

We traveled on until about three o'clock in the afternoon when the Indian called our attention to a white pole about eight inches in diameter and twenty feet high, standing in a great pile of rocks at the edge of the beach. When we passed this pole and monument, the Indian said we were now safe, as the California Siwashes would not dare to come above that pole, for the Coos Bay, Umpqua, Clickitats, and some other tribes he mentioned, would make war on them and drive them back. After resting a little while we traveled on for about two hours and, turning into a little cove, we built a fire and roasted our mussels and ate them. We then took up our line of march and traveled till it was dark and then turned off to our right where we found some dry sand, in another little cove, and all laid down and slept until morning.

As soon as it was daylight we were up and away. That afternoon we reached Coos Bay. The Indians met us more than a mile from their camp and brought us dried salmon, dried elk meat and salmon berries. They were extremely friendly and expressed themselves as being very glad that we had not been killed by the California Siwashes. We stayed all night with these Indians who seemed to vie with each other in doing everything they could for us. In the morning they took us across the bay and landed us about where Empire City now stands. They told us that we would make the mouth of the Umpqua the next day. We bid our friends goodbye and struck across the sand hills and through swamps, where sometimes the water was three to four feet deep. We floundered around in these sand hills and swamps until we were nearly tired out and struck for the beach again. About an hour before dark we reached the beach. The wind was blowing so hard from the west that it made it difficult and unpleasant to travel against, so we left the beach and sought shelter behind some sand hills that rose to more than a hundred feet above the sea. We found some dry pine logs near a thicket of brush and soon had a big fire going. Here we laid down and slept until morning, notwithstanding we were soaked with the mist that had been driven across the sand hills by the gale in the night.

After we had dried ourselves a little by our fire we struck out for the beach. The gale had subsided and the beach, for more than 100 yards in width and as far as we could see up and down the beach, was literally covered with fish that had been driven ashore the night before by the gale. "Luck at last," cried Eagan, "Here is fish enough for a feast for the Gods;" and each one of us picked up two apiece, weighing five or six pounds each, and back we went to our camp where we had left a big bed of coals, where we roasted our fish, eating all we could of one and taking the rest with us. That afternoon we reached the mouth of the Umpqua River. The Indians on watch for us had notified the white men on the other side of the river that the white men, who had shot a keg of nails into the Indians at Port Orford, killing many of them, were on the other side of the river. We could see the white men launching their boats at what was called Umpqua City; at that time it consisted of one house built of sheet iron and one tent. In about an hour they had reached us and taken us aboard. Having a fair wind they hoisted sail and just as the sun was setting on the second day of July, 1851, we were landed and made welcome in white men's quarters, after having an experience that not soon would we forget.

Never did a set of poor, weary, ragged, hungry white men receive a more royal welcome than we did at the hands of Dr. Joseph Drew and his associates at their camp at the mouth of the Umpqua River. We rested there one day and on the morning of the fourth they took us in their boats and, having sailed up the river, they left us at another new town called Scotsburg. Here we landed about one o'clock and after I had eaten some dinner I bade farewell to my comrades and struck out for Portland. The rest were so worn out and footsore that they were compelled to lay by and rest. I traveled as hard as I could and on the night of the fourth I stayed with a man whose name was Wells.

I left his house before daylight and, after a hard day's tramp, I reach the hospitable house of the grand old pioneer Jesse Applegate. He had just received his mail from Portland and was busy reading the account of our fight with the Indians. The conclusion drawn from the account was that we were killed and burned up. I did not interrupt him till he got through reading his paper. I then asked if I could get some supper and a place to stay all night. "I can give you some supper but all my beds and blankets are in use," he said. I told him I was quite hungry and it made very little difference with me whether I had a bed or not as I had been sleeping for sometime without a bed or blanket. He then commenced talking about those unfortunate young men that had been lured into the jaws of mis-representation. "Why," said he, "those Indians down the coast, combined with their brothers, the Rogue River Indians, are the worst Indians on the American continent, and the bravest. Every old settler in Oregon knows that. The man or company that persuaded them to go down with the view of making a settlement at Port Orford was guilty of a great wrong."

"Well," said I, "Mr. Applegate, I am happy to inform you the men were not murdered but escaped, and eight of them I left at Scotsburg yesterday and I am the ninth." I told him my name and then I gave him an account of our retreat and his remark was, after I got through, "Wonderful, wonderful."

Here I must make an explanation. I had written a full account of our first battle with the Indians on Battle Rock and also an account of our last battle, fifteen days afterwards, and closed the account with these words, "We are now surrounded by three or four hundred Indians hungry for our scalps, on one side; by thousands of miles of water on the other; and at least 150 miles from any white man's house. We have but little grub and are nearly out of ammunition and if the Indians should make a night attack and rush on us we certainly could not defend ourselves against so many." This paper I folded up and placed in the back of an old book, went to the stump of the pine tree that we had just cut down, and buried the book in a hole about a foot deep, then scraped of the bark on one side of the stump, just over where the book was, and wrote with a piece of red chalk these two words, "Look beneath."

When the steamer *Sea Gull* reached San Francisco, after leaving us at Port Orford, she was embargoed for debt and tied up, so it was impossible for Capt. Tichenor to return in 14 days as he had promised. Col. John B. Ferguson, then U.S. Mail Agent for California and Oregon, and a friend of mine, learning from Capt. Tichenor that he was tied up for debt and could not return on time, and knowing much more about the Indians on the coast than the captain did, went to the captain of the steamer *Columbia* and dispatched him one day before her regular sailing time, with strict orders to call at Port Orford and take us back to Portland. The steamer stopped at Port Orford the day after we left Battle Rock. The captain and a number of passengers went ashore and found the body of the fellow in the red shirt that we had killed in the first fight and buried in the sand, but the tide had washed him out and he was then as white as could be. They made sure that it was one of us when they went up on the rock where everything showed evidence of a fight. In looking around their attention was called to the words written on the stump and they soon dug up the book and after reading it they were sure that the Indians had wiped us out. As no Indians were to be seen, they concluded to search a little further for more evidence of our fate. They finally found where a big fire had been built and in the ashes they found some human teeth and some charred pieces of human bones. This ended their search as they were now sure that we had been killed and burned. What they really found was where the Indians burned their dead after the first battle with us. They then returned to the steamer in the full belief that we had all been killed and burned, all but the body they found on the beach.

The steamer sailed at once with the account of our trouble up to the time we left

Battle Rock. This was published in *The Oregonian* as soon as possible, and this was the account that Applegate was reading when I reached his house. Nearly all my friends in Portland and all over Oregon really believed that it was all up with me and all my party. Not so with the old mountaineers, Joe Meek, Otway and Wilks. They all said that we would turn up all right yet, and when I reached Portland with the news that my party was all safe they were as happy as men could be. I reached my old quarters in Portland on the 11th day of July, 1851, strong and rugged, having had enough of adventure to do me for some time.

As to my comrades on the expedition, I never saw but two of them afterwards. Eagan settled in Portland, married and raised a family. Palmer settled in Salem, had a saloon, and was quite well fixed. These two men I saw quite often. In 1866, Slater was killed by Indians, on Rogue River. In 1855, Cy. Hedden joined a company under Col. T'Vault and tried to reach Port Orford by land. T'Vault's party consisted of 10 or 12 men and when they reached the Coquille River, Hedden pointed out our trail to T'Vault and told him he was on dangerous ground and must be cautious. He paid no attention to Hedden's warning, but went into camp on a grassy plot not far from where we crossed the river. In the night the Indians surprised his camp, killing the most of his men. Hedden escaped with a man by the name of Williams who had been wounded with an arrow, and when the shaft was pulled out the head was left in his body. Hedden and Williams finally reached Scotsburg where Williams suffered for months but the arrow point finally worked its way out. Hedden stayed and waited on him until he got well.

When I look back over this whole affair I think you will agree with me that, take it all in all, the history of the Port Orford expedition is worthy of a place in the history of the early settlements. As to our fight, considering our inexperience and the arms we had, we certainly did well. There is no other battle in Indian warfare that I know of, that equals it, except that most glorious defense Mrs. Harris made in 1855 on Rogue River in defending her house and home containing the dead body of her husband and her living child, when for more than ten hours she, all alone, stood off at least 100 of the bravest Indians that ever lifted a white man's scalp, killing, according to the Indians' own statement, fifteen. To this little woman we must all give the praise of making the grandest fight, against fearful odds, that was ever made on the continent of America.

It was the first time that the Indians of Port Orford had ever been whipped, usually killing more of the white men than they themselves had had killed. Here they had lost 25 warriors and not killed or captured a single white man. It was the old cannon that did the work. It was an entirely new thing to them as they really thought that we were using thunder and lightning against them. The noise and the fearful execution done by the gun demoralized them. They were not only scared but they were terrified and the killing of their two big chiefs taught them that we were dangerous. I have often thought that our escape was due as much to their fear of us as to our good luck. I can look back over the long stretch of years and feel a generous pride that none of my party were killed.

I know not if any of my old comrades are living now. I was the youngest one in the party and I have passed by three score years and ten. If any of them are living, "God's blessings on them;" if they have crossed the great Divide, then, "Farewell."

Nearly all of the old pioneers of Oregon are gone. No braver, bigger-hearted, or truer set of pioneers ever blazed the way for the march of civilization than they who:

"Belonged to the legion that never were listed,
They carried no banner nor crest;
But, split in a thousand detachments,
Were breaking the ground for the rest. "

My task is done, and I claim no other merit for these recollections than that of truth.

J. M. Kirkpatrick,
Oro Blanco, Arizona
November 29, 1897

7

The Indians and Early Indian Troubles of Southwestern Oregon

If the early history of the Port Orford area, as it is presented here, seems in the first few chapters to be crowded with reports, accounts and narratives of strife between Indians and settlers, it is because the pioneer years of the Oregon Country were devoted to the disturbing activities of Indians. They were ever a topic of conversation and prominent in the news of the day. This was largely due to the prevailing unrest among the tribesmen because of white men encroaching upon their tribal lands and privileges, and the long delays before final settlements of grievances were obtained. There were also many misunderstandings over matters that the far distant authorities in Washington did not view in the same light as the local Indian officials saw them.

Much of the following narrative must be credited to W. A. Langille whose devotion to Oregon history is reflected in the care with which he presented his material.

Prior to the immigration period, the members of the white race the Indians of Oregon had encountered were explorers, or traders and fur hunters who came and went, or bartered for furs. When the settlers began to arrive in numbers, the Indians were entirely ignorant of the white man's ways, his purpose in coming, or the implications involved in accepting the civilization that was being thrust upon them. They were forced to accept new ideas without any understanding or realization of the social and cultural forces, or the physical power, behind them. Some of the tribal chieftains wisely foresaw that the opportunity for them to live their traditional lives had suddenly come to an end, their future was in doubt. They saw their people demoralized and preyed upon by unscrupulous white men without a chance of adequate redress. On the other hand, in each and every tribal band there was a predatory element which was almost continually committing depredations against the white intruders despite the admonitions of their chieftains. Other members of the tribes rebelling against the wrongs inflicted upon them, endured for a while, and when redress seemed impossible, they resorted to vengeful retaliation.

When Joseph Lane, the first Territorial Governor of Oregon under the authority of the United States, reached Oregon City on March 2, 1849, he found the Cayuse War practically ended. In Western Oregon there was a rising tide of Indian discontent, brought about by the menacing border warfare that had been going on for a number of years between Rogue River Indians and travelers over the Oregon-California Trail. Troubles in the Rogue River Valley multiplied as miners crowded into the area. Early in 1850, these troubles became acute. Brought to Governor Lane's attention, he assembled a small force of white men, and with a few Klickitat warriors under Chief Quatley, proceeded to the Rogue River country and called a council with the Indians. Boldly, he arrested their chief as a hostage and stepping forward alone, he struck the weapons from the hands of a group of armed Indians, and two days later concluded a peace treaty that was nominally observed for over a year.

After making this treaty, Governor Lane went to California on a mining venture; he had learned he was to be superseded as Territorial Governor by John P. Gaines.

It was in June 1851, after ex-Governor Lane returned to Oregon that the battle on Stuart Creek took place, in which Lane, now a general, acquitted himself with credit in battle, and effected a peace treaty after capturing 30 women and children and holding them as hostages. This treaty was fairly well respected until 1853, when the Indians again resumed their depredations and by the end of that year practically all the bands of Southwestern Oregon were on the warpath.

In this uprising, volunteers from as far away as Linn, Marion and Polk Counties joined the military in an effort to suppress the maraudings.The Indians had a fortified camp on Evans Creek, where, under General Lane's leadership, they were attacked, fighting so close together that the belligerents could converse. The Indians reproached Lane for the attack and asked him to come into their camp and arrange another peace. Surprising all his men, General Lane stopped the encounter and, although wounded, he marched alone into the Indian fortification where it was arranged with the chiefs that both whites and Indians should return to Table Rock and make a permanent peace. This was accomplished in the afternoon of September 10, 1853, in the shadow of the picturesque, and now historic rock.

This second treaty of peace was no more enduring than the first and the Indian depredations were resumed early in 1855 continuing until the last pitched battle with the Rogue Rivers at Big Meadows (Bend) near the junction of the Illinois and Rogue Rivers. It ended on May 28, 1856 when Chief John (Te-cum-tom) of the Applegate band came in and surrendered to Joel Palmer, Superintendent of Indian Affairs. His surrender resulted in the removal of 2,700 Indians, old and young, to the Grande Ronde and Siletz reservation which had been newly established by Lieutenant Phillip H. Sheridan.

While these incidents were taking place, white men began the settlement of the coastal areas of Coos and Curry counties.

The first of the white men to visit what is now Curry County is a matter of conjecture. In 1812, the Russians, with the consent of the Spanish Governor of California, established a trading post on Bodega Bay, forty odd miles north of San Francisco,which they maintained until 1840, when it was discontinued at the request of the United States government. Before and during this time, the Russians had a foundry at Sitka, Alaska, where they cast bells for the orthodox churches of the Northland, and also shipped them to the Spanish mission churches of California.

In this period of occupation and trading in California, there is little doubt that some of the Russian trading vessels, or even those of the earlier navigators, were driven ashore on the Oregon Coast and wrecked, the survivors accounting for the presence of an occasional alien of white or mixed blood as is cited in the episode of Battle Rock. The descendants of early survivors of Russian and other shipwrecks may account for the presence of men of large stature among the tribes up and down the coast. Also, early visitors report that the coast natives had knives fashioned from iron which they asserted came from the wreckage of vessels found on the beaches.

The first authentic account of white men passing through Curry County was the ill-fated Smith party, which left the San Gabriel Mission with 15 men and 68 horses in May, 1828. The party was led by Jedediah S. Smith who had accumulated a rich load of furs for the St. Louis market. Deep snows precluded crossing the Sierras or using the untraveled Siskiyou route to the Columbia River, and the southern route was unsafe. From near the head of the Buena Ventura (Sacramento) River, they crossed the Coast Range through the rugged, rocky, steep-canyoned Trinity Mountains where horse feed was scarce and a number of horses were lost on the steep, rocky sides of the deep canyons.

The Chetco River was reached on June 24th. The crossing there was made at low tide on June 25th, the ford only saddle-girth deep. When ready to march next day the party discovered, a mule was missing, and three men were sent back to find the animal. On returning, they passed a Chetco village at dusk, and the Indians rushed out with their bows and arrows and "made after them," yelling and screaming as they attempted to surround the trio. The men hastily retreated on their horses, swimming a small creek where the Indians gave up the chase. They overtook the party in camp some 12 miles up the coast at "Thoglas" (probably Whaleshead) Creek. Next morning they found three horses had been wounded by arrows, two of them dying a day or two later. They reached Pistol River on June 26th and Rogue River on the 27th where they found the "Villages of the Tul-tush-tun-tude." They lost 12 horses crossing the Rogue, making 23 lost in three days.

On July 12th, they crossed the Umpqua River. While engaged in this task an Indian stole an axe. He was seized with the intent of tying him to a tree and punishing him. But he gave up the axe apparently without animosity. A short march was made the next day, the party camping nearer Smith River.

On the morning of July 14th, the camp was at rest, awaiting the return of Smith who, as was his custom, had gone ahead to plan the travel route. Harrison G. Rogers, second in command, was in charge of the camp. Contrary to a strict camp rule, but relying upon the seemingly friendly attitude of the "Keli-wat-sets" (Umpquas), he permitted the Indians to come into the camp in numbers. The men were lying about camp and entirely off guard. Arthur Black, a little apart from the others, had been cleaning his rifle and just finished loading it. At a given signal the Indians attacked the party.

When the disturbance started three Indians leaped upon Black, he shook them off. Seeing all his comrades struggling on the ground and the Indians stabbing them, he fired into the crowd and fled to the woods, escaping several pursuers. Returning to camp, Smith met John Turner running frantically toward him through the underbrush. Turner, who was temporary camp cook, told Smith how the chief who had stolen the axe, and had subsequently been humiliated had led his entire band upon the encampment killing everybody but Turner. His escape was due to his great size and unusual strength. When the Indians rushed him he seized a large firebrand with which he valiantly beat off his assailants, knocking down, if not actually killing four of them.

The two men decided not to endanger themselves by trying to recover any of their effects and hastily started up the Umpqua reaching Fort Vancouver in August. To their great surprise, they discovered that Black had reached the post the evening before. He had made his way to the coast and nearly famished, reached a "Tillamook" village, where he was cared for, then escorted to the Hudson's Bay Company Post.

When Smith arrived, Governor Simpson was at the fort, and instructed Dr. McLoughlin to send a strong party to bury the dead, recover the stolen property and punish the Indians. Thomas McKay, placed in charge of this party, returned in October with all of the furs, some of which were recovered from the natives as far away as the Upper Umpqua and the headwaters of the Willamette.

Alexander McLeod was sent out with a second party, which included Smith and his two men, Turner and Black. McLeod succeeded in recovering both the Smith and Rogers journals of their trip from California. The last entry in Rogers' journal was:

"These Indians tell us after we get up the river 15 or 20 miles, we will have good travelling to the Wel-hammet or Multnomah where the Callipo Indians lived." They also found that the Umpquas could converse in the Chinook jargon.

Jedediah Strong Smith, one of his mother's fourteen children, was born in Bainbridge, Chenango County, New York, June 24, 1798. He was an interesting character among the fur hunters and frontiersmen with whom he associated, few of them equalling him in the arts of the wilderness. He was a devout Christian, scholarly for his day, prudently fearless, and a keen observer of every feature of the country he pioneered and mapped from day to day with commendable accuracy. In his comprehensive journals, he recorded all of the pertinent physical and cultural features and all the worthwhile incidents of his extensive, exploratory travels. Most unfortunately, his earlier records, which he had planned to publish in book form, were destroyed by fire.

In 1830, while seeking water for a thirsting party he was leading across the deserts of the Southwest, he was killed by a band of Comanche Indians in an off-guard moment, while watering his parched horse from a hole he had scooped from the almost dry bed of the Cimarron River near Taos, New Mexico. (The incidents Jedediah S. Smith described are from the Ashley-Smith journals.)

Smith River in California, flowing beside the Grants Pass-Crescent City Highway, and Smith River opposite Reedsport in Douglas County, Oregon, were named after him.

There is a dearth of written history concerning the Umpqua River-Chetco River section of the Oregon Coast from 1828 to 1850. It is known that in 1828, soon after the recovery of the Smith furs, the Hudson's Bay Company established a trading post on the Umpqua River at, or near, the present town of Elkton. This was the supply point for the fur brigades that reached down the coast and into California. In keeping with the company's traditional policy of stern justice, their trappers and traders alike lived and traded in comparative peace with all of the natives they contacted, and available records do not indicate there were any serious difficulties with these coastal tribes.

After the Smith massacre, the next Indian difficulty recorded happened just below the Rock Point Bridge in Jackson County in June, 1836. Particulars of this encounter are not available. (Gaston's Centennial History of Oregon, page 404)

In 1837, Ewing Young went to California and purchased 700 head of cattle at three dollars per head, and drove them to the Willamette Valley arriving there with 600 head. Young experienced considerable trouble with the Indians while in the Rogue River Valley, as did many others who traveled the Oregon-California Trail then and in later years.

All the Rogue River Indians were tribes which hereditarily belonged to the

Klamath and Shasta nations and spoke the Shasta dialect of the Athapascan language. The Upper Rogue Indians claimed all the land and streams in the Rogue River area from its sources down to and including the Illinois River and its valley. From there to the sea, Rogue River was known as the To-to-tin, and from the Chetco River to and including the Coquille River to the junction of its south fork, all the Indians belonged to the To-to-tin branch of the tribe,which was made up of 12 bands living in 14 villages. The names of the bands, their numbers and location of their villages as given in the report of Isaiah L. Parrish, Indian Agent of the Port Orford District on July 10, 1854, are shown below.

Of these, the Chetcos and the Coquille bands displayed the most antagonism towards the whites and were the most troublesome, seconded by the bands that lived along Rogue River from the sea to the village opposite the mouth of the Illinois River.

Name of Band	Men	Women	Boys	Girls	Total	Location of Villages
Nah-so-mahs	18	20	10	11	59	Mouth of Coquille
Choc-re-le-atins	30	40	18	17	105	Forks of Coquille
Quoh-to-mahs	53	53	22	23	145	Mouth of Flores Creek
3 villages						Mouth of Sixes River
						Port Orford
Cosutt-hen-tins	9	9	6	3	27	Rhinehart Creek (?)
Equa-chees	24	41	18	19	102	Euchre Creek (?)
Yah-shutes	49	45	24	12	130	South side Rogue River
3 villages						North side Rogue River
						Three miles up Rogue River
To-to-tins	39	47	22	12	120	Three miles up Rogue River
Macka-no-tins	53	58	17	17	145	Nine miles up Rogue River
Shasta-koos-tees	45	61	23	16	145	Above/near Agness
Chetl-essen-tins	10	15	11	9	45	North side Pistol River or
						Crooks Point
Wish-te-na-tins	18	26	12	10	66	Houstenatin Creek just south
						of Ostranders
Chetcos	117	83	22	19	241	Both sides mouth of Chetco
						River

The locations of the lands claimed by the various bands, as nearly as can now be determined, are as follows: The land of the Nah-so-mahs reached from the coast to the forks of the Coquille River and southward an undetermined distance. The Choc-re-le-atins claimed the upper reaches of the Coquille.

The Quoh-to-mahs lived in three villages along the coast. Their north boundary joined the Nah-so-mahs and reached to Port Orford where there was a village. The others probably lived at the mouth of Flores Creek, near the Newburgh State Park, and there was one band at the mouth of Sixes River.

The Cosutt-hen-tins' land touched that of the Quoh-to-mahs south of Port Orford and reached to that of the Equa-chees, which began at a point opposite the Three Sisters (a group of offshore rocks, midway between Mussel and Euchre Creeks) and joined the Yah-shutes land near the mouth of Rogue River. This band had villages on both sides of the mouth of this stream, claiming all of the coast as far south as Cape San Sebastian, and also three miles up both sides of Rogue River, to To-to-tin land; the third Yah-shutes village being on the south side of the river, three miles or so up from the sea. The To-to-tin village was on the north side a mile further upstream. The To-to-tin land reached six miles up both sides of the stream to that of the Macka-no-tins who claimed 12 miles along both sides of the river to meet the territory of the Shast-koos-tees whose village was above Agness, and about opposite the mouth of Illinois River.

The Chetl-essen-tins claimed land from Cape San Sebastian to Houstenatin Creek, just south of the present Ostrander place, where it bordered the Wish-te-na-tins land which went south to Whaleshead Creek, where it met the land of the Chetcos. At the mouth of Whaleshead Creek there was a fair weather chance for unloading the small craft that supplied a trading post located there in beach mining days. The once numerous Chetcos had their villages at the mouth of the Chetco River.

The easterly boundary of all the coastal tribe areas was indefinite, and for all practical purposes immaterial, except where they bordered the larger salmon streams, and included special fishing rights,which the holding bands guarded most jealously.

When the first reporting white men went among these people, they found them living quite contentedly in their land of comparative plenty. The men wore little or no clothing, except the skins of deer or other animals which were thrown over their shoulders in cold weather. The women were attired in skirts made of plaited strands of cedar bark or grass, fastened at the waist and reaching to the knees. The children were without clothing.

A variety of food was quite plentiful. The tide-covered rocks of the seashore held quantities of mussels, the beach sands yielded a variety of clams and whelks, crabs were abundant on the tide flats of the bays and river estuaries. The rivers were a bountiful source of the various salmon and other fish which entered the streams. While some deer and elk were killed for meat and their skins used for raiment, the Indians did not live by the chase. The streams or seashore were their principal source of food.

From the uplands, the women and children obtained camas bulbs and edible roots, and gathered a variety of berries, acorns and other tree fruits. Their cooking was done by roasting before the fire or in water-tight baskets with heated stones.

Their shelters were crudely built of driftwood and forest material. With fire and stone implements, they fashioned seaworthy canoes from forest trees that would carry a dozen or more warriors, and they were expert in their use on stream or ocean. In these they voyaged up and down the coast and hunted the fur clad mammals of the sea. Although they possessed a few old trade muskets, ammunition was scarce and they depended upon their ancient weapons and tools in war, the hunt, or for domestic purposes. Stone axes, knives of flint, clubs, spears and bows and arrows were their dependables.

Like most of the canoe men of the Pacific coast, they were generally short in stature, although early chroniclers mention that some of the men were tall and splendid specimens of physical manhood. Collectively, they were not as well appearing as the inland tribes, and the comparative ease with which they made their living tended to make them indolent. As a group, very few of the women had good figures and they were neither comely or attractive. When it was proposed to remove the Coast tribes to the Umatilla reservation, the Cayuses strenuously objected because of their diseased condition, and habits that were not in keeping with Cayuse standards.

Some writers insist that until the coming of the white man chastity amongst the women of the To-to-tin tribe was insisted upon, and its violation by a female was punished by cutting off her ears, putting out her eyes or, in some cases, by death.

Although most of the To-to-tin tribe objected to the coming of the white man and his rude disturbance of their leisurely existence, it is worthy of note that the greatest animosities developed when the lands most coveted by the usurping whites were the ancestral homes of the natives. If these were adaptable to the uses of the white men, little consideration was given to the hereditary rights of the natives. Naturally, they resented being forcibly dispossessed of what was rightfully theirs, "without just compensation or due process of law." As men have always done, they fought to hold their homes and property, futile as their efforts were. .

Rifle shots at dawn, application of the torch, and the white man was "peaceably in possession." On these grounds some of the retaliatory acts of the untutored Indians can, in retrospect, be overlooked, if not condoned. Unfortunately there are many instances where attacks by Indians were inspired by bloodlust, and pillage was the only motive.

Curry County Settlement

The White man's permanent intrusion of the Curry County coastal area began when Captain William Tichenor put the small steamer *Sea Gull,* into the then recently charted Ewing Harbor, now Port Orford roadstead, bringing from Portland a party of nine men, who were landed on the beach, June 9, 1851, for the purpose of establishing a settlement, an effort which began and ended at the place of its inception, on what became known as Battle Rock. Ewing Harbor was surveyed and charted by William P. McArthur in 1850 and was named after his vessel.

Here, on June 10, the day following the landing a horde of natives gathered on the beach and made an assault upon the citadel, that became known as Battle Rock, (an account of the skirmish is presented in chapter 6).

The day following the escape of the men who were embattled on the rock, the Steamer *Columbia,* for which they'd been waiting, but had missed, piloted by Captain Tichenor, arrived from San Francisco. There were 67 men aboard, well armed and provisioned for a four month stay. They decamped, settled in permanently and Port Orford came into being. When the group from San Francisco found the body of a white person on the beach, the camp of the first band demolished, they assumed all had been killed, and reported them dead. When the steamer returned it brought a detachment of troopers from Fort George, Astoria, in the charge of Lieutenant Whyman, who was accompanied by Anson P. Dart, the first Superintendent of Indian Affairs to officiate in the Oregon Country. Also arriving were Isaiah L. Parrish and H. H. Spalding, newly appointed special Indian Agents.

The vessel also left six horses, and before sailing Captain Tichenor arranged for two parties to seek out a usable pack trail route for the shipment of supplies to the then promising Jackson County mines. The foot party returned in a few days after being hopelessly bewildered. The horse party, under T'Vault, became lost in the maze of canyons and hills at the headwaters of the south fork of the Coquille River and abandoned horses and equipment. Making their way to the coast down this stream, they were attacked by Indians near the Nah-so-mah village, where five of the party were killed and two wounded. The bodies of the dead were so badly mutilated that they could not be identified. Williams, one of the wounded, had an arrow driven into his groin, the head of which was not removed until 1855. T'Vault reached the mouth of the Sah-quah-me, now the Sixes River, where the Indians took his rifle, stripped him of his clothing except a portion of his shirt, then permitted him to go on to Port Orford. He arrived there the second day after the Coquille trouble. A man by the name of Brush, who was partially scalped by a blow from a paddle, arrived the next day. Brush Creek in Humbug Mountain

Park was named after him.

Later in the year, Samuel Culver, Indian Agent, arrived and took charge of Indian matters in the Port Orford area. Dart and his special agents left Port Orford upon Culver's arrival.

Further details of these Indian attacks described here may be read in the interesting articles written by Captain Tichenor and J. M. Kirkpatrick for the *Pioneer History of Coos and Curry Counties,* published under the auspices of the Pioneer and Historical Association of Coos County, Orvil Dodge, historian, which is available in many libraries.

Further Indian Troubles

During 1851 difficulties with the Indians of the Rogue River area were constantly increasing and it became very evident that more troops were needed to keep the coast bands in control, and General Hitchcock in command of the Department of the Pacific with headquarters at San Francisco ordered Lieutenant Colonel Solas Casey with a 90-man force of regulars. A detail of men was sent to the Coquille River to punish the Indians for their attack of the T'Vault party. Lieutenant Stoneman, later Governor of California, was in command. When his mission was accomplished he reported, "a large number of them were killed and the moral effect of the operation was very great."

In this same year, Fort Orford was built and continually garrisoned until the removal of the Indians in 1856 when the post was abandoned. At the time the fort was built, Port Orford was the only settlement on the coast south of the Umpqua River and it was in the area dominated by the treacherous To to-tins from the Coquille River to the Chetco River. They were the people who were contemptuously referred to by Kirkpatrick's friendly Coos Bay Indians as "California Siwashes," a term which included all the Indians of the Curry County coast and the Coquille River area, none of whom were permitted to pass northward of a certain point south of Coos Bay marked by a bleached pole set in a pile of rocks. The word "Siwash" as used years ago was an epithet expressing Indian depravity.

In 1850, the Congress passed an Act to extinguish the Indian title to all lands west of the Cascade Mountains and President Fillmore appointed Anson P. Dart, Superintendent of Indian Affairs for Oregon. At the same time the Congress authorized the creation of a Commission on Indian Affairs. The first members were the newly appointed territorial Governor, John P. Gaines, Alonzo A. Skinner and Beverly S. Allen.

On October 3, 1851, Superintendent Dart reported that treaties had been made with four bands of Indians between the Coquille River and the Oregon-California line covering an area of approximately two and a half million acres. The acreage covered by the treaty was "represented as all being good farm land," the purchase "price $28,500, payable in ten annual payments, no part of which is to be paid in money." The report also states, "The total cost, including the treaty expense, was less than one and a half cents per acre." About this time an Indian reservation was created which extended along the coast from Cape Perpetua to Cape Lookout. This area was later restored to its previous status before being occupied as a reservation.

Further Curry County Settlement

The settlement at Port Orford grew slowly. Mining began in the Klamath River area in 1850, in Jackson and Josephine Counties in 1851. By 1852 prospectors had spread widely throughout Southwestern Oregon and Indian troubles multiplied. The next Curry County settlement was established in the pleasing and productive Chetco Valley July 1853, when a group of 12 men among whom were Christian Tuttle, A. F. Miller, Thomas Van Pelt, James Jones and James Taggart. All of the men figured prominently in later Indian troubles in the lower Rogue River and coastal areas. During the summer and early fall the settlers were busily engaged erecting their houses and building fences on their chosen land locations. Later there was some friction between the whites and Indians that resulted in the burning of the Indian villages early in 1854. Prior to this, Anson P. Dart had been succeeded by Joel Palmer as Superintendent of Indian Affairs in the Oregon Country.

The first half of the 1850s marked a period during which there were many Indian troubles in this vast area. For most of the decade, Joel Palmer was in charge of Indian Affairs in a region that included Oregon, Washington, Idaho and the western portion of Montana. From his Indian agents, scantily distributed throughout this extensive territory of meager communication, he received word pictures of the Indian troubles caused by the invading white settlers. In the same fashion knowledge of the depredations of marauding bands of natives came his way. His tenure of office covered the period of the most serious difficulties with the coastal band of Curry County.

Palmer's reports to the Commissioner of Indians Affairs at Washington, D. C., as printed in Congressional Documents are authentic statements of incidents related in this narrative and have been used when appropriate.

Dated at Dayton, Oregon, September 11, 1854, and printed in Senate Document, Second Session of the 33rd Congress is Mr. Palmer's report on Indian matters in Oregon. The following is a synopsis of the conditions he then found in Curry County:

"On the trail, being the great thoroughfare from Jacksonville to Crescent City, there are houses at convenient distances for the accommodation of travellers. Near the coast and along Smith River are tracts of excellent land, much of it covered with a dense forest of redwood; many trees over 20 feet in diameter. There are a few fertile prairies abounding in various kinds of grass.

"About three miles north of our boundary line a stream empties into the ocean, designated on the map of the coast survey as Illinois River; the Indian name is Chetco. Here are many indication of having once resided a numerous people. In the fall of 1853 one Miller and several associated located land claims in this vicinity. The first built their houses about a quarter mile from the river to which the Indians made no objection. Subsequently, knowing the newly discovered mines would attract an influx of people, they projected a town speculation, formed an association and selected a site at the mouth of the Chetco River. The face of the country is such that the crossing must be at the mouth of the river by ferry; here were two Indian villages on the opposite banks of the river, of 20 lodges each. This ferry was of no small importance. The new townsite included one of the villages, and when preparations were made to erect a house within its limits, the Indians strongly protested; but at last acquiescing, the cabin was built and occupied by Miller. Hitherto, the Indians had enjoyed the benefits of the ferry; but now Miller informed them that they must no longer ferry white people. They, however, sometimes did so, and were threatened with the destruction of their lodges if they did not desist.

"The misunderstanding became so acute that several men who had been fighting Indians on Smith River, in California, were called in by Miller and quartered in his house for nearly two weeks. Becoming unwilling to remain longer they were about to return to their homes; Miller objected to their leaving until they had accomplished something for his relief, as on their departure he would be subjected to the same annoyance as before. The next morning at daylight, the party consisting of eight or nine well armed men, attacked the village, and as the men came form their lodges, 12 were shot dead. The women and children were allowed to escape. Three men remained in the lodges and returned the fire with bows and arrows. Being unable to get a sight of those Indians, they ordered two squaws, pets in the family of Miller, to set fire to the lodges. Two were consumed in the conflagration; the third while raising his head through the flames and smoke for breath was shot dead. What added to the atrocity of the deed is, that shortly before the massacre the Indians were induced to sell the whites their guns, under the pretext that friendly relations were firmly established. In the next two days all the lodges in the two villages were burned, except two, belonging to the friends of an Indian who acted with Miller and his party. This horrid tragedy was enacted about February 15, 1854, and on Mr. Palmer's arrival on May 8, the place was in 'peaceable possession' of Miller. After the massacre the Indians several times approached the settlement, robbed houses and once attacked three men, but succeeded in killing none. In all, 23 Indians and several squaws were killed.

"The other settlers condemned this atrocity and told Miller he would have to face the consequences alone. Miller was subsequently arrested and placed in the custody of the military at Fort Orford; but upon his examination before a justice of the peace, was set at large 'on the grounds of justification, and want of evidence to commit.'

"The details of a similar occurrence at the mouth of the Coquille River have been laid before you in a report of Special Agent Smith. These narratives will give you some idea of the state of affairs in the mining districts of this coast. Arrests are evidently useless, as no act of a white man against an Indian, however atrocious, can be followed by a conviction. The legislators of the provisional government enacted, in its day, a law in these words: 'A negro, mulatto or Indian shall not be a witness, in any court, or in any case, against a white person.'"

In Special Agent Smith's report dated February 5, 1854, he relates, "A most horrid massacre, or rather an out-and-out barbarous mass murder, was perpetrated upon a portion of the Nah-so-mah band residing at the mouth of the Coquille River on the morning of January 28 by a party of 40 miners. The reasons assigned by the miners in justification of their acts; by their own statements seem trivial. However, on the afternoon preceding the murders the miners requested the chief to come in for a talk. This he refused to do. Thereupon the whites at and near the ferry-house assembled and deliberated upon the necessity of an immediate attack upon the Indians. A courier was sent to the upper mines, some seven miles to the north, for assistance. Twenty men responded, arriving at the ferry house in the evening preceding the morning massacre.

"At dawn on the following day, led by one Abott, the ferry party and the 20 miners, about 40 in all, formed in three detachments, marched on the Indian ranches and 'consummated a most inhuman slaughter,' which the attackers termed a 'fight.' The Indians were aroused from sleep to meet their deaths with but a feeble show of resistance; shot down as they were attempting to escape from their houses; 15 men and one squaw were killed, two squaws badly wounded. On the part of the white men, not even the slightest wound was received. The houses of the Indians, with but one exception, were fired and entirely destroyed. Thus was committed a massacre too inhuman to be readily believed."

Later investigations made by Mr. Smith a few days after the atrocity revealed that the few Indians involved, "had only five guns, two of these unserviceable," and they were in no way capable of combating some 300, well armed miners operating in the near vicinity, and even if disposed to try, they would not have risked any attempt of violence against such odds.

There is no doubt that some of the Indians committed petty, exasperating thievery at every opportunity and were annoying in other respects, but it does not appear that they had recently done anything to justify such a wanton, brutal assault as was made upon these practically unarmed, unsuspecting natives, even if their early records were not entirely clear. Also, Lieutenant Stoneman had achieved his grim retribution when he avenged the killing of the five members of the T'Vault party who were seeking to return to Port Orford. It was but a few weeks before the T'Vault incident that the Coquilles had assisted the Port Orford bands in an effort to capture the Battle Rock party led by Kirkpatrick who had been able to escape their clutches only through the aid of a friendly Coos Bay Indian.

These earlier incidents happened prior to any settlement in the Coquille area, and the whites involved had not given the Indians any reason for their attacks. For their crimes of the past the Indians had already paid dearly. The mass killing and destruction of the homes of the Nah-so-mah band by camp followers, and possibly a few miners, was an act equally as atrocious as any perpetrated by the natives and was without any just provocation, although it was masked in the conspired sophistry of so called public meetings and meaningless resolutions, citing certain trivial acts by the Indians.

Following the unjustified massacre of the Nah-so-mahs and the burning of their village at the mouth of the Coquille River on January 28, 1854 was the tragedy inflicted by ruffians upon the Chetcos in mid-February. However, the remainder of the year seems to have passed without recording any other serious encounters between the whites and Indians along the coastal area.

In the Spring of 1855, the Indians of the upper Rogue River grew restless despite the treaty General Lane had made with the chiefs, "John" and "Limpy" at Table Rock in 1853, and there were a number of skirmishes, some quite serious. On the lower Rogue and along the coast there were some disturbances during 1855, in the Chetco area and at Pistol River.

As early as March 8, 1856, the new Captain Abbot, and questionable "hero" as leader in the Nah-so-mah massacre of 1854, had a skirmish with the Chetcos at Pistol River losing several men. When the Indians had his small force completely surrounded and ready for the kill, troops came to his relief driving the hostiles away with heavy loss. On March 20, troops attacked the village of Macka-no-tins ten miles up from the mouth of the Rogue. A few days later they fought the bands of "John" and "Limpy" at the mouth of the Illinois River. The Indians fighting desperately left five dead. On March 27, the regulars again met the Indians on the lower Rogue who after a brisk fight at close quarters fled leaving 10 warriors dead. Two soldiers were severely wounded. On April first, a company of citizens again attacked the village near the mouth of the Coquille River, killed nine men, wounded eleven and took 40 squaws and children prisoners.

About the same time, volunteers led by William Packwood and William Windsor ambushed a party of Indians in canoes when passing through a swift, narrow channel of Rogue River (near Lobster Creek), killing 11 men and one squaw; only one man and two squaws escaping. On April 29, a party of 60 regulars were attacked near Chetco River while escorting an army pack train. Three soldiers were killed or wounded, the Indians losing six killed and several wounded. Active in these campaigns were the "Gold Beach Guards," "Coquille Guards" and the "Port Orford Minute Men."

The letter of Joel Palmer, written to George W. Manypenny, Commissioner of Indian Affairs, on March 9, 1856, and printed on page 750, of Volume 2, Senate Documents, 3rd Session, 34th Congress, states: "That a party of volunteers encamped for some time at the Big Bend of Rogue River, above Agness, returned, and a part of them encamped near the To-to-tin village, three miles above the coast; the remaining portion having passed on to the mining village at the mouth of the river. On the morning of February 22, at daylight, the camp near the Indian village was attacked by a party of Indians supposed to number about 300, and all but two, it was supposed, put to death; one man making his way to Port Orford, the other to the village at the mouth of Rogue River. With one exception, all the dwellings from the mouth of Rogue River to Port Orford have been burned and the inmates supposed to be murdered; five persons, however, had made their appearance, who at first were supposed to have been killed. Benjamin Wright, the Special Indian Agent of the district, is believed to be among the killed.

"Up to the last advices from that quarter, Mr. Wright expressed a confident hope of being able to maintain peace among them; but the extraordinary success of the hostile bands and the ease with which they had invariably gained a victory, inspired a belief that they were abundantly able to maintain their position, and rid themselves of the white population. In every instance where a conflict has ensued between volunteers and hostile Indians in Southern Oregon the latter have gained what they regard a victory. It is true that a number of Indian camps have been attacked by armed parties, and mostly put to death or flight, but in such cases it has been those unprepared to make resistance, and not expecting such attack. This, though lessening the number of Indians in the country, has tended greatly to exasperate and drive into a hostile attitude many that would otherwise have abstained from the commission of acts of violence against the whites.

The avowed determination of the people to exterminate the Indian race, regardless as to whether they were innocent of guilty, and the general disregard for the rights of those acting as friends and aiding in the subjugation of our real and avowed enemies, has had a powerful influence in inducing these tribes to join the warlike bands.

"It is astonishing to know the rapidity with which intelligence is carried from one extreme of the country to another, and the commission of outrages (of which there have been many) by our people against an Indian is heralded forth by the hostile parties, augmented, and used as evidence of the necessity for all to unite in war against us.

"These coast bands, it is believed, might have been kept out of the war if a removal could have been effected during the winter; but the numerous obstacles indicated in my former letters, with the absence of authority and means, in my hands, rendered it impractical to effect. It is hoped the condition of things is not really so bad in that district as the letters referred to might seem to imply; enough, however, is known to convince us that a considerable portion of the coast tribes below Port Orford, and extending eastward to Fort Lane, and very likely those on Upper Coquille (for they are adjacent) are hostile and indisposed to come to terms, and doubtless will remain so, until they have positive demonstration of the folly in attempting to redress their own wrongs.

"A considerable number of the Lower Coquille bands had been once induced to come in, but by the meddlesome interference of a few squaw-men and reckless disturbers of the peace, they were frightened, and fled the encampment. A party of miners and others led by the exterminator Packwood, who had collected at Port Orford, volunteered, pursued, and attacked those Indians near the mouth of the Coquille, killing 14 men and one woman, and taking a few prisoners. This was claimed by them as a *battle,* notwithstanding, no resistance was offered by the Indians. I dispatched messengers to all the upper bands, and they came into camp, and expressed a willingness to remain at any point which might be designated. In reply to questions asked those who had previously been there and fled, why they left, they replied that they were told that one object in getting them there was to put them to death. This impression, by them, appeared to be well verified; for among the number who first surrendered of this band, were two Indians who had been charged with the murder of two white men two years previous. The citizens demanded their arrest. One was taken and delivered to Lieutenant McFeely, Commanding at Fort Orford, and was put by him in the guard house. The other made his escape a few days after. Agent Olney requested the lieutenant to permit him to take the Indian before a civil officer for examination, which request was complied with; when the Indian was turned over by the agent to a mass meeting of the people assembled for the purpose, he was tried, condemned and immediately executed, by hanging. (This execution took place on Battle Rock.) It is proper, however, to state that the Indian is alleged to have confessed his guilt through an interpreter, and very likely deserved death, but that could give no justification for the act of the agent in turning him over and aiding a mob in thus unlawfully condemning and executing him."

It was at the beginning of this last general outbreak of the combined Rogue River and coastal Indians, that the Geisel tragedy took place at midnight on February 22, 1856. Many others were killed on that fateful night, and practically every home of the white residents of Curry County was burned.

A state park known as Geisel Monument was created which embraces the site of the Geisel home. This site is now enclosed by an ornamental iron fence erected by descendants to protect the graves of the family, which are marked by appropriate monuments. By inference, this park also commemorates all the other tragic Curry County deaths that occurred during the last effort of the Indians to rid themselves of the white people who had invaded their lands and despoiled them of their heritages.

The large tribes were greatly decimated by early epidemics of smallpox and measles. Later on, disease, coupled with the almost constant attrition of the tribal manhood in warfare with the encroaching whites, so reduced their numbers that by 1856 the belligerent Southern Oregon tribes were no longer capable of successfully engaging in a war against the available military forces and the greatly augmented, well armed, civilian population which opposed them.

When the Indians' capable leader, Chief John, was defeated in the Big Meadows Battle, at the junction of the Illinois and Rogue Rivers on May 27-28, 1856, and the defiant, scattered elements were all brought in, the pitiable, hopelessly defeated remnants of a once large native population realized that they could no longer combat the overwhelming strength of the forces arrayed against them, and surrendered.

Soon after, all the bands were grouped together and with a military escort to protect and control them, they were transported to the Grande Ronde and Siletz Reservations. As misguided warriors they were reduced to impotency and their careers ended. As tribal units their individuality was lost in their collective segregation with others of their kind on reservations common to all of them.

When the Indians departed from their ancestral homelands, the glamorous, storied mining days of the the early 1850s had almost passed, their romance heightened by the excitement of fighting a brave and antagonistic native foe.

No doubt the transfer of the Indians pulled at the heartstrings of many of them and Chief John's reply to the military commander perhaps expressed the sentiment of the vanquished native: "You are a great chief; so am I. This is my country. My people were here when these great trees were very small. My heart is sick with fighting; but I want to live in my country. I want to go back to Deer Creek and live among the white people as I used to do. They can visit my camp and I will visit their camp; but I will not lay down my arms and go with you to the reservation. I will fight. Good-bye." A week later Chief John's warriors were hopelessly defeated at Big Bend and surrendered unconditionally, to Captain Ord at Rhinehart Creek. The Indian wars in Southwestern Oregon had come to an end.

8

Fort Orford

The Donation Land Claim Act passed by the Congress in 1850 offered pioneer settlers title to 160 acre tracts of land to encourage prospective farmers and merchants to settle the far western territories. Open to settlement were 640,320 acres. Due to the extreme geographic isolation and limited tillable land, the coastal portion of Southern Oregon was of little interest to prospective settlers. The initial attempt to establish a settlement came in June of 1851, when nine men were put ashore at Ewing's Harbor, (earlier named Indian Bay by the Russians and now known as Port Orford) five miles southeast of Cape Blanco, from the steamer *Seagull,* captained by William Tichenor.

Their battle with Indians in the area and their retreat described earlier in detail, had become part of history. Also faithfully recorded was the aftermath of the Battle of Battle Rock which finally resulted in the arrival of a detachment of army regulars.

Tichenor, mindful of the Battle Rock fiasco, returned on July 14th with 67 men, who had agreed to construct a blockhouse in return for title to town lots. This group, made up of itinerant miners who had struck out in the gold fields of California, were primed with stories of abundant riches in the sands and streams in and around the townsite. Tichenor meantime, fearing further attacks from the Indians, pleaded with the army to establish a post near his settlement to insure protection for the settlers and to provide a port facility for deployment of troops and supplies to all of the Southern Oregon coast, declaring that the roadstead was a mere 35 or 40 miles from the Oregon Road and the Rogue River valley to the east. To substantiate this, he sent out an expedition under the command of G. W. T'Vault to locate a suitable connecting route to the Oregon-California Road.

After several weeks of struggling through the dense underbrush and becoming hopelessly lost, the bedraggled party came to the upper Coquille River where they were able to procure a a canoe from a frightened Indian who advised them they could easily reach the mouth of the river. Near the mouth they were attacked by Indians, losing five of the nine in the remaining party. (Thirteen had given up and returned to Port Orford a week before.) Tichenor, backed by public opinion created by newspaper accounts of the attacks, again pleaded with the army at Fort Vancouver.

In September, General Hitchcock, Commanding General of the Department of the Pacific, ordered Lt. P.T. Wyman and 20 men of Company I, First Artillery to Port Orford for the purpose of locating and constructing a permanent post there. Arriving by steamer on the 14th, the men set out to effect 14 buildings on the bluff overlooking the bay from the abundant cedar logs on the site.

On October 22, 1851, General Hitchcock ordered three companies of regular troops, under the command of Lt. Col. Silas Casey to the Coquille River, via Fort Orford, to punish the Indians responsible for the T'Vault Massacre. The expedition, hampered by adverse weather, poor trails and lack of maps, dogged the elusive Indians for weeks before finally attacking a camp on the North Fork, killing 15 persons. Retiring to the mouth of the river, they set up a temporary camp (named Camp Abbeyville) before returning to San Francisco (Benicia) in December.

In January, 1852, the schooner *Captain Lincoln* bound for Fort Orford, laden with troops and supplies, was driven in by a furious southerly gale and beached north of the entrance of Coos Bay. Miraculously, all hands were saved and most of the supplies salvaged. The men made a makeshift shelter of sail and planking which was aptly named "Camp Castaway." Plagued by bad weather and poor communication, an effective rescue was not organized until May. (In 1948, a retired army officer, Col. Preston Rohner, purchased a portion of the old fort site at Port Orford and operated a motel and dinner house which he named "Castaway Lodge" unaware that 96 years earlier, a group of marooned soldiers bound for Port Orford had used the name for their makeshift camp on the north beach at Coos Bay.) Such was the origin of the little post which was truly "West of the West." During the five years the fort was commissioned, the soldier's duties consisted of drilling, stopping leaks, building roads and trails, hunting and fishing. All mail and supplies arrived by boat on a non-scheduled basis, about every fortnight.

Indian troubles began to arise in October, 1855, when Lt. August V. Kautz was attacked while locating a trail between Cow and Grave Creeks near the Oregon Road some 60 miles east of the fort. Two troopers were killed in this battle. Isolated depredations by both factions (miners and Indians) occurred until the night of February 22, 1856, when Indians, incensed over the loss of their ancestral homes, erupted in a violent attack in the area wide around the mouth of Rogue River leaving nearly 30 settlers dead and their homes destroyed. Citizens mustered in "Volunteer Militia Companies" and the regular army dispatched over 300 men in an effort to quell the uprising, which was accomplished in four months of difficult combat. The little fort proved its worth during those tense days as a supply point for the army and a haven for the settlers and the peaceful Indians in the district.

In September, 1856, the little fort was dismantled and shipped, by sea, to the new post at Umpqua City. Included in this operation were two structures housing the officers, the hospital, two barracks, a small blockhouse, several storehouses, planking from the protective wall and all the furnishings. The blockhouse and wall were erected at the height of the Indian uprising. The wall, eight feet high, consisted of a couple planks horizontally placed on posts set eight feet apart. The center space was filled with packed earth and a glacis was constructed around the outside. Several sally ports were provided for the effective use of the four inch mountain howitzer.

Capt. George Meservy of the "Gold Beach Guards" utilized the remaining buildings at the fort as a base of operations for the rounding up of stragglers for transporting back to the reservation at Grande Ronde. A short time later, R. W. Dunbar leased the site for a period of ten years (at no consideration) in hopes of being appointed to the post of Collector of the Customs. Capt. Tichenor, still envisioning Port Orford as a second San Francisco, and having more political influence than Dunbar, was awarded the post. He immediately requested permission to occupy the site. The issue was tossed around in typical bureaucratic fashion as Dunbar had possession of the lease; Meservey was squatting on the grounds; Tichenor had the customs appointment and the site of the fort was within the boundary of Tichenor's Donation Land Claim. Situation normal, all fouled up.

Eventually, all was resolved as the parties moved on to more rewarding pursuits and finally the Great Fire of 1868 reduced all vestiges of Fort Orford to ashes, memories and memoirs. A historical marker was placed by the Curry County Historical Society at the southwest corner of Sixth and Oregon Streets marking the northeast corner of the fort compound. History buffs who stay at the Neptune Motel in Port Orford will sleep near where the guardhouse once stood. The five acre compound commanded a spectacular view of the roadstead. Oregon Street, which runs north-south, forms the east boundary while an extension of Seventh Street would form the northerly limits. Graveyard Point, the site of several unmarked soldiers' graves, lies on the westerly side and the Pacific Ocean marks the southern boundary. The following is a composite of the post returns of Fort Orford which were filed at Fort Vancouver. Months that are missing were originally reported as "no change in personnel."

September 14, 1851 - First Artillery, Company I. Twenty men transferred from

Astoria, Lt. P. T. Wyman in command. Fort Orford established pursuant to order number 15, Division of the Pacific, August 19, 1851.

October, 1851 - No change in personnel. A letter of October 1, from Adj. Gen., Pacific Division, gives instruction concerning Indian affairs and the military reservation at Fort Orford.

October, 1851 - Field return of a detachment of United States troops en route for the Coquille River, Oregon Territory. Silas Casey, Colonel, U.S.Army., in command. Companies A, C, E, First Dragoons. 191 men, 11 officers. No wounded. Officers: Capt. Elias Klaus, Quartermaster; John Campbell, Asst. Surgeon; Henry Stanton, 1st Lt., First Dragoons; Horatio Gates Gibson, 1st Lt., 3rd Artillery; George Stoneman, 2nd Lt., First Dragoons; Robert S. Williamson, 2nd Lt., Corps of Engineers and Thomas Wright, 2nd Lt., First Dragoons.

November, 1851 - No change in personnel at the fort.

November, 1851 - On detached service, Brevet Lt. Col.Silas Casey. First Dragoons, Companies A (64 men), C (63 men), E (71 men); Third Artillery, Company I (1 man); Second Infantry, Company G (1 man). Company A encamped at the Coquille River, Camp Abbeyville, Oregon Territory; Company C exploring a route to the Oregon Road from Fort Orford. A. J. Smith, Stanton, Bradford, Couts exploring, Stoneman at Abbeyville.

December, 1851 - Ninety two men under Horatio Gates Gibson, 1st Lt., Third Artillery. First Dragoons, Company C, 63 men; First Artillery, Company I, 21 men. Five temporarily at the post. Officers: Gibson, Kaus, August V., Wyman present. Smith, Stanton, Serrel, Stoneman, Williamson absent.

February, 1852 - Command changes to Henry W. Stanton, 1st Lt., First Artillery. Stanton joined from detached service, 19th February, 1852.

March, 1852 - Command changes to Lt. P. T. Wyman, 85 men. Lt. Stanton to Camp Castaway March 2nd with 15 men. Lt. Horatio Gates Gibson transferred March 11th. Smith, Stanton, Stoneman and Williamson still on detached duty.

May, 1852 - Stanton assumes command, May 12th. 83 men.

June, 1852 - Wyman assumes command, June 20th. Stanton to explore route to the Oregon-California Road.

August, 1852 - Stanton assumes command, August 27th.

September, October, November, December, 1852 - No changes, 80 men.

January, 1853 - No changes. Ordinance Sergeant Kelly joins, January 24th.

February, 1853 - Capt. Andrew Jackson Smith assumes command, February 18th. Stanton to Wyman, February 4th. Wyman transferred, February 18th. 73 men, one natural death.

William Tichenor, founder of Port Orford, and the propeller-driven steamer, "Sea Gull."

Drawing of Port Orford in 1859. Courtesy of author.

Port Orford about 1943.

Scenic view of Port Orford with Oregon Coast Highway 101.

Old country tractor at Sixes River about 1913.

Port Orford area harvested much timber as indicated by the rig pictured about 1922.

W. G. T'Vault, Postmaster General.

Hauling salmon from the Sixes River about 1910.

Chief Te Cum Tom (Old John), head of the Port Orford Quo-To-Mahs Indian tribe.

General Edward O. C. Ord, Captain Company B, 3rd Artillery, in Rains' expeditions 1855; Company K, Wrights expedition 1858; in command at Fort Vancouver, March 31 - May 7, 1861. Photo courtesy of Oregon Historical Society.

Louis Knapp, builder of the famous Knapp Hotel. He was a pioneer and member of the Oregon State Legislature.

Captain J. M. Kirkpatrick, leader of the nine heroes of the battle of Battle Rock.

Artistic rendition of Indians attacking Battle Rock, Port Orford.

The Hughes Ranch House near Sixes River about 1900.

Early auto road, Langlois, Oregon about 1910.

Cape Blanco Lighthouse, Oregon Coast Highway.

Joaquin Miller "Poet of the Sierras" in buckskin costume.

S. S. Cottoneva beached at Port Orford (see chapter on Shipwrecks).

Port Orford salvagers removing timber that floated ashore from one of numerous wrecks that occurred off the rugged Pacific Ocean coastline.

Elk River School about 1915.

District 15, Grammar School at Cape Blanco, Hughes Ranch, about 1895.

*Gilbert Gable and Van DeGrift about to
blow the heads at Port Orford in 1935.*

Gilbert Gable and party at Floras Lake near Port Orford.

Jetty dedication with Oregon Governor Martin and Secretary of State Snell — 1935.

The S. S. Shasta swings to her mooring at Port Orford's new breakwater dock – the only natural deepwater harbor in a thousand miles of the west coast. Port Orford, Oregon, Labor Day, 1935.

Cheese factory at McMullen's, Denmark, about 1915.

Survivor Bob Adams of Salt Lake city, Utah points out the area where his ship, the Richfield Oil tanker S. S. Larry Doheney, was torpedoed by the Japanese Submarine I-25 near Port Orford on October 5, 1942.

The Richfield Oil tanker S. S. Larry Doheney was torpedoed by the Japanese Submarine I-25 on October 5, 1942.

The 350 foot Japanese submarine I-25 was one of a small flotilla that patrolled the west coast during the early stages of World War II, sinking merchantmen, a Russian submarine and shelling targets at Long Beach, California and at the mouth of the Columbia River.

U. S. Naval Institute photo of Chief Flying Officer Nobuo Fujita – the only pilot to bomb the U. S. Mainland. Fujita has visited this area twice on good-will missions and in 1962 presented his samurai sword to the City of Brookings.

Old Roosevelt Highway at Hubbards Creek about 1920.

The famous Port Orford Lindberg House about 1914.

Adolphson's Mill at Elk River, located west of Marsh Ranch. Team on the left driven by A. J. Marsh.

Axtels, one of the early families in the Port Orford area at their ranch on Elk River.

Dance pavilion Port Orford Agate Carnival 1914.

"Crankin' her up," about 1914. The Zumwalt boys watch the parade of feed and seed trying to go by. First Masonic Hall was above the drug store located where Orford's parking lot is today. Note steps going up to Leslie Tichenor's old home place at the end of the street.

Turn of the century shoppers at unidentified Port Orford dry goods store.

Two unknown turn of the century women.

Lightering freight at Rogue River about 1915.

March, April, May, June, July, 1853 - No changes. 60 men.

August, 1853 - Stanton relieved A. J. Smith August 15th. Williams relieves Stanton, August 27th.

September, 1853 - No changes. 14 men.

October, 1853 - No changes. 11 men.

November, 1853 - Command changes to August V. Kautz, 2nd Lt., 4th Infantry.

December, 1853 - No changes. 9 men.

January, 1854 - No changes. 7 men.

February, 1854 - No changes. 6 men. Private Dan Fall to Presidio, accidentally injured by the falling of tree whilst cutting fuel for use at the garrison on the 4th of February.

March, 1854 to March, 1855 - No changes with the exception of the arrival, on May 10, 1854, of Company B, 3rd Artillery, 24 men. J. Milhaus joins in June, 1854.

April, 1855 - Command changes to John Milhaus, Asst. Surgeon, September 11th. Kautz on detached service.

May, 1855 - Command to Kautz May 7th. Milhaus to Fort Vancouver.

June, 1855 - No changes. 26 men. Rodney Glisan, Asst. Surgeon joins, June 21st.

July, 1855 - Command to Glisan, July 22nd. Kautz to Coos and Umpqua Rivers.

August, 1855 - Kautz in command. Kautz and Glisan attending a council of the surrounding Indian tribes at Myrtle Grove, Rogue River, Oregon Territory.

September, 1855 - 51 men and officers. Company G, 4th Infantry and Company H, 3rd Artillery. 48 men. Officers: August V. Kautz, 2nd Lt., 4th Infantry; Rodney Glisan, Asst. Surgeon; John Chandler, 2nd Lt., 3rd Artillery. Detached: John F. Reynold, Bvt. Maj., Capt. 3rd Artillery. On detached service commanding Company A, 3rd Artillery. Ordered to join per General Order #77: James Hardie, 1st Lt., 3rd Artillery; Richard Arnold, 1st Lt., 3rd Artillery; John Drysdale, 2nd Lt., 3rd Artillery.

October, 1855 - Command to John Chandler, 2nd Lt., 3rd Artillery. Lt. Kautz and detachment of Company H, 3rd Artillery on reconnaissance of road from Fort Orford to Fort Lane, Oregon Territory, October 2, 1855.

November, 1855 - Kautz in command. Reported back November 18, 1855. 49 men. October 25th, Killed in action: David Adams and John Hill, Privates, 3rd Artillery. October 31, 1855; Wounded in action: Phillip Eggley, Pvt., 3rd Artillery. Kautz slightly wounded in an affair with Indians October 25, 1855, six miles from the Oregon Road between Grave and Cow Creeks, Oregon Territory.

December, 1855 - No changes. 49 men.

January, 1856 - Command to John F. Reynolds. August V. Kautz to Fort Stillicum. Lts. Chandler and Drysdale on the field.

February, 1856 - No changes. 47 men. Letter authorizes Lt. Chandler to remain at post until completion of buildings he is engaged on. (Stockade, wall and glacis.) Lts. Chandler and Drysdale joined post February 14, 1856.

March, 1856 - No changes. 175 men, 1 musician. Company H, 3rd Artillery, 85 men. Company G, 4th Infantry, 83 men. Officers: Robert Buchanan, Col., 4th Infantry; John Fulton Reynolds, Capt.; Robert McFeely, 1st Lt., 4th Infantry; John Chandler, 2nd Lt., 3rd Artillery; John Drysdale, 2nd Lt., 3rd Artillery. E. A. Hillman employed at the post. Letter assigns Col. Buchanan to the command of the District of Southern Oregon and Northern California and directs the troops therein to open attack against the Indians. Dated March 8, 1856. Order March 8, 1856, orders movement of troops from Fort Orford, Fort Lane and Crescent City to the mouth of the Illinois River.

April, 1856 - Command to Robert McFeely. Wounded: William Nash, Sgt., 3rd Artillery, Co. B, in an affair with Indians on Rogue River, March 26th. John Mahoney, Pvt., same. Pvts. Dave Kennedy,William Garry and Kenny Hugh all wounded in an affair with Indians at the mouth of the Illinois River, March 23, 1856. Circular relating to the firing of the ball cartridge. Buchanan, Glisan and Agur in the field. Reynolds, Hardie, Drysdale and Arnold to the field, April 2nd. Nine civilians employed at the post during the month. Viz: five carpenters, four laborers. Rate of compensation $5.00 per day for carpenters and $3.00 per day for laborers. Civilian physician E. A. Hilman discharged by reason of expiration of contract, April 14th.

May, 1856 - Command to R. McFeely. 51 men. Paymaster here May 30th. A. Coffee, Bvt. Lt. Col., and Capt. R. E. Clary, Quartermaster. Buchanan, Augur, Kautz and Chandler out since May 1st. May 24th, pack train to the Illinois River.

June, 1856 - 244 men. Company C, 1st Dragoons, 83 men. Company G, 4th Infantry, 123 men. Temporarily at post 31 men. 728 Indians mustered. Letter of June 16th relative to the hanging of a Port Orford Indian and disapproving of Agent Olney's course, etc., etc. June 2, a detachment to the Rogue River, Oregon Territory. Officers: R. Buchanan, Colonel; J. Chandler, 2nd Lt.; G. Ihrie, Lt.; C. Crane, Asst. Surgeon; R. Glisan, Asst. Surgeon; J. Milhaus, Asst. Surgeon; A. J. Smith, Captain; R. McFeely, 2nd Lt.; N. B. Sweitzer, 1st Lt. Battle of Big Bend: Killed in Action: Frederick Cannon, Pvt., 1st Dragoons (9 additional KIA's were reported by Capt. A. J. Smith in post returns of Fort Lane, near Table Rock, Jackson County.) Wounded in Action: Christopher Frazer, Pvt., 1st Dragoons; Joseph T. Caag, Pvt., 1st Dragoons; Michael O'Leary, Pvt., 1st Dragoons; Charles Quail, Pvt., 1st Dragoons; Joe Crinian, Sgt., 4th Infantry; Ed Cavanaugh, Pvt., 4th Infantry; Timothy Murray, Pvt., 4th Infantry; Patrick Roack, Pvt., 4th Infantry; Bernard Weaver, Pvt., 4th Infantry; John White, Pvt., 4th Infantry. Medical Nurses: John Wersale and Daniel McLeary, Pvts., 3rd Artillery, and John Barry and

John Schmidt., Pvts., 4th Infantry. Cook: John Schmidt., Pvt., 4th Infantry.

July, 1856 - R. McFeely in command. 26 men.

August, 1856 - Glisan and Reynolds detached, August 13th.

September, 1856 - 4 men. Indian rifles sent to Benecia, California. General orders announcing the death of Bvt. Brig. Gen. Henry Stanton. (Killed by Apaches.) Post abandoned on August 22nd, pursuant to General Orders Number 19, Department of the Pacific.

Treasury Department, September 11, 1862 - Refers to correspondence relative to occupancy of Fort Orford as a custom house. Says that the lease to Dunbar was without consideration and that the decision of the question rests entirely with the Secretary of War.

Treasury Dept., Sept. 11, 1862

Sir,

I have the honor to acknowledge your letter of the 5th instant and enclosures relating to the occupancy of Fort Orford, Oregon, for the use of the Customs, and requesting me to take such action as the case seems to require. The collector at Fort Orford made application to me to occupy the buildings of this old fort for the customs, no buildings being as yet provided for him; and on 24 March last, I requested, "if there be no objection to such occupancy you would so instruct the Commanding Officer of the Department." And on 2 April, Gen. Thomas wrote to Gen. Wright to, "comply with the request of the Secretary of the Treasury if it can be done without endangering the securing of the post."

It has since been discovered that this Fort was leased to L.W. Dunbar for ten years from the 1st of May, 1860, (a lease without consideration) unless the premises should, previous to that time, be required for military use or it would be deemed advisable to sell them.

It does not appear that the buildings of this old fort are required for military purposes, and if this be so, it would seem fitting that the United States should have the use of this property if not for military, for civil purposes.

But this is a matter outside of a power possessed by me, and whatever cause shall be adopted by the War Dept. will be acquiesced in by the Treasury.

With great respect,

_____

Secretary of the Treasury

To: G. E. M. Stanton, Secretary of War

Fort Orford, Oregon Territory, July 14, 1856 - Enclosed contracts for transportation on the steamer *Columbia* from that place as follows:

1. Company F, 4th Infantry to Portland. Forty (40) dollars each for the officers and twenty (20) dollars each for the men.

2. Company B, 3rd Artillery to San Francisco. Fifty (50) dollars each for the officers and twenty-five (25) dollars each for the men.

3. A number of Indians (prisoners) to Portland at ten (10) dollars each. Also orders pertaining thereto. BH 39

Fort Orford, Oregon Territory, July 14th, 1856

Gentlemen:

I have the honor to transmit herewith contracts made with W.L. Dall, Master of the steamship *Columbia* for the transportation of troops and Indian prisoners of war; and the order pertaining thereto.

I am Gentlemen, Very Respectfully

Your Obedient Servant,

Robert MacFeely, 1st Lt., 4th Infantry, AAGM

Headquarters, Fort Orford, Oregon Territory, District of Southern Oregon and Northern California, July 4th, 1856 - Order number 5. Directs acting Adjutant General McFeely to furnish transportation for companies F, 4th Infantry and B, 3rd Artillery and Indian "prisoners of war."

Headquarters, Fort Orford, Oregon Territory, District of Southern Oregon and Northern California, July 4th, 1856 - Order number 6. (Extract) 2st Lt. Robert McFeely, 4th Infantry. Acting Adjutant General McFeely will furnish transportation for the commands of Captains Ord and Floyd-Jones, making a separate contract for the passage and fare of the Indians to Portland. By order of Bvt. Lt. Col. Robert C. Buchanan. (J. S. Chanoler)

Lt. Ihrie, Fort Orford, July 3, 1856 - Encloses the following papers: (Accounts) for 1st (dr): Monthly papers for March, 1856. Duplicate contract with Robert Whitman to furnish 82 pack mules at $3 per day. Order assigning him to perform the duties of acting Assistant Commanding Officer. Copy of order assigning him to the duties of acting Commanding Officer.

Fort Orford, Oregon Territory, July 3rd, 1856

To Bvt. Maj. Gen. Thomas S. (Dewulf), Quartermaster General

U.S. Army, Washington, D.C.

Sir:

I have the honor to acknowledge the receipt of a copy of "Regulations for the Quartermaster's Department" on the 11th.

I also have the honor to enclose authority for duties of A. A. R. M.; duplicate copies of contracts; monthly returns for March, 1856, and Quarterly Returns for the first quarter of 1856.

I am, Sir, respectfully your obedient servant,
George S. Ihrie, 2nd Lt., 3rd Artillery, A.A.G.M.
Copy of "Special Orders Number 2" assigning Lt. Ihrie to duties of A.A.G.M.

Headquarters, Crescent City, California, District of Southern Oregon and Northern California. March 8, 1856 - Special order extract: 2nd Lt. George P. Ihrie, 3rd Artillery will perform the duties of acting assistant adjutant General to the District of Southern Oregon and Northern California. By order of Bvt. Col. Robert C. Buchanan. Signed, George P. Ihrie, 2nd Lt., 3rd Artillery, A. A. G. M.

Washington, D.C.
July 1, 1923
Postmaster
Port Orford, Oregon
Dear Sir:

In October, 1851, I was ordered to Port Orford on an expedition against hostile Coquille Indians, and I later built the military post out of the abundant timber thereabouts. I left it in March, 1852, and wended my way to Eastport, Main ... the two extremes of the continent. Later in 1855, I stepped ashore there on my way to the Columbia River. I have not seen it since, but would like a picture of it as it is now. I recall the names of some of the officers there, more or less temporarily; General Silas Casey, George Stoneman, Lt. Stanton, Capt. Kane and others that I do not recall. Can you send me photographs of the town as it is now? It was then a wilderness of forest.

I was then in my 25th year and I am now in my 96th year, but I look back to my sojourn there and with the Coquille Indians with much satisfaction. I also built the military post of Fort Bragg, California and of Fort Churchill in Nevada. I have views of the former as it was and is. The cost of the pictures I shall be glad to remit to you.
Very sincerely yours,
Horatio Gates Gibson
Brig. Gen. U.S.A., Ret.
Washington, D.C.

The following is a brief description of the buildings as shown in the drawing on the opposite page. Present day location is south of Seventh Street and west of Oregon Street at the south edge of the city, Port Orford, Curry County, Oregon. The grounds are now occupied by the Neptune Motel, the old Port Orford High School, the remains of

Castaway Lodge and one single family dwelling.

The headland in the background of the drawing is Graveyard Point which extends in a southerly direction and forms the western side of the roadstead. About 30 percent of it has been blown away for use as a jetty (which subsequently washed away). The building in the foreground is the officers quarters as the building beyond (center) is the officers mess. These and the two buildings at far left (barracks) were dismantled and moved to Fort Umpqua. The remaining buildings of the row were storehouses for supplies and ordinance. The guardhouse stands just to the right of the flagstaff on the bluff. The stockade and walls are not pictured. The building on the extreme right is a canvas covered stable and blacksmith shop. The two small buildings at center and upper right center are the post backhouse and a small cabin respectively.

9

Geology And Flora And Fauna

The area from Humbug Mountain to the Sixes River comprises the northernmost limits of the Klamath Mountains, a complex range which runs diagonally across the Oregon and California border areas. The river bottom lands upon which the larger ranches of the area are located and the marine terrace lands around Cape Blanco and Port Orford are, geologically speaking, recent deposits laid down during the Pleistocene Age (the age of man). The massive Otter Point formation of Blacklock Point and the headlands at Port Orford date back to the Upper Jurassic Age, or about 145 million years ago. A mental trip spanning 160 million years of chaotic geological occurrences might be summarized as follows:

160   Galice formation; a rock base formed in a trough that stretched from the Klamath Mountains to the Wallowas.

135   Nevadan Orogeny; a mountain building period caused by the tectonic movement of the oceanic plate under the continental plate. Gold, copper, serpentine, gabbros and diorites were emplaced during this dramatic period.

90   A volcanic trench occurred or developed near the present coastline. Thrusting reoccurred in surges over a 70 million-year span from the Nevadan Orogeny which left the Galice and Otter Point formations in disarray and heavily fractured.

65   The Cretaceous Age. Erosion had reduced most of south-western Oregon to sea level and eventually a tropical ocean covered the region.

38   This period (Eocene) was highlighted by another span of plate tectonics which brought about folding and faulting of the rocks, and of course more confusion to the future geologists.

15   The upper marine terraces were formed during the Miocene and Pliocene Ages and eventually uplifted. These terraces are made up of marine sediment of upwards to 3,000 feet in depth.

2   Lower marine terraces formed which at one time extended many miles (25) to the west. Wave action and rising ocean levels caused by the receding glaciers of the Ice Ages have eroded this terrace to its present coastline.

This erosion continues to chip away at the terraces and low lying sand dikes end eventually, as the ice packs at the poles recede and ocean levels rise, the river bottom lands will become salt water marshes and Garrison Lake will once again evolve into a salt water lagoon or a shallow bay. Oceanographers predict this eventuality by the year 2050.

Fourteen soil types are found in the Port Orford-Sixes River area and include: Bayside (Be), Sixes River Pasture; Blacklock (B1), cranberry bog and Christmas tree lands near the airport; Duneland (Ad), adjacent to coastline; Ebson, Orford, Sebastion and Trask found on the upper reaches of the Sixes and Elk Rivers; Ferrelo (Fe), lower Crystal Creek and Sixes bottom; Gardner (Ga), flat river bottom lands along Sixes and Elk Rivers at Woodworth's Litterell's and Hughes' ranches; Langlois (Lg), tidal flats at Sixes; Knappa (Kp), well drained soils mainly sited north of Elk River on lower McKenzie Ranch; Nehalem (Nh), upper river frontage on Sixes and Elk and lower Elk river bottom lands; Netarts (Nt), stabilized dunes at Port Orford; Winchuck (Wc), along Sixes River above Dry Creek.

Flora and Fauna

There are no less than 179 species of birds observable around the Port Orford area of which 59 are resident while the others are seen seasonally or as they migrate. Bird lovers are treated to the best of many habitats as migrants pass by or are driven shoreward by gale winds at sea. The Bonaparte's gull is very noticeable in May as thousands stream by on their trek from the Yucatan to Alaska, while magnificent whistler swans can be seen in pairs or flocks. Bald eagles sometimes feed at the surf line and the resident gulls badger them in flight. The eagles, drenched with water by their fish-catching dives, shake vigorously, almost dog-ike as they attempt to gain altitude to clear away from the swoops of the pesky gulls who in turn seem always to manage to keep a wing-length away from the fierce talons of the hungry eagles.

Forty years ago murres were common along the rocky coastline and Battle Rock was a favorite nesting site for the birds, if you can call a rock ledge a nest. Today they are rarely seen as humans have encroached on their domain. Aside from the high winds which make walkers and standers out of the flyers, the feathered population of the area fare pretty well in the wild, with human assistance of feeders and tender loving care. There are still some hunters,however, that must prove their shooting skills and raise havoc by indiscriminate killing of non-game birds and animals. Only education and understanding will eradicate that problem.

Around the turn of the century a market for murre eggs was developed in San Francisco by George Forty who gathered upwards of 200 dozen of the irregular-shaped, blue-mottled gems from off shore rocks each week during the egg laying season.

Nearly 40 species of mammals are to be found in this area headed by the magnificent whales which are plentiful during the migrating season, May through September. Roosevelt elk, reintroduced within the last 20 years, thrive along the upper reaches of Elk River but do on occasion wander down river to range on the ranch lands. These deep forest denizens provided Indian and settler with easily obtained sustenance — so easy that in a few short years after white settlement the herds were decimated and were unable to sustain their numbers. The graceful blacktail deer range throughout the area and are probably beneficiaries of human encroachment as they thrive in logged-off areas, cleared farmlands and, of course, they know every orchard and garden plot in the area. Whether pet or pest, they are a favorite subject for artists and shutterbugs. Although rarer, one may occasionally sight cougar, ringtail cats, marten, weasels, fox or northern flying squirrels. (See "Resource Analysis of the Elk and Sixes Watershed," Marianne Sandstrom-Schultz, Appendix 5, pp 14-18)

The Port Orford area, at the time of the first settlement, was heavily timbered. The bottom lands along the rivers were shaded by the huge, limby spruce and the mountainous hinterlands were covered with huge stands of fir, hemlock, alder and cedar. The Quo-to-mah Indians were well aware of the easily worked durable wood and used it almost exclusively for the construction of their houses (wickiups) and canoes. The first sawmills in the area began cutting and shipping cedar lumber as early as 1854. The harvest of the prized tree has continued ever since and Japan has purchased millions of board feet of cedar logs since the early 1920s, paying astronomical prices for it.

Within the last 20 years it has not been the saw that has threatened the Port Orford Cedar but rather a water born spore of the pathogen Phytophthera Lateralis which attacks the root of the defenseless tree and is usually always fatal. Although difficult to control, efforts being made to minimize the spore damage include careful drainage and slope management and appear at this juncture to be successful in saving the Port Orford Cedar from extinction.

10

Land Acquisition Methods And The Hughes Ranch

There were several methods of acquiring the government lands that were available under the Homestead Act. The Homestead Entry allowed a citizen 160 acres (320 after 1909) of non-timber, mineral or irrigable land to prove upon by residency and improvement within three years. When proven up, a patent was granted. After 1909, a filer could, after 14 months, pay $1.25 per acre in order to obtain title thereby commuting the three year requirement. Other methods of securing lands were cash entry, timber cash entry, soldiers warrants or script, Indian allotments and Donation Land Claims. Only two of the latter were filed and patented in the Port Orford area, that of Tichenor's at Port Orford and the Dyer's claim at the mouth of Elk River.

It was during this period that the larger ranches began to be blocked in and cleared. Although the Great Fire of 1868 destroyed a great deal of brush and timber in the hills, most of the bottom lands along the Sixes and Elk Rivers were covered with large stands of spruce. As this wood had little marketable value, these great monarchs were drilled and burned, the stumps blown and rooted out with teams of horses. Brush was cleared by hand, the labor for which was contracted by the acre. Several families of Sixes and Elk River Tututnis left the reservation, living unmolested along the rivers and working, from time to time, on the Joe Ney, McKenzie and Hughes Ranches. Aside from meeting local beef requirements, stock was sometimes driven over the mountains to the railhead at Roseburg … a long and costly drive. Dairy operations blossomed in the 80s and 90s. The Zumwalt, Marsh, Forty, McKenzie and Hughes Ranches began building fine dairy herds from which butter was produced and marketed in San Francisco in 25 pound boxes. It should be noted that the early trade developed between San Francisco and Port Orford rather than Portland.

The Hughes Ranch

Since the enrollment of the Hughes House upon the National Register of Historic Places in the early 1980s, a great deal of interest has been generated concerning the development of the ranch and the people responsible. In the interest of keeping the story as close to the facts as possible, I decided to record and publish the information compiled and held by me as a fourth generation member of the Hughes family.

My grandmother, Alice (Hughes) Masterson, was the eldest Hughes daughter, born to Jane and Patrick Hughes at Port Orford in 1864. She resided on the ranch for nearly 50 years until her passing in 1929. My father, John Patrick Masterson, was closely associated with the ranch for nearly 36 years and moved there with his bride, Vernice, in 1921, residing in the main house for a year until their new home was completed. It was located where the Park Manager's residence is now.

It was in this comfortable home that I was raised along with my brother Jack and sister Martha. Of the Hughes offspring, I knew five of the seven, as James and Alice had passed on before my arrival on the scene.

I truly regret not having the opportunity to learn from Edward, the eldest Hughes brother, first hand of the early days on the ranch but I was too young for that sort of thing. I learned much information from my parents, Annie (Doyle) Hughes and neighbors. Ranch records, school reports, old photo albums, newspaper clips and personal correspondence have added to and enriched the interesting story which I relate to readers in the following pages.

The Hughes Ranch was located close to Oregon's oldest and most famous landmark ... Cape Blanco. Sighted and named in 1603 by the Spanish explorer, Martin D'Aguilar, sailing the little vessel *Tres Reyes,* this historic cape could have possibly been the one seen by Bartolome Ferell(o) 61 years earlier in 1542. In any event, the windswept majestic cape is the oldest landmark in Oregon. Captain Vancouver renamed it Cape Orford in 1792, but his attempt to anglicize it's name failed to take hold. Cape Blanco was for many years the farthest west point in the United States, but when Washington gained statehood in 1889, Cape Alava on the Olympic Peninsula bumped Blanco to second place, although Blanco is the farthest west one can drive to.

The cape is, geologically speaking, an ancient marine terrace that at one time extended much farther west, eons ago. Tectonic activity and erosion have interacted over the thousands of years to form what we see today. Historians have concluded that the early Spanish captains dubbed the cape "white" for the chalk cliffs (which are in reality non-existent), or for the layers of shells seen on the south side. These shell layers are barely discernable at a close distance let alone far out to sea. Unless a mariner is inside the formidable reefs, west of the cape, the prominence is difficult to make out, and if he is due west only the light from the lighthouse, built in 1870, gives away the cape's position. No matter really ... the cape is a special place which is enjoyed by land-lubbers and feared by seafarers.

To the north of the cape lies the Sixes River which forms the northern boundary of the lower Hughes Ranch. The bottom lands near the mouth are made up of poorly drained lands which are for the most part unproductive for agricultural purposes aside from marginal pasturing of sheep. Wildlife thrives there in abundance in a delicate balance of nature. Soil scientists classify the lands of the lower river as Nehalem, the cape as Knappa and the balance of the ranch as Langlois type. In summary, this means that without intensive drainage of the bottom lands and continuous clearing and burning of the uplands, the property is best suited for sheep pasture. The heavily tussocked areas one sees today were productive hayfields in the 1930s.

Each ranch in the Port Orford area has it's own common names for certain areas depending upon the geographical features or the use of the structures. The following are some that I recall, or have heard described:

The Cape – That area from the cemetery to the lighthouse. This area was heavily timbered until the 1950s with spruce and pine. The state highway was constructed in the 1920s and evidence of the Old Cape Road which traversed the land from north to south is still marked by wagon wheel ruts west of the cemetery.

The Island – The large hummock situated to the right (north) of the main road as you cross the first bottom. This area was left unfenced and provided sanctuary for the stock in times of high water.

The Church – The small mission church named "Mary, Star Of The Sea, built in 1892 on the cape. It was the farthest west church structure in the United States.

The Orchard – Located just east of the island near the river, this large orchard provided apples, plums, pears and cherries for the ranch families as well as many neighbors and friends but is now nonproductive.

The Orchard Hole – Features a large rock in the middle of the river that provided an excellent swimming and diving spot, as well as a well-fished haven for the wily chinook, steelhead and trout.

The Ford – The shallows located just upriver from the Orchard Hole was used as an animal and equipment crossing to the James Hughes Ranch north of the river.

The Boathouse – A commercial boat rental and landing facility located at the first bend of the river and operated by Pat B. Miller and Dolly Smith in the 1930s. A slaughter house was located to the east of the main house on the river and used in the late 1800s to prepare fish netted commercially.

The <u>Swinging</u> <u>Bridge</u> – A narrow suspension bridge located near the first bend, connected the Hughes and the Sweet Ranches and provided a precarious walkway for the Sweet family school bus on the south side.

The <u>Garden</u> – A fenced area about 1/2 mile from the house near the old original barn and farmstead. The deer loved it.

The <u>Potato</u> <u>Patch</u> – An acre or so of ground a little west of the island that produced a bountiful crop.

The <u>Mines</u> – An old cabin and spring on the beach, south of the present park parking area. The original mine was further south towards Elk River but this area was used until the mid-1940s.

<u>Duffy</u> <u>Place</u> – Farmstead of Michael Duffy, and close Irish friend of Patrick, who worked in the mines and on the ranch. Property now held by the VanLoos.

<u>Sullivan's</u> <u>Gulch</u> – A low swampy area near the original mine unproductive for the most part. It is an ancient river bed now named Beaver Marsh.

The <u>Barn</u> – The main barn located 14 mile east of the house. Built in 1905, the complex included a separator room and creamery.

The <u>Tin</u> <u>Barn</u> – Metal barn located just under the hill as you come down the first grade. Used for winter hay storage.

The <u>Shed</u> – A large machine shop and storage facility sites just south of the cut of the roadbed at the Island. Old tractor stored there.

<u>Castle</u> <u>Rock</u> – The largest rock at the north beach, known also as Thomas's Rock.

<u>Riverside</u> – Name Father Hughes used for the ranch. He always addressed his envelopes with this term on the lower left hand side.

The <u>Light</u> – The term applied to the lighthouse. You always "went up to the light."

<u>Cape</u> <u>Blanco</u> <u>University</u> – Name given to the one room schoolhouse of District 15, on the cape by the Hughes's. Built in 1882.

The <u>Chapel</u> – The small room at the head of the stairs equipped with a small altar and religious statues and used by Father Hughes during his visits.

The <u>Wash</u> <u>House</u> – Bunkhouse, washroom, potato and tool storage west of house.

The <u>Smoke</u> <u>House</u> – Two-story structure between the main house and the smaller residence used for meat and fish smoking.

Flora and Fauna

Nature endowed the ranch with a wide and diverse cover of flora. One can identify dozens of varieties of delicate wildflowers on the cape along with huckleberry, strawberry, salmonberry, thimbleberry, blackberry, blackcaps, salal and blueberries flourishing next to rhododendrons, azaleas and other beautiful shrubs. The overstorey consists mainly of Sitka spruce, shore pine, fir, hemlock and cedar. Large chittums are found in the western end of Sullivan's Gulch. This bark along with the blossoms from the digitalis (foxgloves) were harvested and sold as they possessed medicinal qualities.

When the Hughes Ranch was settled, all the bottom lands were covered with huge stands of Sitka spruce trees. They were so thick that it was nearly impossible to drive a team and wagon through them. Even the extreme edges of the steep bluffs at the cape were covered, and when Louis Knapp, Sr. cleared the land for the construction of the lighthouse in 1869, he managed to push the trees over the bluffs and burned them on the rocks below. The uplands near the church, school and cemetery were not cleared until the late 1940s and '50s when Bud Hall began to clear and fence the lands for use as sheep pasture.

In 1928, Fred Lockly, the "Journal Man," interviewed Father John Hughes for his column in that Portland paper. John was quoted as observing, "When I was a boy, Curry County was a hunter's paradise. The hills were full of deer, bears, cougars and the streams were filled with fish." I am sure that during the early years the Hugheses took wild game for their larder, but in their later years I cannot recall any of the uncles taking any game except salmon. (The only exception was the occasional skunk that invaded the smoke house.) My father did some trapping in the 1920s but it seemed he caught more skunks than mink or martin, and he would then feel sorry for the mustiledae and make pets of them, making mother and uncles somewhat unhappy. The deer population was pesky as they consumed the saltlicks placed out for the stock and made short work of planted flowers and garden vegetables. On any night the ranch came alive with the nocturnal critters … especially the orchard. No one bothered them except an occasional poacher who was promptly ordered off the ranch. Even the stock dogs were not upset by the numerous animals that roamed the ranges.

From the vantage points on the cape, one can observe the great grey whales as they migrate from Alaska to Baja and the Gulf of California. These magnificent creatures are favorites of locals and tourists and from time to time an older whale will take up residency in the local bays where he is watched, named and adopted by the natives. On the reefs, west of the cape, Stellar sea lions gather to feed and an occasional pup will wash ashore as will the sick or injured adults. Adult sea lions and seals enter the lower river to feed on salmon and eels, much to the chagrin of the sport fishermen.

Indian Occupation

Evidence of the everyday activities of Indian life are readily found and identified on both sides of the Sixes River. These Native Americans were made up of the linguistic stock of Athabascans, descendants of early migrations from Siberia through Alaska and Canada down as far as Arizona, perhaps 25,000 years ago. They were the Quo-to-mah bands of the Tu-tu-tunnes or Rogue Rivers and they occupied the lands from Humbug mountain to Floras Lake with large village sites at Hubbards Creek, Elk River, Sixes River and Floras Lake. A census report made by the Indian Agent Parrish, in 1854, reported 144 adults in the bands led by the headman named Hap-hult-a-lan who resided at the Sixes and a sub-chief name Tag-o-no-cia at Port Orford. The band name, Quo-to-mah, translated "people who live on bay," while the Kaltsergheatunne village meant "people who live on a point of land that extends far out into the sea." Another village site as yet not identified but associated with the Sixes River band was called Siksestunne and was the probably origin of the name Sixes. It translates "people of the far north country," and may refer to the village site at Floras Lake.

These people lived in permanent plank houses or wickiups which were placed over pits dug out three or four feet deep. Early settlers and soldiers dubbed the villages "rancheros." Stick houses of limbs and brush were used at the food gathering sites and used as temporary shelters. They harvested acorns, fished the rivers with spears and traps, gathered shell fish and killed elk by means of pit-traps placed along the known animal trails. The occasional whale or seal lion that would wash up on the beach provided a special treat. The life expectancy of the Indians was under 30 years and after the early settlers and miners made contact vast numbers died from smallpox, measles and other diseases for which they had no immunity.

After the close of the Indian War in 1856, several families returned to the Sixes River area from the reservation 150 miles on up the coast. (Siletz) They lived along the rivers, and in Port Orford, working from time to time clearing land for the ranchers, but most of the time they eked out a meager living gathering fish and acorns. Edward Hughes told of one old headman (tyee) who would examine the fish landed by the younger men along the river bank. On occasion he would throw back a nice bright fish exclaiming that it was a "Tituna" or Elk River fish and unfit to eat, thus maintaining his status as Chief. Tools, stone implements and arrow points lost by these ancient peoples were found with regularity on most areas of the ranch while the main village site on the north side of the river was excavated by amateur pot-holers many years ago.

Captain George Vancouver came to anchor near the heads at Port Orford in April, 1772, and before long, several large, dugout canoes came alongside his ships, the 340 ton

Discovery and the armed tender *Chatham.* The occupants began to barter skins and smoked fish for trinkets, iron and clothing. Vancouver noted that these people were well kempt, clean and honest. His observations give us the first credible description of the Quo-to-mahs, the roadstead and headlands at Port Orford and the cape. Jedediah Smith, leading a party of trappers and one hundred head of horses and mules, traversed the area in 1828. His unfriendly and harsh treatment of the natives (he dismantled wickiups at Rogue River in order to build rafts for the crossing) led to the nearly complete annihilation of his party at Smith River near the Umpqua River. At the mouth of the Sixes he observed only two natives, but you can be sure most of the village observed his party. The last "tyee" of the Quo-to-mah bands was "Port Orford Jake" who passed on in 1912.

Pioneer Settlement

The first white settlement occurred on the beaches south of Cape Blanco where miners set up long-toms in order to extract the fine gold occurring in the black sand deposits at Sullivan's Gulch and on the beaches. From 1854 on individuals purchased lands around the lower river and began the slow arduous task of clearing them for limited agricultural use, limited for the most part to subsistence farming due to the lack of transportation opportunities. All commerce relied on vessels plying between San Francisco and Portland and in times of adverse weather, weeks or even months might pass by without a ship risking a stop at the roadstead at Port Orford.

Patrick Hughes was born near Castlecaulield in southeastern Tyrone County in 1830. Tyrone is in present day Northern Ireland but in ancient Irish history the area was known as O'Neill Country. While most historians attribute the mass migrations from the area to the great potato famine there is ample evidence that the British "overlords" confiscated the most productive lands and left the rocky unproductive slopes to the Irish peasants. Coupling that with economic, political and religious harassment, most of the energetic young people chose to leave. Whatever the motives, Patrick Hughes took leave of his native land and immigrated to Boston where he worked as a laborer from 1850 till 1854. He married Jane O'Neill, also from Tyrone, in 1853. They decided to go west and subsequently sailed to Panama, crossed the Isthmus on horseback and sailed north to San Francisco by steamer. Jane had worked in a lamp factory in Boston, but while in San Francisco she toiled as a domestic while Patrick worked in the gold fields. He came north to Oregon in 1857, working as a laborer and prospecting for gold. The "fever" took him all the way to the Frazier River in Canada in 1859. Finally Jane wrote to him that she was coming north on the Oregon-California Road and they met at Oregon

City. In the fall of 1859, they were at Deady, Oregon, near the present day Roseburg, and in 1860 they wended their way to northern Curry County ... he still looking for gold and Jane looking for a place to start a family.

Patrick's mining interests continued for ten years until he began purchasing lands at the mouth of the river. His first recorded purchase was at the original mine site known as Sullivan's gulch (recently renamed Beaver Marsh) in 1868. The period from 1860 to the early 1880s are sketchy as there were no local newspapers or coverage in the larger metropolitan papers of happenings on the remote south coast. As noted earlier, Hughes began acquiring titles to various parcels of land around Cape Blanco in 1868. In the 1870s, he served a term as County Commissioner and served on the first County Road Viewing Committee and assisted in locating the first road surveyed from the north county line to Port Orford.

During this period nine children were born to Patrick and Jane, seven survived. Paul died in infancy and is buried on the slopes above the original farmstead. Edward, the oldest son, was born in Deady, Oregon, near present day Roseburg (Winchester), as Jane made the trip over Camas Mountain to insure medical assistance for her first birthing. The remainder of the children were born at the ranch or at Port Orford ... the records are unclear about this. Edward was born in 1862, and the youngest, Francis, entered the world in 1877. The author's grandmother, Alice, was born in 1864.

Educational opportunities for the Hughes children as far as formal local schooling was concerned were nonexistent in the late 60s and 70s. Edward was sent to a small Catholic academy at Vancouver, Washington Territory, by the name of Holy Angels College in October, 1876. There he learned the rudiments of English grammar, mathematics and history, along with, of course, catechism of the Roman Catholic religion. Upon his return to the ranch it was his duty to teach and pass on his knowledge to the younger brothers and sisters.

A small school was constructed on the hill above the farmstead in 1882, financed by the levy of a tax upon the ranches that made up the tax roll of District Number 15. In the beginning years of the district the boundaries were vague and thus the census varied from year to year. In 1889, there were 47 school age youths reported. They were from families which included the Posts, Pierces, Limpachs, Devilbliss, Ayers (Applebees) Moltons, Cornwalls, Jurgensens, McKenzies, Langlois, Hughes, Goodmans, Fitzhughs (6), and Allens. Upon the creation of new districts up river, the census leveled off as travel to the small schools was an important factor in determining the location of the school facilities. Teachers were paid $30 to $40 a month with room and board. The school terms were usually in the seasons of good weather and lasted three months. Total tax receipts rarely exceeded $160 and expenditures included firewood, chalk, an occasional book or two and teacher's salary. Textbooks were rarely lost and were used over and over. One teacher's report noted there was no dictionary at the school while another reported that the school grounds comprised of "hundreds of acres!" Another teacher reported the wood shed was very leaky and that the ventilation was more than adequate. The students referred to the little school as Cape Blanco University. A partial list of the teachers who toiled there include J. S. Hodgin, E. A. Hargreaves, A. G. Thrist, Katie Warren, W. S. Guerin, J. A. Tyler, J. J.Stanley, and Stella R. Smith. The School was closed in 1896.

Father John C. Hughes – Mary, Star of the Sea Mission

Patrick, following Irish tradition, encouraged his third son, John, to study for the priesthood. He was sent to Baltimore and Montreal and after many years of schooling became the second native Oregonian to be ordained in 1895. In 1892, Patrick decided to erect a small mission church near the cape and contracted Johan Lindberg to build it. Although never consecrated it was blessed by the bishop of the Archdiocese of Portland in 1894 and was used sparingly due to the difficulty of travel. The last occasion it was used was for Jane Hughes's funeral in 1923. It withstood the severe cape weather for nearly 70 years and was finally piled and burned in the early 1960s. It was located between Patrick's headstone and the group of markers at the old cemetery. All the remains were exhumed from this cemetery and reinterred at Mount Calvary Cemetery in Portland in the winter of 1938-1939. There were two unmarked graves in the area however … those of two children who died in infancy, born to the Charley Fortys. John served many years in Portland as parish priest at several locations. During his annual visits to the ranch he would always gather up the youngsters for an enjoyable outing. He never expounded upon religious subjects but used his time enjoying a good chew of tobacco and reliving his childhood years on the ranch he truly loved. The little chapel at the head of the stairs was kept in order for his daily mass when he came to visit which was always a great treat for his brothers, sisters, and family.

The following is a list of the Hughes children and their marital status:
Patrick, 1830 - 1901 married Jane O'Neill 1833 - 1923
Edward, born 1862 at Deady, Oregon. Remained a bachelor.
James, born 1863 at Cape Blanco, married Laura McMullen, two daughters.
Alice, born 1864 at Port Orford, married P.J. Masterson, one son and one daughter.
Paul, born 1867 at Cape Blanco, died in infancy.
John, born 1869 at Cape Blanco, ordained priest.
Mary, born 1873 at Port Orford, married Frank McMullen, five daughters and one son.

Thomas, born 1874 at Cape Blanco. Remained a bachelor.
Francis, born 1877 at Cape Blanco. Married Annie Doyle, one son.
One child died at birth.

Death of Patrick Hughes

One evening in late June, 1901, Patrick rode out on a large team horse toward Sullivan's Gulch to bring in several stray cows loose in the area. He failed to show up for the evening meal, and about seven o'clock Edward saddled a horse to go out to locate his father. He did not find him for three hours when he finally discovered him pinned under his horse in a drain ditch. Patrick was crossing a log bridge when the horse lost it's footing and fell into the ditch on top of Patrick. As the horse struggled it became apparent to Patrick that he must destroy the animal lest he be killed by the frantic kicking and struggling. He managed to extricate his pocket knife and cut the horses throat but after that was accomplished he could not struggle free. After Edward finally found him it was several more hours before help was gathered and Patrick finally freed. He was carried to the house where he died several days later on June 27th, of massive damage to his head and chest. His funeral was one of the largest held at that time in the county and was attended by friends and relatives from all over southwestern Oregon.

After the death of his father, Edward took over the management of the ranch and in 1905, a butter creamery and large barn were constructed and butter was produced, boxed in 25 pound containers, and shipped by sea from Port Orford to the San Francisco markets under the Hughes Ranch label. When the Mendocino, Marin, and Contra Costa County California dairies supplied the market the Hughes Ranch butter could not compete due to high transportation costs. Local cheese factories developed in northern Curry County supplied by milk from large dairies on the Sixes River, Elk River and Floras Creek. With the advent of World War II, the ranch found it difficult to obtain steady help to manage the large dairy and as a result the lands were used for sheep and beef cattle. By the 1960s most of the standing timber was logged and mismanagement had taken its toll. The fourth generation had become disinterested and the property was sold to the State of Oregon whose Parks Department was interested in establishing an overnight park at the cape. The old buildings were long gone and the old house was slated for demolition until pressure of sorts was brought to bear and the Parks Department began the slow process of restoration. It was then placed on the National Register of Historic Places in 1980, and is today operated as a museum by the Friends of Cape Blanco as an example of 1900 Victorian architecture and furnishings.

Anecdotes of the Hughes Ranch

In the early 1880s Patrick Hughes signed an agreement with William Windsor to deliver salmon to the "fish house on the Sixes" for the price of 25 cents apiece for fish 10 pounds or over and 10 cents for smalls. Commercial netting of fish continued on the river until the mid-twenties when it was outlawed.

In December, 1919, the Standard Oil Company tanker *J.A. Chanselor* ran aground just north of the mouth of the river in heavy fog. Aboard were 35 men, 30 of whom drowned including the son of the owner of the *Oregon Journal,* a large Portland daily newspaper, Mr. Jackson. Mrs. Jackson hired John Masterson, who was home on Christmas vacation from Corvallis, to walk the beaches each day in hopes of finding the remains of her son. He was never found. Upon the death of the father it was willed by him that his ashes be spread upon the waters where the ship foundered.

In 1860, Joaquin Miller, the celebrated "Poet of the Sierras," made a fast trip into northern Curry County and swept Minnie Myrtle Dyer, neighbor of Jane Hughes, into matrimonial bliss. So fast was the romance that the beautiful and talented Miss Dyer had no time to prepare and as a result had to borrow her wedding night attire from Jane Hughes. Jane cherished the outfit and handed it down through the family. It was displayed in time at the Hughes House. The marriage didn't last, the nightgown did … so much for whirlwind romances.

Besides the untimely death of Patrick Hughes, two other tragedies worthy of mention occurred on the ranch. In 1932, Doctor Roland Leep, husband of Agnes Hughes, was accidentally shot and killed in a hunting accident on the reef off Cape Blanco and in 1939 or 1940 Frank Cook, who worked and lived on the ranch took his own life after learning that he was rejected for enlistment into the U.S. Army. His cabin was located under the hill near the tin-barn.

There is some confusion as to the location of the school house at the ranch (District 15). In the 1920s Vernice Masterson tutored Joseph Hughes and Verlun Moore, the former the only son of Francis, while the latter lived on the James Hughes place across the river. The lessons were held in her house where the state caretaker/manager lives now. At the end of each term the boys were taken to the Sixes School and given tests to insure proper schooling. As stated previously, the one-room school was on the cape near the church.

As a very young boy, my memories of the ranch during the 1930s and early 40s are very vivid. Not long ago, a traveler stopped in Port Orford for lunch and in casual conversation mentioned that during the depression he and his family camped "on a gravel bar on Sixes River next to a large orchard." He had traveled down the coast looking for work and had found none and as a result his camp was indeed hardscrabble. About four o'clock, an older man came riding up on a black horse, examined the campers and rode away. An hour or so later he appeared again astride his horse on which was strapped bags of potatoes, onions, bacon and some fresh milk. The rider beckoned the camper to come over and he gave him the victuals.

I questioned the man regarding the appearance of the benefactor and it was indeed Edward, the eldest Hughes brother. But this was typical of this generation of the Hugheses and for that matter most of the ranching community of southwestern Oregon.

My recollections of the "uncles" leave the impression that they were mild mannered, gentlemanly, somewhat, but not overly pious (not even Father John), honest, caring and if alive today they would certainly fit into the mold of sensible environmentalists. Edward and Thomas, the bachelors, were for the most part opposites. Edward was reserved, contemplative … the type who planned ahead while Thomas was far more outgoing, humorous with a zest for life, taking advantage of the good things like nice clothes, fast horses and Buicks. Edward's dedication to the operation of the ranch did not allow time for much serious romance. Thomas was engaged to be married but a death in his bride-to-be's family forced her to take on the responsibility of raising several children and she eventually married her sister's widower. I am sure Thomas was very disappointed but in those days that was the way of life. Both brothers took their vacations in the city, usually San Francisco, combining business with pleasure on at least one trip by ship a year. They would return with new photographs, gifts for all and of course supplies and implements for the ranch. My mother told of their purchases of the newest kitchen utensils which resulted in the best equipped kitchen in the county.

The kitchen was a special place and always the center of daily activity. The large wood stove and grill had several large cast iron warming ovens above it and a large hot water tank elevated on the left side. The pantry and larder was always stocked with canned fruits and vegetables, bulk flour and sugar and usually there were several pies or loaves of bread cooling in the window. Butter was stored in brine barrels while fresh milk and cream were stored in a small, cool unfinished basement under the west side of the house, under the kitchen. Family dinners at the big house took several days to prepare and consisted for the most part of home grown morsels … except the olives which Edward loved and I hated, but as he was the patriarch, I was sure to take several when they were passed.

Electric power never reached the ranch until about 1942, and so I grew up to the hiss of the pressurized kerosene lanterns and battery radios that worked only at night and then it seemed they picked up more static than signals. It is hard to select a favorite haunt for each place of activity that I recall now has special meaning. The wash house was more than a place to clean up. Upstairs there were small sleeping rooms for ranch hands and storerooms which contained a fascinating sailing ship model, a large apple cider press and old tools by the dozens. Near the doorway leading to the washroom a musket and octagon-barreled long rifle were propped against the wall undisturbed for years while above the sink a life ring from the *Chanselor* served as mute testimony to that 1919 disaster.

The old smokehouse was rather interesting. It was two storied with a staircase and walkways inside the perimeter walls while the center was unfloored with a large fire pit. Bacon, hams, beef and salmon were hung on large hooks or racks throughout the spacious building. The warm fire or coals would occasional attract a civet cat or skunk which in turn would cause a controlled panic. The unwelcome guests were coaxed out with warm milk in order to preserve the contents of the building.

The barn which was huge by any standards offered many varied experiences to a young boy. On the walls hung harnesses, yokes, saddles, bridles and tools of a bygone era and in the east end a courting buggy and utility wagon collected the dust of many years of non-use. Near them were two large Belgian draft horses used in earlier years to pull stumps and general work, but as they aged no work was required of them and in the rainy season they stayed in the barn or corral … pampered like the pets they were. In the Spring their duty was to wander about the lower fields mowing the Canadian thistles which they relished. The peak of the barn housed the track and trolley for the hay lift. When the hay was loaded on the wagons in the fields, rope slings were lain across the load as it was built up and upon unloading the slings were attached to a mechanism that was raised by use of a pickup and pulley to the high track and when the load drew over the hay mows the trip line was yanked releasing several hundred pounds of hay in a cloud of dust and seed, thistles and weeds, and pray that you weren't caught under it. The barn ceiling was also a favorite spot for the barn swallows to build their little upside down, igloo-like mud-daubed nests and they were not to be disturbed under any condition.

Stanchions in the barn held about 60 head of dairy cows although only one side was used during my time. The herd was hand milked although an old gas DeLavel milking machine was tried but proved unsatisfactory. The herd was made up for the most part of temperamental, small teated Jerseys, but they always proved to be top butterfat producers. During the butter producing years the milk was transported by a narrow gauge rail to the creamery down towards the river where it was churned by a large steam driven paddle apparatus. The facility, although intact was never operated in the thirties. We were never allowed to play in or enter the machine room, however, the large rock outcrops near there provided us with delicious licorice fern root … real honest to goodness home grown candy.

Trips to the "orchard hole" for picnics and swimming were much fun as were the horseback rides to the beaches around the cape. Harvesting of potatoes, apples, garden vegetables and wild berries was always topped off with an impromptu picnic lunch as the resource was usually far removed from the houses.

Each December the profits for the ranch were divided equally among the family. The womenfolk fared as well as the men and for the most part the ranch was always prosperous, considering the fact that all subsistence, fuel, rents, taxes and insurance was furnished by the ranch fund. There was always funding available for the younger people to attend schools at high school or college levels … providing they maintained proper deportment and grades. The first and second generation of the Hughes family were benefactors to many church and community projects.

Special mention of Annie (Doyle) Hughes is indeed appropriate in this work. She moved to the ranch in 1905 after marrying Francis and honeymooning at the Lewis and Clark Exposition in Portland. I do believe that she hardly took her apron off her entire life save to go to church or to a rare trip to Bandon or Port Orford. Her domestic duties were never ending and covered washing clothes, cleaning house, cooking, mending or whatever for the entire family. To the Hughes brothers she was indeed a saint.

My favorite ranch-hand was a tall, willowy man named "Beany" Welch. He was always good at playing tricks or other schemes to amuse us but at the same time he kept a watchful eye out for our safety around horses, cattle or equipment. Up until World War II he had worked for many years on the ranch.

It saddens me sometimes to visit the ranch as there are very few mementos of the past, save for the old house, left that I knew. The fact that it is still there is somewhat of a miracle as the state seriously considered razing it in the early 1970s. There are parts missing or replacements that aren't quite the same but all in all it does reflect somewhat pioneer life on a ranch in the isolation of southwestern Oregon.

Shipwrecks

More often than not, a shipwreck contributes more than folklore to the local history of a given area. For isolated Curry County this fact was especially true. The earliest known wreck occurred at Port Orford in the 1830s when a Russian whaler became stranded. Russian charts, which pre-date any British or American work, indicate that soundings were made southeast of Battle Rock, perhaps during salvage operations of the wreck. The red-shirted leader of the Indian assault on the surveyors at Battle Rock in June of 1851, may have been a survivor of this early wreck who chose life among the natives to the hardships of service as a sailor for the Tsar. Since that first wreck, there have been more than 30 major mishaps near Port Orford and more than 50 along the Curry coastline, not counting numerous small boats of the local fishermen which got into trouble.

Three ships, under contract with the U. S. Army to bring supplies to Port Orford, wound up on the beach during the early 1850s. They were the *Anita,* the *Iowa* and the *Francisco.* A fourth, the *Captain Lincoln,* was driven in by a fierce gale and wound up on the north spit of the entrance to Coos Bay where 45 survivors, including 35 dragoons of "C" Company, 1st Dragoons, set up Camp Castaway, and waited three months to be rescued. (Dodge, pp. 114)

On September 6, 1895, the British steamer *Bawnmore* grounded just off Floras Lake. An engineer prospecting a port at the lake for a San Francisco firm was able to secure a lifeline to drift logs on the beach by which the crew, passengers and captain were removed from the grounded steamer across a 700 foot span. The lifesaving crew from Bandon, having to travel over 20 miles of beach, hauling their boat and equipment, arrived too late of be of "… any material assistance in saving the crew."

The vessel carried a quarter of a million dollar cargo which included live cattle, most of which were lost. The salvage rights were purchased by the engineer who first spotted the ship. The cargo included 900 tons of flour, 200 tons of potatoes, beans, onions, rice and canned goods, hardware and paints and a grand piano in a hermetically sealed container. Using a Montgomery Ward catalogue as a price guide, the salvaged goods were sold at 50 percent of value, while the flour went for $15 to $5 per ton. Local ranchers built hog pens on the beach and fattened up the critters on water-soaked spuds, rice, beans and flour, all of which was boiled and made into splendid hog food.

Also included in the cargo were numerous drums of Pacific Rubber paint of excellent quality. Needless to say, every house and barn "for a couple of hundred miles" was given a fresh coat of yellow paint. The salvage continued for nine months and eventually an auction was held and the salvage sold, including a fancy "coupe" buggy.

The *Chanselor*

According to Neonta Hall of Port Orford, a great ship disaster took place December 18, 1919, at Cape Blanco when a large oil tanker, *J. S. Chanselor,* owned by Associated Oil of San Francisco, struck a submerged rock in heavy seas and darkness, breaking it in two, the stern sinking almost immediately with great loss of life. Having delivered a cargo of 30,000 barrels of oil to Portland, at the same time assisting other vessels in breaking the ice jam in the Columbia River, she was on her return trip to San Francisco. She left Portland on December 17, 1919. The *Chanselor* was a steel vessel built in Newport News, Va. in 1910, 378 feet long, 52 feet wide, with a depth of 29.5 feet, and gross tonnage of 4,938. Ordinarily, she carried a crew of 48 men, however, on this return trip, she had a crew of 38, all of whom were lost except for the captain and two others.

One of the survivors, Earl Dooley, reported later that as soon as the distress signal sounded he rushed to the forward deck. In less than five minutes the ship had broken in two and the stern sank. Most of the sailors, engineers, oilers and steward crew were aft and all went down with that section. At the first sign of distress a life boat was launched and an attempt by the wireless man to call for help did not succeed. Ten of the men, including Captain A. A. Sawyer, got away in the life boat which drifted all night in a cold rain storm. The next morning they picked up two more of the crew who were clinging to a gang plank. Dooley, who survived the tragic wreck, had joined the *Chanselor* in Portland as a member of the steward's department. Among the ten who climbed into the lifeboat were the chief steward, a sailor named Charles Connally, two oilers and other sailors whose names Dooley did not know since he had not been aboard long. The wreck occurred at 5:55 p.m. Francis Jackson, eldest son of publisher C. S. Jackson of the Portland *Oregon Journal,* was sailing as a second assistant engineer. He was 32 years of age and went down with the stern section.

John Masterson, a student at OAC in Corvallis, was home for the Christmas vacation and told his uncle, Edward Hughes, that he "would help get the cows in for milking" on Friday morning, December 19th. John and Edward discovered the wreck in the early morning hours and immediately notified James Hughes, the keeper at the Cape Blanco light house who in turn notified proper authorities in Port Orford and the Bandon Coast Guard station. James Hughes reported the *Chanselor* almost submerged and washed within 400 feet of the shore near the mouth of the Sixes River. Only part of the bridge and the tip of the bow were above water.

Deputy Sheriff Howard W. Jetter, with Eugene White, Carl White and Clarence Wright, all of Port Orford, took George Forty's double ender surf boat, known as the *Grass Belly,* thought to have originally come from a whaling ship, and brought it over-land to the mouth of the Sixes River. Sheriff Jetter and his crew attempted to cross through the breakers to open sea north of Island Rock and hoped to reach the sinking vessel. They gained but a short distance when a heavy breaker struck the little craft and capsized it. Jetter, failing to keep his head above water, drowned. The others, managing by desperate efforts to keep afloat, were literally washed ashore. Eugene White was known to have suffered for years with lung problems due to this accident.

A telephone message was sent from the J. S. Hughes Ranch near the scene to Captain Robert Johnson of the Coast Guard station in Bandon telling of Sheriff Jetter's drowning. His body was recovered about an hour after the accident and men at the scene worked hard to resuscitate him but all signs of life had fled. The *Grass Belly* also came ashore at that time. Deputy Sheriff Jetter was a well known resident of northern Curry County and he had been placed in charge of the beach patrol. Two life buoys were washed ashore which bore the name, *J. A. Chanselor,* establishing the identity of the wreck. The twelve men in her life boat drifted aimlessly throughout Friday with strong winds and bitterly cold rain. Two of the men died. There were a few sea biscuits and no water. Darkness had started to approach when they sighted shore and agreed to try for it. The first wave upset the boat and all were pitched out. Dooley later reported that he lost his life belt but could swim and finally came by the overturned boat and managed to get hold of it. Captain Sawyer also reached the overturned boat as did a German sailor named Kahler. "We did not see any of the others except the head steward who was drowned later while swimming for shore. Most of the men were drowned by the first sea when we entered the breakers." The boat came to shore north of Bandon at Whisky

Run. Three reached the beach still alive and later three bodies were picked up, the other four still missing. Among the survivors was Captain Sawyer who was taken to Bandon Hospital. Quartermaster Kunkle was taken to a private home and Earl Dooley was taken to the Bandon Light House.

Captain Johnson of the Bandon Coast Guard, learning of the wreck, sent men to the scene to aid in recovering the bodies. Jacob Kamm and James Robb, friends of publisher C. S. Jackson and family, also came, and Johnson made arrangements to take them to the Sixes River area. The Jackson family also asked John Masterson to patrol the beach in search of bodies and to locate their son, Francis Jackson. Later when Masters returned to Corvallis and OAC he received a check from Mrs. Jackson for $25 as payment for his efforts.

The bow of the ship was in very strong currents and sinking deeper in the sand. Within a day or two it was completely submerged near Blacklock. A black cat clung desperately to the mast for many days. For years the mast could be seen at low tide, finally disappearing altogether about 1980. Two other sailing schooners, *City of Napa* and *Anna Hormine* wrecked at Blacklock in 1884 and 1886.

A great many people from the area visited the scene of the *Chanselor* wreck daily, most arriving on horseback. The ship was handsomely furnished in hardwood, the top of a library table in the captain's cabin being inlaid with silver valued at $400. By late January it still had not been accounted for. A splendid hardwood door that came ashore with scarcely a blemish was disfigured with an axe in order for the axeman to secure the brass lock! Canned goods, dishes, pots and pans came ashore along with much lumber which was immediately packed off.

Captain A. A. Sawyer stood for investigation of the wreck in Portland in March, and was found "guilty of failure to properly navigate his vessel." He was suspended of his license for two years.

John Tucker of Bandon took a team and wagon to the Whiskey Run area and brought the steel life boat back to Bandon, placing it on the upper bluff area overlooking the lower Coquille River and Lighthouse, where it remained for many years. It bore the name *J. A. Chanselor.* Piercy Sweet and other young people remember spending a few hours of youthful play on this lonely relic.

After the death of C. S. Jackson, Mrs. Jackson brought his ashes to Cape Blanco (sometime in the 1950s) and by helicopter, sprinkled them over the area where the *J. A. Chanselor* wrecked and her son, Francis Jackson, was drowned.

More Shipwrecks

The *S. S. Joan of Arc* came to rest in the harbor at Port Orford in mid-November of 1920, after striking the Rogue River reef. All hands were safely removed to the city of Topeka after she struck and the deserted hulk drifted north, coming to rest just west of Mill Rock between Hubbard Creek and Battle Rock. The cargo of railroad ties was salvaged and eventually the hull washed up on the beach and was burned to obtain the iron bolts and hardware. She was built at Rolf, California in 1918.

The Chamberlin owned *S. S. Phyllis* was carrying 800 tons of general cargo when she ran aground between Retz Creek and Humbug Mountain on March 9, 1936, during a heavy northwester which she had bucked all the way from San Francisco. Tom Hatcher and Charley Davis pioneered a cat road down to the wreck site where John Marsh, Jack Kronenburg and Fred Caughell salvaged the cargo of sugar, oil, canned foods, grain and dozens of five gallon containers of malted milk mix. Thus, the mishap provided the youngsters of northern Curry more malted milk than those who were were forced to drink it would care to remember. Henry Axtel purchased the hull, hoping to erect a tourist trap out of it but after he cut it in two, a storm came up and planted the pieces upon the beach.

The following year the 113 ton steamer *Cottoneva* was caught at the dock at Port Orford on February 9 by a moderate southerly. Her stern-hold was nearly loaded with lumber, causing the bow to rise and act as a sail. Although headed seaward, she failed to get up enough steam to clear the roadstead and was driven to the beach just east of Battle Rock. The ill-fated crew were saved by a "breeches buoy" or sling anchored to the hill near the beach. The old vessel, built in 1917, was salvaged by Orris and Louie Knapp, who built a large barn from the timbers at their Elk River ranch.

On December 2, 1941, the lumber schooner *Willapa* out of Coos Bay, encountered heavy seas off Port Orford. After losing her deck load, deck and wheelhouse, she came ashore at the foot of Humbug Mountain on the south side. All 24 of the crew were rescued by the efforts of Commander Flake's Coast Guard crew and heroic action by Jim Combs, a local fisherman who launched his small skiff into the raging seas to provide shuttle service from the Coast Guard vessel to the dock. The larger vessel dared not approach the piling due to the heavy surge and Combs ferried the survivors, two at a time, to safety. Harry Strahan, Crawford Smith, Donna Reauburg and other fisherman assisted in the daring rescue. The crew had spent nearly 12 hours clinging to the wreckage and life-lines. For First Mate Stablebaum it was his second harrowing experience at Port Orford as he was the skipper of the *Cottoneva* previously mentioned.

Less than a year later, Commander Flake had another task facing him as his life-saving crew put to sea in response to an SOS from the torpedoed tanker *Larry Doheney* just south of Port Orford. Northbound, she was holed by the submarine *I-25* but remained afloat for some time. A "Q" boat, an old wooden-hulled Olsen boat jammed full of logs and equipped with hidden guns much like the German "Raiders," happened on the scene and with lights ablaze, circled the strickened tanker all night, hoping to lure the *I-25* to the surface. The six man navy gun crew stayed aboard the *Doheney* as the gun on the stern was not awash. Five crew perished when the oil ignited. The captain of the ship was lost during rescue operation. The oil-soaked men were brought to the Port Orford dock by Commander Flake's motor lifeboat where they were cared for by the local chapter of the Red Cross.

Within the last several years (1980s) sport divers have converged on the roadstead at Port Orford and have made some interesting finds. In an area just southeast of Battle Rock ship machinery can be seen at low tides and upon further examination it was determined that a total of four shipwrecks are stacked ... one on top of another! The bottom remains, it is believed, are from the Russian whaler that beached there in the period from 1820-30. The other three are in all probability the *Anita,* the *Iowa* and the *Francisco,* army transports which wrecked in the 1850s. Most of the salvaged materials are hauled away without much documentation or analysis.

Shipwrecks Along the Curry County Coast

Russian Whaler, name unknown about 1830, Port Orford.
Hagstaff, 1849, Rogue River.
Anita, January 1852, Port Orford.
Iowa, May 19, 1856, a U.S. Army supply vessel, Port Orford.
Francisco, June 6, 1856, Port Orford.
Friendship, 1860, North of Sixes River.
Bunkalation, June 1870.
Northwestern, January 3, 1875, Rogue River bar.
Milo Bond, November 21, 1875, Rogue River bar.
Johanna Brock, February 17, 1877, off Rogue River, drifted in at Ophir.
Willamantic, November 3, 1875.
San Buenaventura, ?
Bawnmore, September 6, 1895, between Blanco and Floras Lake.

Washcalore, May 21, 1911, Cape Sebastian.

Irene, ?

Majestic (bark), June 21, 1921.

Maid of Oregon, November 22, 1895.

Emily, ?

Harriet Rowe, January 28, 1876, Port Orford.

Brother Jonathan, July 30, 1865, Point St. George.

Esther Colos, October 21, 1879, Rogue River bar.

Victoria, March 28, 1883, Cape Blanco.

Mose, May 25, 1884, Port Orford.

Ocean King, April 1887, Cape Blanco.

Gray Hound, December 14, 1887, Port Orford.

Thistle, January 13, 1889, Rogue River.

Alaskan, May 13, 1889, Cape Blanco.

Rosalind, February 18, 1890, Otter Point.

T.W. Lucas, October 24, 1894, Port Orford.

Ella Laurena, December 23, 1895, Cape Blanco.

South Portland, October 1903, Cape Blanco.

Wasp, May 21, 1911, Cape Sebastian, recovered.

Bandon, August 30, 1917, Port Orford, recovered.

Sinola, June 15, 1917, Cape Blanco, recovered.

Rustler, August 24, 1919, south of Rogue River.

J.A. Chanselor, December 19, 1919, mouth of Sixes River, Standard Oil.

Joan of Arc, November 16, 1920, Rogue River Reef, in at Port Orford.

Bella, December 23, 1920, Christmas candies, etc., en route to G.B.

Hugh Hogan, May 18, 1922, Cape Blanco.

South Coast, September 16, 1930, 16 miles west of Cape Blanco.

Cottonevea, February 10, 1937, Port Orford.

Phyllis, March 9, 1936, Retz Creek, just north of Humbug Mountain.

Willapa, December 4, 1941, just south of Humbug Mountain.

Larry Doheney, October 5, 1942, Cape Sebastian.

Susan Olsen, November 1942, Southern Oregon Coast.

Enido, December 22, 1941, off Blunts reef, drifted into Crescent City.

Zarembo III, September 13, 1947, WSW of Cape Blanco.

Alice H., September 23, 1950 near Port Orford.

Ommaney, October 6, 1951, 80 miles west of Cape Blanco.
Barge #14, Sause Brothers, January 1956, south of Humbug Mountain.
Fulton, February 1904, Port Orford.
Napa City, 1887, North of Cape Blanco.
Active, June 1870, Floras Lake-New River.

12

Disasters

"In Curry County where the winds often blow over 100 miles an hour ... live the most independent people in the state of Oregon." This line was used to begin a magazine article several years ago and it is quoted to point out that visitors often remember more about the weather and the character of the people than the beautiful coastline, wild and pristine landscapes or the much sought after isolation of the area. Winds up to 100 mph tend to frighten the valley folk but are considered old hat here. When they peak out at 150, with gusts at 190, well, that's another story ... and that they did on Columbus Day, 1962. (see *Oregonian*)

A day or two before, a freak storm hit Gold Beach damaging the Riley Creek School and tipped over several trailers and airplanes but the worst was yet to come. A funeral was held for Judge Fernley Long in the Presbyterian Church at Gold Beach that morning and about 200 persons gathered to pay their last respects. By 11:30 a.m. the wind was roaring so hard no one could hear the minister and many were not listening, for the building was hardly a safe place to be. The widow finally said, "Fernley would not want us to continue under these conditions," and the congregation was excused and they dispersed into the most fierce windstorm ever recorded in Curry County. The next four hours were beyond belief. This writer was blocked from making it into Port Orford by a canyon full of uprooted trees at Humbug Mountain. Parking alongside the highway just north of Beartrap Creek, I watched the roofs of the Humbug Lodge restaurant and store pop off like corks of champagne bottles. Huge old growth fir trees high on the south spur of the mountain were shedding tops of 30 feet or more ... snapping like match-sticks. Six hours later a crew had chain-sawed a single lane through the canyon and as I proceeded north, Rumpty Kreutzer, southbound in a Johnson lumber truck, shouted out ... "no use going to Port Orford, Patrick, there's nothing left!" Upon entering Port Orford I observed what looked like a war zone ... trees wrapped in power and telephone wires, roofs off, buildings collapsed, windows of plywood; and sea gulls, the ones that survived, walking around in a daze. There were two or three candles lit however. Aden Chapman, Otto Pitcher and Mrs. Hand were dispensing tranquilizers in liquid form at Orford's, Pitches, and the state liquor store. Needless to say they were not in need of customers. Fortunately, no one was hurt in this end of the county but the beautiful greenery at Port Orford was wiped away. Houses once surrounded by stately windbreaks were now conspicuously alone on their lots, most with windows shattered and roofs off or damaged. The Dykes trailer north of town literally exploded and the Herzig building next to Tucker's Market imploded and collapsed. Boats on the dock were tipped and turned and four buildings between Jackson and Washington were blown off their foundations while the old Lindberg-built house at Sixth and Jackson did not lose a shingle! Trees that were not blown over were wind-burned so severely it would take years for them to regain their green composure. Believe it or not, even the hardy rhododendrons were uprooted!

Buildings in the hinterland sustained similar damage. Barns and outbuildings were toppled but in an unusual pattern and timber was felled in a like manner. The winds acted more tornado-like than a normal and predictable sustained southerly and the damaged areas occurred in a crazy-quilt pattern.

The storm did have a beneficial effect on the people as they methodically pooled their resources to make do. Billy Woodward set out with his power saw to buck logs that blocked driveways. Refusing payment, he worked steadily for days at his self appointed mission. "Ting-a-ling" McCall, the local telephone serviceman, struggled 20 hours a day for ten days restoring service as best he could while the crews from Coos-Curry Electric, under the direction of Jim (Ready-Kilowatt) Wilson and Roy Carr, met the emergency head on restoring service and lining up generators needed by stores and shops which required power for freezer units. The town survived and although considerably altered in appearance, the only loss of life was Tony Wahl's chickens up on Langlois Mountain. Georgina figured that the folks in Bandon should have had chicken and dumplings for about a year as she watched several thousand flightless birds heading (or tailing) north. Clara Miller was saddened by the loss of her green stamps which were sucked out the blown-out rear door. A week later a neighbor living a mile north returned them. When Lou Griffy's roof came completely off, the suction brought clothes, radios and the like with it and the piano was moved some 30 feet inside the house.

The fire of 1868 destroyed the whole town of Port Orford save for Cap Tichenor's house located on the hill above the dock. That huge fire was not confined to this area and in fact the whole coast was engulfed. Ships were prevented from approaching the coast at Yaquina (Newport), Coos Bay and Port Orford due to the heavy smoke. Fortunately, this area had few families and they survived by retreating to the beach. One family, the Unicans living several miles north of town, holed up in a 25 foot dug well to save themselves. That conflagration was a good case for instant urban renewal.

~ ~ ~

The following is a letter written by Mary S. Pugh, wife of Dr. Lonner R. Pugh, about the tragic fire which burned Bandon in 1936, and is a grim reminder of what happened further south of Bandon. Dr. Pugh was local fire chief in Port Orford at the time.

(This appeared in the *Port Orford News,* April 27, 1961 and is now in Neonta Hall's scrapbook.)

Port Orford, Oregon
September 1, 1936

My Dears:

Saturday was the hottest day I have ever seen in Port Orford, 104 on the back porch and 80 in the shade. No wind at all in town. About three o'clock Lon got word the Sea View Ranch (Ena McKenzie) barn was burning. A salesman had his car out front and the two jumped in; they stopped at the firehouse long enough to pick up an extinguisher and then speeded. By the time they had gone the six miles there the barn was all gone and the house was half gone. The house, a big affair, had been built of lumber from the beach and was furnished with things that could have come around the Horn and other things which had been obtained from boats wrecked in the early days. Some of it was lovely.

Lon came home and had not had supper yet when word came that Zumwalts were in danger. I gave him a sandwich on the run and he was gone. They fought hard there with the flames within 100 feet of the house and big cedar grove. Their backfire flared in their faces, but they saved the place. By that time word had come that Bandon was in flames; that Brush Prairie was in flames; that fire was raging on Starvation Ridge. Finally a friend took me out the highway — we went about seven miles and it was getting hotter all the time. Out there the wind came in little whirls which fanned the fire and pushed it on. Madden Butte, heavily timbered, burst into flames with a roar louder than the ocean at its top and in 15 minutes the whole butte was burned. That fire spread over the highway and burned out several families. I came home with Lon about midnight with fires apparently under control. We had just got to sleep when someone pounded on the door and said Zumwalts were again in danger. He fought out there again. Many people in that vicinity moved out but eventually those homes were spared. Two families on Starvation Ridge were burned out. Lon came back that time about 3:30. Before breakfast Lon was called again; all Sunday it was spasmodic fire fighting.

About this time we began to get reports from Bandon. A friend had gone to Coquille to meet her mother. On the way back they stopped her at Bandon and said she could not get through. Fifteen minutes later a gas tank exploded on the highway. She went to the hotel and registered for the night; 30 minutes later the hotel was on fire. She had her mother and two small children with her; she took them down on the beach. The smoke and sparks were falling badly so she kept moving them to rocks farther out. About that time the tide turned and she had to start moving them in again. A boy from here saved her car for her. He drove it through flames onto a hillside that was already burned. The paint was not injured much but the upholstery was black.

Saturday afternoon Alice Adams gave birth to a baby boy at the home of a friend in Bandon. (Alice is the sister of Earl Pugh's first wife.) When the friend's house burned they took Alice to the hotel, in fact she arrived there while Mrs. Medford was there. Half an hour later that was burning; they tied Alice and her baby to a cot and lowered her into a life boat and took her out to the lighthouse tender, the *Rose*. There they gave her the captain's cabin and she stayed there until Monday morning and when she was moved to the Coquille Hospital. I think her baby was the third reported born that night as I could not locate any of the others when I tried to outfit them with baby clothes. I think she appeared so many places they had the baby born in each.

Sunday we drove through Bandon. There isn't a good looking house left in Bandon. The funny thing is that there are no ashes or debris. Just fireplaces, like a graveyard. I wanted to pick up one of the poor homeless things and bring it home.

Both Saturday night and Sunday night our electricity went off. Since then they are only giving us power half the time as the water power will only generate that much. All streams and rivers have dried up alarmingly. Until today the wind has been in the south which protected us. Today it is north but the fire is apparently under control unless something new comes up.

Sunday, Lon commandeered two truckloads of CCCs and sent them to save the Sixes school house. By ditching and backfiring they saved that. Fifty of them sent to the new Lake school house apparently had no boss, so they stood and let it burn — it was a nice stucco building.

Monday we went to Bandon and took soap, clothes, etc. Helped sort clothes and found a lot of fine baby things. Went on, took them to a young mother in Coquille who had been moved there from the burned out district. At Coquille which was almost under martial ruling as fire was so close, they were doing a nice job of work. Had beds fixed up in their community building for women and children. In the rest room older girls were putting the smudgy little refugees under the shower; little girls from two to six, and they came out fresh and shining to be dressed in clean clothes. So many things have been donated, many of them lovely. On the way back we picked up a roll of Red Cross diaper cloth and brought it home; tore it up that night and peddled it around among my friends. We hemmed over six dozen diapers that night which I took back the next day. We also put up a bunch of bottles of cough syrup which I took for Miss Fasnacht to hand out; so many have developed colds. In fact they were dreading a flu epidemic now.

Lon keeps going out on tours of inspection; yesterday a lady asked me when the dentist would be in. I said I imagined after the first good rain!

One day I outfitted a woman and her children with things I had collected and reported her to Lucille Parsons who took care of bedding for her. Lon thinks we are safe now but we have been kept on the edge pretty much with various reports, many of them false.

After Ena McKenzie burned out they brought her to the hospital as she had completely collapsed. I saw her the next day and instead of grieving over all she had lost, she said, "I am a Red Cross nurse and subject to call; I should be in Bandon helping instead of on my back here." Everyone is like that. Dr. Lucas is usually so spotless. Monday he was laughing about his shirt, his only one to come through the fire. Tuesday I congratulated him on a clean one he had acquired somewhere, probably Coquille.

The first relief we could help in is over; now Red Cross, army, Salvation Army, etc. are all there and prefer not to be bothered unless they ask for something definite.

> Much love,
> Mary S. Pugh
> Friday, October 2nd

The sun was out — the first I had seen of it except as a red ball on Sunday, since Saturday. Tonight the moonlight is lovely. Today I have felt fairly safe.

Fire Department

In view of the fires that visited Port Orford, a brief look at the Fire Department should be helpful. The information presented here was prepared by Sally Prince, a local writer who gave her permission for the use of her words. Some comments have been added.

Every Monday evening the serenity of Port Orford is pierced by the wail of a fire siren. Promptly at seven, the local volunteers gather at the fire hall for a weekly meeting and routine equipment check. The community is proud of their well-trained fire fighters and modern fire equipment.

During Port Orford's earlier years, however, the town had to make do with what was available. The men relied on "on the job" training. Their equipment was whatever was available.

Bob Ostrander, now deceased, was interviewed by the local newspaper some years ago. He served the community for many years as a volunteer firefighter. Here is his account of those early days with the fire department.

"As I recall, the town's first fire truck was a Model-T with a tank on the back to hold the water. Then, we had a hose trailer, a two-wheeled rig. It was man-powered.

"We'd park the old Model-T on the hill — the fire house was over by the old jail on Jefferson Street — this was sometime during the 20s.

"Well, as I said, we parked the truck on the hill 'cause in order to start it we had to release the brake, then pop the clutch as it rolled down the hill. But the darned thing never went very far. We had to get out and push it to the fire.

"We didn't have an organized bunch of firemen in those days. We just came a-runnin' when we smelled smoke or heard a lot of hollerin'."

Ostrander remembers the time consuming job of filling the tank with water. "We'd push the truck to the lake or a nearby creek, but shucks, by the time we got back to the fire again there wasn't nothin' left to fight. We just put out what was still burnin'."

In those days fire fighting was with the hope the fire could be contained quickly and not spread to other building. Ostrander said there was little hope of saving whatever was on fire. Families living outside the city limits battled the blaze on their own.

"But when a home was destroyed," he continued, "everyone in town pitched in to help out the family. In two days we had a home built for them. The lumber yard donated all the wood. The store donated all the hardware, and the people gave food, furniture and clothing. The fire victims usually ended up in better straights than beforehand."

It was sometime in the late 1930s that Ostrander remembered the volunteers going to Coquille to be fingerprinted. "I guess you could say that's when we got organized. That's when the regulations and building codes started gettin' strict. We had to put metal jackets around chimney flues — just couldn't stick pipes through shingles anymore."

B

Schools

The expression "three Rs" (readin', ritin' and 'rithmetic) was coined as a result of a basic need for the early pioneers to erect small one-room schoolhouses in which the rudiments of penmanship, math, science and grammar could be offered to nearby students. To the little school at Cape Blanco the three Rs aptly could have stood for "rain, ragin' winds and repair."

Established in the early 1880s, the little school house of District 15 was located on the ancient terrace of Cape Blanco among the dense forest of pine and spruce trees with salal, blue flag and wild strawberry as it's natural landscaping. Not far from the now abandoned cemetery and only a mile or so from the western extremities of the cape the, little structure had to withstand some of the severest weather on the Oregon coast with rainfall measured by inches and winds that exceeded 100 miles per hour several time in a winter season.

The first census of the district listed 47 persons of school age ranging in ages from four to 20, and included 14 pioneer families in the vicinity. Nine students actually attended the three month session. The next year only three families were recorded; the McKenzies, Langloises and Hugheses, with a total of 13 youngsters. This was due to the construction of other schools in the upper Sixes area closer to those they served. In 1890, there were only nine registered voters in District 15.

The first year of operation the district received $317.36 in tax money and paid out $163.50 of it for the teacher's salary and the little school operated without "apparatus" or even a "Webster's Dictionary." The water closet was located out "among the trees" until 1896, when one was constructed. The last year of operation was 1898, when only one student showed up and she, Grace Langlois, attended from November through February.

And so over the years "Cape Blanco University," as Thomas Hughes wrote of it, faded into obscurity. All that remains are a few dog-eared text books, one ink bottle and one photograph which will have to provide future generations a brief but interesting glimpse into the colorful history of northern Curry County.

The little school of District 15 was only one of several one-room school houses that emerged in Port Orford in the early 1880s. Schoolhouses were build at Port Orford, Elk River and Sixes, and teachers were hired for terms of three months during periods of good weather. Wintertime school terms were not possible due to the lack of roads and bridges. Describing Curry County in 1878, J. Upton writes … "Curry County had not a single mile of legally established highway … there were less than half dozen wheeled vehicles … the county seat was visited by one mail a week carried on horseback and whose prompt arrival was difficult and problematical during the winter season on account of the frequency with which our 'bridle trails' encountered unbridged streams with rapid currents swollen by current rains."

The locations of the schools after districts were organized, as best as can be ascertained, were as follows:

Port Orford - On the hill at Ninth and Jackson. This building still stands and is used as a private home. A second structure was located at Eighth and Washington where the school playground is now located. (1913)

Elk River - The "downriver school" was located near the present day Marsh Ranch while another was constructed near Adolphson's second mill site several miles up the river. The lower school was attended by Port Orford children from time to time. Louis Knapp, Nick Marsh, Sr., Ima Johnson Strahan share memories of this institution.

Cape Blanco - attended by Langlois, Hughes, Sullivans and other children in the area, was located on the Old Cape Road about 1/2 mile southwest of the now abandoned cemetery.

Sixes - One structure was located near Dry Creek, one on the hill above the Farrier Ranch and one, the most recent, just east of the Sixes Hotel and stage house now owned by Sam and Viola Cuatt. Mention is made of the Round Grove school in the *Port Orford Tribune,* December 11, 1894, in a report by Mr. Capps who was the teacher. Its location was presumably in the Sixes or Lower Floras Creek area.

All of these elementary schools were supplied with meager teaching aids and textbooks which were used over and over again. Annual budgets rarely exceeded $150 per year with the bulk of the taxes raised going for salaries which ranged from $35 to $50 per month. The teachers boarded at the nearest ranch and were certified by the County

School Superintendent after an extensive examination was passed. The "State" Paper Exam included subjects as penmanship, history, spelling, algebra, reading, school law, written arithmetic, theory of teaching, grammar bookkeeping, physics, civil government, physiology, geography, mental arithmetic, composition, physical geography, botany, plane geometry, general history, English literature and psychology. This exam took three full days as did the County Paper Exam although the latter covered fewer subject areas and the certification was good for first, second and third grades. In August of 1901, W. S. Guerin granted County Certificates to Miss Camilia Lorentzen, Miss Pearl Walker, Miss Mary Bossen, Mr. W. Gardner and Miss Dora Taggart. Miss Rose Long was an applicant for the State Papers.

Teachers Institutes were held annually as three day learning and socializing events. Teachers presented papers in the various subject areas that were their strengths, thereby all teachers in attendance were exposed to a smattering of specialized theories and subject matter.

Teachers were required to fill out reports which, although abbreviated, contained some interesting questions relating to the condition of each particular school, its grounds, facilities and furnishings. Visits by the County Superintendent were rare and this official undoubtedly relied on these reports to verify the maintenance of state standards. J. J. Stanley, reporting with characteristic brevity on the commodiousness of the Cape Blanco School at the Hughes Ranch, said that it contained "hundreds of acres." In 1889, Stella Smith reported that the ventilation of the same school (where 100 mph winds are not uncommon) was "extra good." That year 47 school age youngsters appeared on the census rolls while only seven attended school at Cape Blanco University which did not reflect lack of interest but rather the degree of difficulty encountered in getting to the school.

District boundaries were non-existent in the early days as evidenced by a letter from County School Superintendent Frank Stewart to the District Clerk, E. Hughes in 1889: "The records of the boundaries of the various districts are in (sic) inexactable confusion, hence I have not written them in any of the Books of Records." Stewart's misspelling of the word "inextricable" probably went unchecked, for the Cape Blanco school did not, according to the official records, possess an unabridged dictionary. Certified teachers moved from district to district according to, for the most part, the weather and other circumstances. A partial list of the pioneer teachers include, W. S. Guerin, Ran Tichenor, J. J. Stanley, Stella Smith, J. S. Hodgin, E. A. Hargreaves, Alex Thrift, Katie Warren, Clarissa Merriman, Ames Johnson, and Mary Masterson.

In Port Orford, Randolph Tichenor conducted private classes in the 1880s and from time to time would publish the achievements and deportment of the students, as did

Ames Johnson, at the turn of the century. There was no need to hide your report card if your folks subscribed to Walter Sutton's *Port Orford Tribune*. In those days they "told it like it was."

In 1913, a two story school was constructed at Tenth and Washington which was to serve all grades until 1927, when Port Orford Union High School was built at Sixth and Oregon on property which once served as the site of Fort Orford. The grade school was in service until the present school was built. The old school had seen two world wars, a depression and periods of prosperity but its image conjures up the memories of the old bell, oiled floors, wood stoves, May poles, sack lunches and dedicated teachers. A partial list of the teachers include Mrs. Grant, Katherine Smith, Mrs. Dunbar, Mrs. Rice, Mrs. Hoggatt, Mrs. Russell, and Effie Sweet Parsons. Despite the somewhat primitive conditions which were average for the times, the end products could read, write and number with the best.

The high school was the pride of the town. Situated on the hill which once served as an army fort, it beckoned to those who desired self improvement and Ruth Clark, its first principal, instilled seeds of accomplishment by intertwining scholastic, athletic and cultural activities with strong moral fibers. The gymnasium was constructed a year or two later with donated lumber and labor and the students raised enough money to furnish lights and a light plant (purchased from Koblenzars at Ophir) for the stage and playing court. Gilbert Gable modernized the stage and gym lighting in 1936. The beautiful stage curtain was sewn by the girls of the school under the direction of Nettie Toole. This building soon became the cultural center of the Port Orford area and was the scene of county wide competition of sports and drama and of course graduation exercises which always featured formal attire and a beautifully decorated stage and hall featuring cedar, rhodies and other wild flora.

In 1957, the Langlois and Port Orford districts combined to form a consolidated joint district. A new high school was built midway between the two communities. Divided opinions spurred emotions to run high but the student bodies combined with a minimum of difficulty and as one who served on the faculty observed, "The kids could have suffered from the raging controversy between the factions but they proved up the claim by setting aside any prejudices and proceeded to concern themselves with more important things … such as choosing a school name, colors, nickname, cheerleaders and student body officers. As they accomplished this, they soon forgot whether or not their friends came from Langlois, Port Orford or Timbuktu … "

The new high school was able to offer an enriched curriculum which included physics, several foreign languages (including Russian), trigonometry and other courses not available in the two smaller high schools. Athletics were expanded to include football and wrestling and the school found itself competing in the old Sunset League with Coquille, Myrtle Point and other much larger schools in the State's toughest AA league. One coach lamented, "Sometimes it made you want to hide the game ball." The population of the district has declined over the years due to the closure of most of the mills (there were 12 operating in 1957), and the school population decline has brought about major adjustments in the operation of the district. The population now tends toward the retirement age, making the passing of the school budget quite difficult as many of the patrons have no school age youngsters. The school personnel strive to maintain high standards under adverse conditions and are succeeding according to test results.

14

Churches
And Lodges

Roman Catholic: Followers of the Roman Catholic Church have worshiped in four churches in Port Orford and one in Langlois. The first was at Cape Blanco where, in 1892, Patrick Hughes erected Mary, Star of the Sea, a quaint American Gothic structure which was dubbed the farthest west church in the United States. Used for nearly 30 years, it finally fell to the ravages of time and weather.

A small church was established on Sixth Street between Washington and Oregon streets in 1922. This hillside location was used several years then discontinued.

In 1944, Edward Hughes donated the present site and a small church was built by A. Shaw and James Studley and son Jerry. This structure was removed in 1968, the congregation shared St. Christopher's Episcopal Church until 1983, when the present church was dedicated. Its present status is a mission.

Church of Jesus Christ of Latter Day Saints: The Mormons organized in the Port Orford area in 1949 under the direction of Charles Saxton who in turn served as the first branch president. The first church was purchased from Carl Leonard and was a theatre structure built by the late Gilbert Gable just prior to his death in 1941. It was moved to a site on Oregon Street just east of the old high school and was used until May, 1976, when the new church was dedicated at 21st and Jackson. A disastrous fire nearly destroyed the building in February, 1979, but it was repaired and a year later was rededicated. Today the tidy church presents a simple but beautiful scene to its nearly 100 members.

Zion Lutheran: This church was organized in 1952, and the first building efforts began in 1957, although a smaller chapel-school was used nearby and later converted to a residence for the pastor. The present church at 20th and Washington was erected by volunteer labor and features local wood products including beautiful Douglas fir laminated open beams and myrtlewood trim.The Edstrom Memorial Chapel and bell tower added later were designed by architect Donald Hill, son of one of the original members. The Reverend Ole Larson is presently pastor.

Port Orford Christian Center: This congregation formed in 1936, meeting after revival services at the "Grove" on the Frank Morris property during good weather and in various homes in bad weather until the church was built in 1938, at 11th and Washington. Many improvements and alterations have been made to the structure which include kitchen facilities, two classrooms, a fellowship hall, restrooms, pastor's study and outside improvements.

Port Orford Community Church: Port Orford's largest congregation was organized in June of 1930, although services were conducted prior to that time but were unrecorded. Reverend McVicker conducted services in the Episcopal church until the Gillings store at Fifth and Jackson was purchased in 1943. Arising from humble beginnings, the congregation constructed the present structure in the years 1960-1961 and today the complex includes a parsonage and modern facilities on a half block area.

Jehovah's Witness: A congregation of Jehovah's Witness was established in Port Orford in the early 1950s. Meetings were held in private homes until the old Post Office was rented. The group then rented a portion of the Jensen Center (Port and Starboard) until 1960 when the Kingdom Hall was constructed on Myrtle Lane where congregational meetings are held.

Lodges

Woodsmen of the World: Active near the turn of the century, this movement was active in the area and held regular meetings and social events in an upstairs portion of the Kane Building in Langlois. The group included early day loggers such as A. J. Marsh, A. Jamison and others who assisted surviving families of loggers killed in the dangerous wood harvesting occupation. No records could be located of the dates or officers of the movement other than newspaper announcements.

AF and AM #170 Masonic Lodge: This lodge was chartered in 1919, and met for many years on the second floor of a store building between Seventh and Eighth Streets, although the original meeting hall was located on the second floor of a building on Sixth Street near the present day Silver Door. The present building is located at 12th and Tichenor and was built in 1944-1945. Over the years this lodge has maintained active programs including Eastern Star, and youth activities and the membership contributes to various scholarship and other worthwhile funds within the community.

Sixes Grange: Organized in 1936, the grange has, over the years, been the focal point of rural activities and during the depression years of the late 30s it served as a ray of hope by sponsoring farm-oriented projects, social events and offering low-cost insurance policies to its members. C. H. Brooks compiled a history in April 1979, in which he listed 34 people who originated the first meeting of Sixes Grange #856. These included members of the Woodworth, Hays, Hull, Welch, Steiner, Vorhees, Dewey, Capps, Johnston, Sweet, Zumwalt, Correll, Thomas, Fox, Stites and Tyson families who met in the Sixes School until fall when they moved to a building at Denmark. The Home Economics Club of the Grange was formed and met at Mary Woodworth's home. Active participants included Mary Woodworth, Adelea Welch, Ruth Hull, Ada Capps, Betty Steiner, Noma Thomas, Thelma Stites, May Ward, Juanita Johnston, Lola Post, Hazel McKenzie, Fern Welch, Docia Sweet, Evelyn Rowan, Lena Moore, Frances Kennedy and Mabel Fox.

The Grange purchased a site on the Sixes River from C. C. Woodworth for $100 (which he donated back to the building fund) and work began on the building. The wrecked schooner *Cottoneva* at Port Orford provided much salvaged lumber for the hall and work was done by volunteer labor which turned the building over to the membership in April 1939. The Grange aided in securing electrical service into this area, regular freight service, telephone service, road improvements and other worthwhile facilities while also donating financial support for school functions, church construction and park development.

The Juvenile Grange was active in years past and under the direction of Ken Thompson sponsored many activities for the youth in the 1950s.

5

Cemeteries

The first survey of grave sites in Port Orford was conducted by a party financed by the Smithsonian Institution in the mid-1870s and covered the coastal area from Floras Lake to the Winchuck River. The efforts of the surveyors though hampered by adverse weather conditions, were focused upon graves of the Native Americans. The results of this expedition can be found in a report published in the *Curry County Historical Society Newsletter* of September 1975. Most of the graves of the Indian people are found at the sites of their villages or rancheros usually located at sheltered areas in close proximity to small streams or rivers. After more than 5,000 years of continuous occupation, it is likely for anyone poking around to uncover remains almost anywhere there are diggable soils.

Pioneer cemeteries are found scattered upon private lands and many unmarked sites have long been taken back by nature. The Port Orford area has many of these. The Port Orford Cemetery Maintenance District was formed to care for the Masonic-Knapp Cemetery southeast of town on the Old Coast Highway. Roy Mills was the first paid caretaker and now Ed Hansohn performs that duty. The Tichenor Cemetery, located on "Boothill" Road off Coast Guard Hill Road was the area's first. Occupying a beautiful hill top which Captain Tichenor used as a lookout for passing ships (Spyglass Hill), this site commands a sweeping view from Rogue River to Cape Blanco, although the southern vista is blocked now by trees and brush. In Tichenor's days, the headlands was, for the most part, void of trees and brush and was covered with natural grasses.

Captain Tichenor's resting place is marked with a simple, unpretentious stone, while Elizabeth, his wife, is remembered by a beautiful obelisk. To the captain's left lies a sister who was the first occupant of the cemetery in 1854. Other family members include the McGraws, Windsors, Purdins and Ellen (Tichenor) Quick.

The Hughes Cemetery at Cape Blanco has been restored by the Oregon Parks Department and is the site of the old Catholic church, "Mary, Star of the Sea" constructed in 1892, by J. Lindberg. Although the remains of all the family members were reinterred in Portland's Mt. Calvary Cemetery in the winter of 1938-1939, the stones remain and serve as a reminder of an early pioneer family. There are two unmarked graves of infant sons of Charles Forty at the site however while across the river a single marked grave of a member of the Crew family is identifiable. Many Indian graves occupy the areas north of the mouth of the Sixes River, the final resting place for the Kaltsergheat-tun band of the Quo-to-ma Indians.

The Jake Summers family graves were established on Battle Rock in the summer of 1928 when the remains were moved from upper Floras Creek by Grover Tichenor, Lonner Pugh, Mack Saures and others in conjunction with the dedication of Battle Rock State Park and the Roosevelt Highway. Summers was an original defender of Battle Rock in June 1951. Two unmarked graves on the rock are those of two Indian men hanged on separate dates. A Coquille River brave was given a "kangaroo court" verdict in April of 1856, and executed by the miners, while "Enos" Thomas, a Canadian half-breed was charged and convicted of aiding and abetting the belligerents during the Rogue River uprising. He was hanged by an unruly mob after the prime witness, Mrs. Geisel failed to appear at the scheduled trial. The miners plied "Enos" with John Barleycorn, extracted a "confession," led him to the rock and his gallows where his life came to a violent end. Both men were buried beneath their gallows.

There are three lost grave sites in Port Orford. Two soldiers, privates Adam and Hill, who died at Fort Orford in the 1850s are buried somewhere on Graveyard Point just above the dock a Mr. Long, the first settler in Bandon, was brought to the fort during the Indian troubles where he died of natural causes and is buried near the old fort grounds.

The Curse

At the time of the hanging of the Coquille Indian, the fort was used by those peaceful Indian persons as a haven from war. The condemned man's family was with him at the time of his arrest and after the execution the mother sat upon the bluff on Fort Point and wailed for two or three days in mourning for the loss of her son. The miners and pioneers interpreted this action as the placing of a curse upon the town and it's early settlers. (Many say it is still in effect!)

16

Mining, and Observations On Oregon By A Nineteenth Century Writer

While this chapter is chiefly about mining, I thought it would be helpful to the reader to get a glimpse of Oregon and Port Orford as it was in the middle of the 19th Century from the viewpoint of a journalist who visited Northern California and Southern Oregon in the days when men who came into the Port Orford area were mainly interested in the mineral riches of the land. The following excerpt from a personal narrative of adventures in Oregon by a seasoned writer for *Harper's New Monthly Magazine* was taken from an article published in the late 1850s. Penned by William V. Wells, the story exposes people, places and events of the frontier Port Orford general area in an appealing and historically faithful manner. Such treatment adds value to this interpretation of "West of the West," and it sets the stage for an exploration of the mining activities that occurred.

~ ~ ~

Early in October, 1855, with an old companion of my peregrinations — one of those golden-tempered, delightful traveling companions with whom to associate is a perpetual treat — I found myself on board the staunch steamship *Columbia,* bound from San Francisco to Oregon.

On the evening of the second day we came in sight of Trinidad, a little hamlet situated about 200 miles north of San Francisco. It was quite dark as the steamer came to, near a black, sea-beaten rock, through whose caverns the sea roared with a dismal moan. An inhospitable coast is that of California and Oregon, where, from San Diego to Puget

Sound, a distance of 1300 miles, there is found but one port — that of San Francisco — to which the dismantled ship may fly for refuge in a gale from seaward. Trinidad is a "port"; but justly regarded with terror by the mariner in times of tempest. The fog limited our observations from the quarter-deck to a few dimly-discerned huts far up the bank, and the only sound of civilization was the distant crying of a child ever and anon mingling with the surf's roar. Freight was discharged, and a speedy leave taken of sorry-looking Trinidad.

On the following morning the discharge of a gun from the bows brought us to the deck, when we found the steamer heading into the bay or roadstead of Crescent City. This, like most of the harbors on this coast, can only boast of its capacity. It extends from the houses of the inhabitants entirely across the Pacific. It is proposed to build a break-water here, and so form a natural harbor. An indefinite number of millions of dollars are named as an estimate of the cost. Crescent City is three years old, situated on the sea-beach, backed by a dense mass of pine and cedar forest, inhabited by several hundred traders, packer, Indians, dogs, and mules. A brisk ride to Cape St. George, taken during our stay here, satiated our curiosity. The country becomes uninteresting after the forest and green undergrowth of the coast trees have ceased to be novelties. The men were mostly "Pikes" of an exceedingly rough cast, and the Indians, who were the first speci-mens of the Oregon savage we had met with, were decidedly to us the lions of the town.

Wandering out toward a rocky promontory north of the town, and designated as the Battery, we found an encampment of the Chetkoe tribe. Three old women among them were quite blind, and, squatting in the sand, were feeling nervously around for some bits of willow which they were fashioning into baskets — time out of mind the Indian's occupation. Several young squaws accosted us in broken English. One of them was really pretty, and but for some barbarous tattooing, nose and ear pendants, and a villain-ous smell of decayed salmon, would have been a very Fayaway. This young lady was in "dishabille" as we passed, and, though making her toilet with otter fat, glass beads and shells, did not shrink at the unexpected visit. The entire party wore a dress composed of equal parts of cheap blankets, cast-off coats and shirts, and the usual savage finery. The men sported the bow and arrow armor with a coyote or fox-skin for a quiver. All had the ears or nose split, and one or two coquettish young jades of squaws wore fish-bones through their nostrils, and were otherwise scarified and marked.

On the same afternoon we bade adieu to Crescent City, and were quickly again on our way to the northward. On the following morning the ship's reckoning showed us to be opposite Port Orford, and this being our proposed landing-place, we watched with some curiosity for the lifting of an impenetrable vail of fog which shut out all view of the coast. The speed was slackened, and the "blue pigeon" kept constantly moving.

Suddenly, on our starboard bow, appeared a lofty rock looming out of the mist. It was a grand and startling spectacle. Though the sea was comparatively calm, the ground swells surged up around its base in piles of boisterous foam, roaring among the caverns and gulches, and rushing up to the height of 40 feet; then, as the swell receded, the whole surface presented a bold front of yeasty rivulets, white as milk, and trickling down the rough sides of the rock in hissing cascades, as one might imagine they would down the furrowed cheeks of some awful giant of Scandinavian romance. Clouds of birds hovered around the peak, screaming and dipping down to the waves, and scolding at our sudden intrusion. Our new acquaintance disappeared astern almost as soon as we had descried it. It is the southwestern point of Port Orford harbor, and is one of the enormous boulders rolled by some convulsion of nature from the steeps of Humbug Mountain, which rears its head far above the surrounding country. We could now run with some degree of certainty, and heading boldly in, a gun was fired, the echo of which had scarcely done rattling through the coast-range when it was answered from on shore. A moment after the shrill scream of a rooster came across the water, and the fog lifting, opening to our view a bluff bank, perhaps 40 feet high, upon which was situated a small town, with some 40 houses, half-deserted, and standing at the verge of a bank of lofty foliage, forming the great fir and pine region which skirts the Oregon Coast from the California line to Puget Sound.

From under the lee of a promontory know as "Battle Rock," and the history of which we shall presently review, a boat put forth through the surf, into which we bundled, and grasping the hands extended in kindly parting, we had soon made our first landing on the Oregon coast. As we rounded the point we looked back upon the steamer heading out to sea, and pursuing her way to the Columbia River.

We landed at a little lumber wharf, whence a short walk brought us to the United States Barracks; and entering the house of Dr. Glissan and Lieutenant Kautz, we were soon engaged in conversation with a party of educated gentlemen, whose cultivated talents show the more conspicuously in the wild region that duty had made their place of residence. About 300 yards from the government reserve, and hidden from it by an intervening range of hills, is situated the little town of Port Orford. Its history is that of the sudden and too ephemeral growth of the coast villages of Oregon.

In 1851, a party of men from Portland, Oregon selected this spot for the site of a town, depending upon its roadstead and the facility of communication with the interior for the basis of its success and growth. The discovery of the auriferous sands of Gold Bluff, which were found to extend along the entire coast, from Rogue River to Cape Arago, also augmented the progress of the place. The original party consisted of 18 men; but finding their stock of provisions becoming exhausted, and there being no means of supplying the deficiency, half returned to Portland, leaving nine of their number to await their return. At that time the character of the country between the California line and the Columbia River was unknown. Its deep rivers, bays, tribes of Indians, and topography, were a sealed book, save to a few venturesome old hunters and trappers who had wandered down the coast even to the Humboldt; but their accounts, vague and uncertain, were unknown.

This section of Oregon contained about 2,000 Indians, divided into numerous tribes who soon became aware that the white had settled their country, and, with savage hostility, determined to crush the band at Port Orford. Their rapidly increasing numbers alarmed our little garrison, who retreated upon what is now known as "Battle Rock" — a natural fort showing three precipitous sides toward the ocean, and only accessible from land by a regular causeway. The parapet of this fortification stands not less than 50 feet above the tide. Here they encamped, and barricading the only vulnerable point, they directed a brass six-pounder field-piece from a port-hole left for the purpose, and, loading their rifles, prepared for the worst. The precaution was well timed. The day following this removal, the tribes from the Umpqua, Coquille, and Rogue River, congregated, and mustered nearly a thousand braves. Armed with bows and arrows, and ignorant of the deadly qualities of the American rifle, they advanced up the passageway with yells that made the little band within quail with apprehension. The besieged were under the command of a Tennessean, who restrained the men until their tattooed assailants had approached in an irregular mass, four or five deep, to within a few yards of the field-piece, when the order to fire was given. My informant, who was one of the party, described the scene in Texan vernacular, which I regret I am unable to repeat. It would depict the scene a thousand-fold more graphically than I could write it.

In loading the gun, which was done with slugs, stones, and bits of iron, to the muzzle, they had exhausted their slender stock of powder to two rounds of pistol and rifle charges. As the eyes of the savages gleamed through the chinks of the brushwood barricade, the death-dealing discharge tore through their ranks. This, followed by a well-directed volley from the rifles and revolvers, of which every shot told, sent such of the Indians as were not wounded pell-mell back. What with the roar of the cannon, the cracking of the fire-arms, and the yells of the wounded, the whole mass took to their heels and fled affrighted into the forest. Numbers were dashed into the boiling surf below, or killed among the rocks in their descent. This was the first and last volley. No estimate was made of the slain. Indeed they stayed not to count, but after a hurried consultation, and fearful of the return of the Indians in still greater force, and knowing their own want of ammunition, they abandoned the fort, and taking to the forest, traveled for several weeks, entering the Willamette Valley, and so reaching Portland.

It was a bright sparkling morning, the sun pouring down a flood of radiance after the rain of the previous night, when we mounted two shaggy but strong Indian ponies, and set out for Empire City, at Coos Bay. Every leaf seemed to glitter in the light, and dew-drops sparkled in every bush. It was a morning to make one "love to live," as the lungs expanded with the respiration of spirits like that following the inhalation of laughing gas. The characteristic dryness of the Autumn months of California is not found among these verdant woods. Green and fragrant heath-blossoms adorned the sides of the road, and at times we crossed some noisy rivulet, scolding its way toward the sea, half concealed by an overhanging drapery of verdure fed by its waters.

This continued for some miles, when we came out upon the sea-shore; and now, joined by a couple of horsemen bound to some point above, we scampered over a hard sand beach until we reached the Elk River. Hillman (E. E. Hillman, civilian physician under contract to U.S.Army) having passed this way about a year before, and anxious to display his knowledge of the route, selected the ford, and dashed in, but was soon up to his middle, and reached the opposite banks, having partaken of a cold bath much against his will. The rest, more cautions, mounted the tops of their saddles and escaped with only wet feet. This river during the winter months is impassable. The distance from a log-house standing on the bank to the Sixes River is some six miles, the road leading through a thickly-wooded country. On the route we crossed Cape Blanco, which, until the completion of the recent coast reconnaissance, was supposed to be the most westernmost point of the United States. Cape Mendocino, however, in California, is believed to be a mile or two farther seaward. Our new friends had left us, and we galloped along the verge of the beetling cliff, where we paused to "breathe our horses," and gaze off into the blue ocean beyond.

Here, since the creation, these foaming breakers have chafed, and the rocks skirting the base of the precipice have dashed them defiantly back. From the pitch of the cape a dangerous reef of rocks, standing high above the water, stretches out to sea; the rocks, as we stood and held our hats on in the face of the sea-breeze, were sometimes hidden in the toppling foam. A line carried directly west from where we stand would nearly touch Jeddo, and meet with no impediment on the way. All is "deep blue ocean" between. Here the footsteps of a young American must pause a while. From this point we may look back upon the continent. The cape is a prominent landmark to the mariner, and from here the land trends away to the northeast, giving to the headland the appearance of a shoulder thrust far into the sea. The bluff, crested with pine trees, standing almost upon the very brink, and sloping thence inland, forms a plateau, or piece of table-land, finely wooded, across which the sharp sea gales whistle with unchecked fury. From the cape to "the Sixes" is about two miles. The country slopes to the northward, forming a valley through which the river flows to the ocean. The Sixes has not yet been traced to its source, though it takes its rise not above 40 miles in the interior. It can be ascended with canoes about 12 miles, and is said to wind among fertile bottoms and reaches of the prairie land hitherto only traversed by Indians and wild beasts. It empties into the ocean under the lee of a huge rock, but the bar is impassable even for a canoe. From seaward no entrance can be discerned. At its mouth stands Dan's cabin.

"Dan is an old Norwegian sailor, whose half century of adventures have carried him thrice around the world. He has sailed under every flag in Christendom, has fought in numerous naval engagements, and has been often wounded. Among the otter and bear hunting community in which he is now located, and who never saw salt-water or ship until their journey across the continent to the Pacific shores, he is regarded as a curious ocean monster, to be listened to respectfully, and heeded with more than ordinary awe. His fearful oaths — almost unintelligible, from the Dutch jargon with which he mingles them — his rough outlandish appearance, his undisputed courage, and kind simplicity, have made him notorious, and the traveler along the coast looks forward with sharpened appetite to the roasted salmon or roiled bear steak at 'Dan's.'"

We arrived at the ford at dead low-water, and Hillman determined to push across, though the quicksands are said to be dangerous at that point. However, we plunged in, and by dint of spurring and shouting, reached the opposite side. Dan's hut is about 200 yards from the northern bank. We rode up to the door of a log cabin situated at the mouth of a ravine, and partly embowered in its tangled foliage. From this issues a rivulet discharging into the river; and here the old Northman has decided to pass the rest of his days, within hearing of the ocean's roar — just near enough to be reminded of his many adventures, and yet secure from its dangers.

Dismounting, we tied our horses to a post, while the door opened, and a long-haired, sober-faced trapper, with a face like leather and with the seriousness of a parson, gazed out upon us with Indian stoicism. He was about 35 years of age. Around his head was a dirty handkerchief, the ends of which hung negligently down his face. Slashed buckskin pants, hunting-shirt and moccasins made up his apparel, while the short black pipe, which he held firmly between his teeth, showed that our arrival had disturbed him in the enjoyment of the hunter's Elysium. He regarded our operations with silence and indifference, and when we inquired for Dan, replied by throwing open the door, which hung on wooden hinges, and re-entered the cabin, leaving us to follow if we pleased. After fastening our animals we entered, and found the trapper already stretched before the fire, gazing immovably at the smoky rafters, and pulling gently at the digestive pipe. It was evident that an attempt to disturb our new acquaintance again would be useless, so we shouted, "Dan! Halo there, Dan!" whereupon a savage growl from one of the hide beds in the corner announced that the lord of the manor was taking an early snooze.

"Can you get us something to eat, Dan?" said I, in my blandest tone.

"Are you Coos Bay people?" asked the voice from the bed.

It flashed across me that a slight fib in such a strait would be excusable, and thinking that the Norwegian might have a peculiar regard for the denizens of Coos Bay, I replied, "Yes!"

"Well, get out o' my cabin den, you bloody sneaks! Da don't no Coos Bay man get no grub in my cabin — they're mean enough to pack their own grub!"

It was evident I had made a mistake, and I hastened to explain, when Hillman, who had known Dan, came to the rescue.

"Dan! Don't you know me? It's the doctor; Dr. Hillman, that cured you of the rheumatics last year. Don't you remember me, old fellow?"

At this the heap of bed-clothes began to move, and the old Norwegian, grunting with pain, came out of his lair. He speedily knew the Doctor, and welcomed him, but without deigning me a word or look. The sight of a fat haunch of elk hanging from the ridge pole obliged me to smother my feelings.

Without a dozen words he got to work, and in another 10 minutes was roasting several fine steaks before the fire, which crackled in a huge chimney of mud and stones. Silence seemed the order of the day in this hermit's abode, so, without saying, "By your leave," I stepped over the prostrate body of the trapper, and took down from the fire-place notch a soot-begrimed pipe, half filled with the "dear wee," coolly lit it by an ember, and puffed away.

Dan said nothing. Thus encouraged, I addressed a few words to him with a view of opening a conversation, but without success, and a garrulous attempt upon the still motionless trapper was equally without avail. Foiled so far, and determined to draw the old fellow out, as I learned he had a fund of anecdote, I produced a flask of brandy, saved as a precious relic of San Francisco, and taking a swallow to prove it was not poisoned, passed it silently to the old sailor. He smelt at the mouth, and immediately took a strong pull at its contents, uttering a prolonged and satisfactory "a-h!" as he returned it. The fountains of his loquacity were opened at once, and turning a curious glance toward me, he observed,

"You didn't get dat at Port Orford, no how!"

"You say right," replied Hillman.

And therewith commenced a conversation of an hour's duration; but the trapper, though paying his respects to the flask, said nothing. Throughout this class of men it will be observed, that being alone and in the silent forests or mountain solitudes the greater part of their lives, they acquire a taciturn habit, which seldom leaves them.

We found, by actual experiment, that the sand in the bottom of the rivulet near the house contained gold in fine particles. Dan hobbled out and washed a pan of earth, in which were hundreds of minute specs of the precious metal.

The whole ocean beach of Oregon is thus impregnated with gold, to a greater or less extent. Among other facts, Dan stated that a law went into operation last winter in Oregon, prohibiting the sale of liquors except by the payment of a quarterly license of $50. No sooner had the law gone into effect than the Deputy Sheriff started from Coos Bay, and traveling rapidly through the country before the law could become generally known, had taken every place in his route where liquor was sold, and imposed the fine for selling without a license. Dan's was among the proscribed number, and to this day he heaps anathemas on Coos Bay and its entire population, not one of whom need apply at his door for entertainment. This explained his ominous question on our entrance, "Are you Coos Bay people?"

We gradually grew to be good friends with both Dan and the trapper, and both took particular pains to direct us on our route. By the time our horses were rested we had learned all the necessary facts regarding the country, and paying our score, we mounted and started away to the northward, Dan's old white mare breaking away as we dashed past, and he and his companion performing a series of indescribable gyrations to arrest her evident intentions of following us. We soon reached the ocean beach, where the nature of the sand admits of no faster motion than a walk. The sky to seaward began to thicken, and soon we were riding through a fog so dense that the banks of surf, a few hundred yards from us, were scarcely visible. After an hour Hillman's black beard was sparkling like hoar-frost; the glittering drops standing upon his mustaches as in a winter's morning in New England. The fog was driven inland by a keen wind that searched every seam and opening. It was like riding in the rain. Such weather may be counted on two-thirds of the year along the Oregon beach.

While on the route we met Ben Wright, the sub-Indian agent, an experienced hunter and trapper, whose life has been passed in the mountains and on the western frontier. He was a man of some 32 years, with black curling hair, reaching, beneath a slouched Palo Alto hat, down to his shoulders; a Missouri rifle was slung across his back, and he rode a heavy black mule with bear-skin machillas. Altogether, he was a splendid specimen of a backwoodsman of noble stature, lithe as an eel, of Herculean strength, and with all the shrewdness and cunning acquired by a lifetime passed among the North American Indians. Almost disdaining the comforts of civilized life, and used to the scanty fare of the hunter, he seemed peculiarly fitted for the office he held. I am thus particular in the description of Ben Wright, as his name has just been published among those who were butchered by the Chetkoe tribe at Rogue River in February last. He was in company, when we met him, with several others, any one of whom would nearly answer to this description. Some of them have shared his fate in the massacre above referred to.

Mining Days

Documentation of early (1850s) mining activities in the Port Orford quadrangle is difficult to locate as most activities were reported in newspaper accounts in the *Alta California, Crescent City Herald* and the *Oregonian* and were subject to a good deal of exaggerated claims. Tichenor used "gold fever" as a method to lure the first contingent of settlers from the streets of San Francisco with handbills proclaiming "gold for the taking" on the beaches near his Donation Land Claim at Port Orford. His motive was to procure labor to operate his planned sawmill as not many men would volunteer to sail up the coast to an unsettled, wild part of the Southern Oregon coast to work in a sawmill. The possibility of a rich strike was a "horse of a different color" and he lured 65 men from the raucous saloons and flop houses of the Barbary Coast to make the trip north. Once they arrived, the prospectors found very little promise as the gold bearing black sands on the beaches required the use of mercury to extract the fine gold and the deep gravels along the beaches of the rivers required major undertakings to remove the overburden.

J. S. Diller wrote in 1903, "Nearly all of the gold which has thus far been obtained in the Port Orford quadrangle has come from placer mines, some of which are along beaches in marine deposits and the rest in river gravels, especially along the South Fork of the Sixes ..." Early beach miners included William Sullivan and Patrick Hughes who worked the area south of Cape Blanco for many years. This area was worked continuously until the early 1940s. Jake Summers, one of the original defenders of Battle Rock, mined for years on the south fork of the Sixes. His activities attracted other miners and a fair sized settlement grew up around the diggings ... large enough to be designated as the Summerville Precinct in early elections. Randolph Tichenor, among others, secured a spiritous liquor license for the town.

The Blanco Mine at Madden Butte (near Pacific High School) and the Sixes Mine two and one half miles south of Denmark were developed in the 1870s and were excavations into ancient ocean beaches that yielded platinum and gold-bearing black sands. Charles Jamieson, Mr. Corbin and Mr. Divilbliss were operating mines in 1903 along the Sixes River. The geologist Diller estimated that nearly one million dollars had been taken from the Sixes drainage by 1903, and this estimate was quoted in various schemes to raise monies to operate dredges and open new mining ventures. The figures were questioned in several articles written by John Fitzhugh and M. G. Pohl. Fitzhugh estimated that no more than $50,000 had been extracted, while Pohl's estimate totalled $280,000. Pohl also named some early miners which included the Guerin brothers, Louis Turner, Alboid, the Gatchel brothers, Wilson brothers, C. Morris and a group of Chinamen. Both Pohl and Fitzhugh were knowledgeable on the subject and their estimates were probably more accurate than the promoters.

The Divilbliss and Jamieson operations utilized hydraulics as a method of washing away the gravels as did the Madden Butte (Blanco) Mine. Jamieson's operation was known as the Big Jewel Mine.

In the 1920s mining activities were rekindled by the Inman interests which included a variety of proposals to mine, harvest timber and and construction of a flume to carry logs to the Port of Port Orford which the Inman interest hoped to acquire. The crash of 1929 brought a decline in mining ventures on a large scale but the various ares were honey-combed by "Coyote" mining activities of individual prospectors. In 1933, Gilbert Gable rekindled the mining campfires along the Sixes River with a dredging and placer operations. He constructed a camp on Edson Creek near where the recreation area is now. Then it was a four mile pack above the Plum Trees. Dolly Smith, Bert Hoggatt, Airel McDonald, Lorna Lacey Fruitt and Murial Spoon were a few who worked at the mine. Gable later turned his interest to Port Orford, purchasing the Port property and establishing Trans-Pacific Lumber Company. The actual gold production of the Sixes River venture is unknown.

Today's mining activity is limited to individuals using small dredges in the main streambed. It is probably safe to say that production using this technique is as high as the old hydraulics were in the early days.

While the total production may not have been impressive, a spot check of the day book of the P. J. Masterson store for the year 1897, shows the following miners selling dust at $16 per ounce: Bailey, Corbin, Divilbliss, Brainaird, Hughes, F. Stewart, Fitzhugh, Telby, Patton, Wilson, C. Haines, C. Green, Wattens, Morse, Sullivan, Keller, Platts, A. Jamieson and Zahnizer. Haines sold the greatest volume but never over three to four ounces at a time. Conclusion? Check the records to locate his claim ... maybe he left some. Gold dust did provide a meager livelihood for some. No diamond stickpins but much needed bacon and beans and an occasional brandy.

Blanco Black Sand Mines

Mining, considered one of the leading industries of Curry County in the early pioneer years and the one industry which brought the early settlers to the West, is now carried on by only a few dedicated prospectors working singly, as no large operations have prospered in the northern part of the county in the last 30 years.

One of the larger pioneer mines, located two miles north of Sixes on the main Highway 101, was the Blanco Black Sand Mines, owned and operated by the man who discovered gold in the vicinity, Cyrus Madden. In later years the mines became known as the Madden Mines and the steep hill in the background as Madden Butte. During the time the mines operated, the main highway (county road) was farther west from the present state highway. Deep undergrowth has covered over what visible remains there are of the mines, which were in operation for more than 40 years.

Cyrus Madden was born in Ohio in 1832, and started for the west in 1858, after graduating from Denison University. He taught school in Kentucky, at the same time taking a law course, and was admitted to the bar in that state in 1860. In 1861, he crossed the plains, driving a mule team to San Francisco where he taught in the public schools. Prior to coming to Oregon, he worked for more than three years at the Salmon River mines, then came north on a prospecting trip. Madden knew "pay dirt" when he saw it and eventually acquired around 300 acres of mining land. Being an efficient operator, he used improved methods and equipment developing one of the most valuable mines in the county.

John Fitzhugh, U.S. Deputy Mineral Surveyor, made a complete survey of the Blanco Black Sand Mines. The survey and special reports were recorded with the county clerk, J. H. Gauntlet, on July 24, 1871.

The survey notes mentioned that timber of any size was all dead. The undergrowth of young fir, spruce, alder, hemlock with the brush and briars is very dense, making the survey extremely difficult. The surface of the claim is generally third rate soil with a very small portion being second rate.

Gilbert E. Gable

Gilbert Gable, mentioned earlier as an operator of dredging and placer operations along the Sixes River was featured in the December 5, 1941 issue of the *Port Orford Post* along with William Tichenor. These men were brought to the attention of readers because of their efforts, 80 years apart, to develop Port Orford. Their goals and methods had striking similarities. (The photos of them were published in the *Post* in conjunction with Gable's untimely death and an old timers contest.) Tichenor, the founder and Gable, the promoter. Both men dabbled in mining ventures, operated sawmills, promoted land sales, pushed for port and breakwater development but neither lived to see his aspirations succeed.

Gable first came to Curry County in 1933 after a varied career in publicity, motion pictures, exploration and radio broadcasting.

For several years his energies were directed towards development of a gold mining operation on the Sixes River and it was there that he came into contact with the plans and engineering design drawn by George Walker of Bandon for the Inman interests that had attempted to purchase the Port Orford Port several years previously. The scheme called for the alteration of Graveyard Point, a 400 foot wharf served by a railroad and protected by a jetty straight out from the point. Seven existing rocks would serve as moorings for large vessels. With a cash injection of $300,000, supplied by Mrs. Elizabeth Cunningham, a wealthy Cincinnati widow, Gable began to develop Inman's dream. He convinced bankers and contractors of the feasibility of his over-all plan and the Trans-Pacific Mill and Port Orford Dock and Terminal Company had its beginning. He purchased the wharf site from the Port Commission by agreeing to amortize the outstanding bonds which the Port was unable to pay. The mill site, Buffington Part, was purchased from the Inman interests and in short order a large, modern sawmill was erected.

During this time, Gable had constructed, on the bluff overlooking the dock, a large somewhat pretentious administration building which was to serve his "Gold Coast" empire. In 1935, he blasted the outer portion of Graveyard Point, utilizing the material for the breakwater. The breakwater-dock facilities lasted less than a year as the material used failed to withstand the westerly surges of the first winter storm. Although the mill continued to turn out excellent grade lumber for six or so years, the port development failed to materialize. The Widow Cunningham, upon advice of a private investigator, Col. Paddock, took a complete loss ... about six million by today's standards. In a later court action, the judge observed "... the influence of Mr. Gable, not only over Mrs. Cunningham, but also over the defendant, Capitol National Bank (Sacramento), and the plaintiff corporation, Gorman-McDuffee, appeared to have been almost hypnotic, or a mesmerization, and accounts for many of the peculiar business performances on the part of both the bank ... and corporation." The court concluded "Seldom has a factual presentation been made, or a story written which equals the recital contained in this record of the power which one man, by reason of his overabundance of optimism, was able to exert over bankers and contractors." Such was the M.O. of Gilbert Gable. Despite the bias from the bench, he won the case!

Using topographical maps, Gable projected a railroad right-of-way south from Port Orford through Lobster Creek and up Rogue River connecting to the mainline of Southern Pacific near Wolf Creek. After several years of pushing applications and stock, the undertaking was denied by the powers that be. This denial was the inspiration for the State of Jefferson Movement. Over the years, many individuals have taken the credit for the initiation of the "State of Jefferson" Secession Movement in 1941. But it was Gilbert Gable, Elmer Mankus (Brooking), C. H.Buffington (Gold Beach) and the Curry County Court, headed by Judge Boice who opened talks with California officials in October, 1941, to discuss the possibility of joining that state. Judge Boice appointed the afore-mentioned men to a special commission and they met with California Governor Culbert Olson, on October 30, 1940, and he, in turn scheduled a hearing before an assembly com-mittee on governmental affairs. These men, tired of the empty promises for development aid from the Oregon politicians were dead serious.

Gable's credibility was severely damaged after he appeared before the Portland Chamber of Commerce in November and told the group of a "mystery metal" which lined the beaches of Curry County … a metal harder than steel. *The Oregonian* gave this story a full page. A month later, Gable was dead and the secession movement deteriorated into the "State of Jefferson" circus, headed by Randolph Collier, a state senator from Northern California. Pearl Harbor came next and the issue died.

But while Mr. Gable was plagued with legal and financial difficulties, he never lost his enthusiasm for Port Orford. After leading the battle to incorporate the town he worked tirelessly to upgrade the water system, fire department, library and the over-all image of the city he adopted. Mrs. Gable was active in the culture and arts of the com-munity and helped found the *Guild* and Art Association among other things, including scouting, kindergarten, the "Cinderella Players" featuring a cast of forty, chorus, band, ladies aid and on and on. The Gables were very energetic and Port Orford is certainly the better for their having passed through.

In 1979, Robert (Bobby) Gable visited Port Orford to dedicate the Mayor Gable Council Chambers which he had generously funded as a memorial to his father. There one can see the artifacts of a dream in the form of photos of the mill, administration build-ing, railroad plans and the hand-made myrtlewood council chairs (made by Doug Johnson) which, as hard as they are, will, undoubtedly serve forever.

17

Lakeport

The Impossible Scheme

The following report by Sally Prince appeared in *Oregon Coast Magazine,* October/November 1984. It is reprinted here with permission of the author.

~ ~ ~

The serenity surrounding Floras Lake, in 1908, was suddenly swallowed up by two land sharks with an impossible scheme. Just how they happened on this particular spot is now forgotten. What took place, after they conspired to use the lake and its encompassing wilderness to their own advantage is recorded in history.

The schemers, still remembered as "those two ex-army engineers named Crittendon and Lee," envisioned the fresh-water lake as a coastal harbor. All that was needed to make their vision a reality, they reasoned, was a canal through the 30-foot high sand dune ridge that separated some 25 square miles of lake from the ocean. This channel would create a protected harbor for ships. It would bring world trade to Curry County.

The feasibility of such a project was never considered. Instead, their fantasy included a town of tremendous growth, booming industries, and of course, great wealth for themselves. Within a year's time the peaceful wilderness, located some ten miles north of Port Orford, was transformed into the largest and busiest town in the county.

To give their scheme the support and credibility it needed, Crittendon and Lee formed a corporation, the Lakeport Investment Company, with offices in Portland and

Spokane. Shares were quoted at $100. Using promotional literature, with maps showing the lake to be many fathoms deep, and extensive advertising, the hook was baited. When ads appeared with lake-front lots selling for $12.50, it wasn't long before the promoters were reeling in buyers by the hundreds. Within a short time, lot prices increased to $25, then $50, and finally $300. Opportunity seekers, hoping to make their fortune in this soon-to-be seaport of the world, came from the East, Midwest, and Pacific Coast states. They sold their ranches, homes, and businesses to flock to what was now called Lakeport. Because this enterprise was considered the fastest-growing development on the Pacific Coast, the name was soon changed to Pacific City. Most people, however, continued to refer to it by its original name.

These gullible buyers did not question the promoter's plan. It sounded good to them, and it looked good on paper. They gave no thought to the dune's shifting sands, or to winter storms that would play havoc on the proposed canal entrance. No one inquired if a jetty might be needed. Nor did they ask about transportation for immediate inland shipping. The nearest railroad was 40 miles away, and roads were in poor condition. Heavy winter rains turned them into rivers of mud. All they could see was a big city and an active waterfront lined with warehouses. Their dream: prosperity for all.

To nurture these dreams, immediate development was started by the schemers. Streets were staked out, cleared, and graded. Water pipes were laid. Carpenters worked long hours building shacks, and later, permanent housing. The lumber was milled from the timber felled to clear the land. The sawmill grew from a 25,000 daily board-foot capacity to a 60,000 daily board-foot capacity.

The *Floras Lake Banner*, a seven column newspaper, was established and began publishing the opportunities awaiting those who came to Lakeport. A schoolhouse was built. A post office was established. A bakery, livery stable, freight sheds, a hardware and grocery store, and several eating places opened for business. Professional men, lawyers, doctors, and dentists set up offices.

Withing the first year the town's population swelled to 500, with more arriving each day. The monthly payroll reached $20,000.

It took more than a year's time for the excitement of the new town to wane. When it did, the townspeople began to ask the all important question: When was the canal going to be dug? After all, didn't Lakeport's survival depend on becoming a seaport? The promoters stalled for time. They said they were having difficulty obtaining permission from the government to dig the canal.

Eventually permission to dig the canal was received. It didn't take long for the surveyors to discover the flaw in the scheme, something Crittendon and Lee may, or may not have known. But had they done some investigating before incorporating, they would have learned that Floras Lake was 40 feet above sea level! A canal would drain the lake into the ocean. The bad news spread quickly, and gloom covered the town. Some suggested canal locks might be built, but the cost was prohibitive.

Crittendon and Lee vanished within a few days. It is reported they were never apprehended. Almost overnight Lakeport became a ghost town. Everyone that could leave did so. Those who had no place to go, and those who refused to give up their dreams lingered on for several years. The post office remained there until 1915.

In March 1916, Curry County brought tax suits against the Lakeport Improvement Company and some 150 property owners. The city's 6,000 lots were sold for taxes. Bids ranged from one cent to six dollars for a lot with a house on it. Not a trace of Lakeport can be found today, but there are those who still remember it.

Charlie Jensen will be 84 this year and lives only a few miles from Floras Lake. He remembers his father helped to build Lakeport.

"I was about nine years old," he says, "when my dad ran the only motorized boat on the lake. They didn't have motor boats then, so he installed a one-cylinder gas engine, with a drive-shaft and propeller, and used this to haul lumber and pilings across the lake. He earned about 30 cents an hour for doing this and felt pretty good about bringing home $3 a day. Most of the others were getting only a $1.50 for a ten-hour day.

Charlie's mother told him the family received a letter from Crittendon and Lee asking that they lease their farm to them. Fortunately, the Jensen family did not lease the farm. Charlie and his family continue to live on it today.

He recalls the hardship the Lakeport scheme brought to the Ned Thompsen family. "Thompson owned the hardware store. He sold everything they had in Minnesota to come out here and lost it all."

Chauncey Woodruff did sell his property to Crittendon and Lee. He owned a large ranch and dairy farm near Floras Lake, but he fared much better than the Thompsen family when Lakeport folded. He was quick to foreclose on the company for back payments and reclaimed his property.

His oldest daughter Gladys Woodruff Henry, who now lives in Eugene, was away at school during Lakeport's heyday. When she returned to the farm, she attended the Lakeport School.

"It was just a bunkhouse. All the grades in one large room. A small woodstove heated the place in winter, and I remember we all drank from a community dipper out of a bucket of water. We all stayed healthy though, even with everyone using the same dipper."

Her younger brother, Ed, lives in Coquille, and he grew up on stories about Lakeport. Ed enjoys telling about some of the town's more colorful characters who stayed around after the Lakeport scheme collapsed.

"There was old man Murphy. He had the mortgage on the big hotel and wanted to protect his property. He was crippled and people took advantage of him by stealing from him every chance they could.

"He chewed tobacco, and he sure got his money's worth out of it. After he chewed it for a time, he'd put the cud on top of the woodstove to dry. When it was dry he rolled it and smoked it. He always had a whole line of cuds a-sittin' there and dryin'.

"That hotel of his was quite a building. It was three stories high and had plush carpets. There was a bathroom on the end of each floor. Most every other place had outdoor privies. It had a bar, dance floor and dining room. It was the place for big social gatherings.

"Old Murphy had a lady friend who stayed there with him named Belle. She was quite a gal, I hear, and they called her 'The Bell of Lakeport.'

"Our family always had plenty of meat off the ranch, but there was a fella who'd drive a wagon through town sellin' fresh meat. He'd kill an animal one day and hoped he'd sell it the next. The meat was in the back of the wagon on some canvas. He would cut off whatever you wanted and roll it up in some paper. Them days there was no sanitation laws and no refrigeration.

"When people began to tear down the Lakeport buildings for the lumber, my dad trucked off the hotel lumber with his team. As far as honesty was concerned about taking the lumber, well, in those days it was just a matter of principle that you helped yourself. No one thought anything of it."

After the hotel was gone Ed would sit on the cement foundation and shoot rabbits.

The natural setting of woods and water has been restored to Floras Lake by time. A dense growth of salal, berry bushes and fern cover the once busy streets of Lakeport. Scrub pine and spruce have taken possession of what was once a thriving community. The placid lake is used for fishing and boating, and a number of homes with private boat docks surround it. Although birds continue to find refuge there, the wild swans and geese that Gladys Henry recalls as once "covering the lake" are gone.

Winter storms lash out in fury at the dunes and continual coastal winds arrange the sand in interesting patterns. Those who visit the lake enjoy its serenity. In fact, Floras Lake is pretty much as it was before the impossible scheme.

18

Saw Mills At Port Orford
Past And Present

The following report on the sawmills of Port Orford was written by Frank B. Tichenor in 1940.

In pioneer history, Port Orford holds a thrilling and sacred place. In and about this hamlet surged the wild forces of race conquest and heroic achievement. Not until the present set-up, the Trans-Pacific Company, did this community commence to grow in numbers and security. Port Orford at the present time is a busy scene of lumber and milling and shipping.

The first sawmill arrived at Port Orford on the schooner *San Diego* in 1854. The proprietors of the mill were Rufus and H. B. Tichenor, who located the mill at what is now known as Silver Butte Creek, and at a later date moved and located between what is now Jackson and Oregon Streets and 17th Street. Eighteen days after the *San Diego* unloaded the machinery, the mill was in operation. This first mill gave employment to 25 men, and had a capacity of 500 feet every ten hours. William S. Winsor, of honored pioneer name, was the mechanical manager of the mill and was the one to prepare the first shipment for market. He gave it the name of Port Orford cedar, and by that name it is still known to the world. Mr. Winsor, his wife, and son Charles are buried on the Heads at Port Orford. In 1857, Rufus Tichenor drew out of the firm and returned to new York, and the firm of H. B. Tichenor and Company was formed.

A plank road was made to the mill and covered with sawdust. Every few hours in the day great teams of Percheron horses easily and smoothly drew tremendous loads over such roads and down to the beach where the present wharf is located. There the lumber was loaded on sailing vessels by lighters and brought $125 a thousand board feet at San Francisco.

Mr. Gould built a mill at Hubbards Creek in 1875 one mile east of Port Orford. A tramway was built out to the mill rocks where lighters were loaded and were towed out to schooners. Mr. Gould ran the mill for several years.

While in the mill business, Mr. Gould was elected as Joint Representative in 1878. The mill sawed the pick of cedar from Hubbards Creek to the Elk River. A small town sprang up in a short time. A store, warehouse, blacksmith shop, and some thirty shacks and the mill pond (sic) was located where the Knapp field is now. Small sailing vessels carried the output of this mill to San Francisco. Two and three schooners were often anchored at once during the summer months waiting their turn to be loaded. The cedar lumber was of the best, free from knot and rot. Tramways ran up both branches of Hubbards Creek and through to the Forty Ranch. Oxen were used in hauling the logs to the pond, trees were chopped down and the workmanship was perfect. The ax men in the '70s and '80s prided themselves in their work. The mill employed 60 men in all. Mr. Gould lost one million dollars in this enterprise. After two years of operation, Mr. Gould sold out to Mr. Lurensen, who in turn sold out to Diamond and Dixon. Dixon was drowned in the mill race, and Frankie Roice, older brother of our present County Judge, was drowned in the mill pond. Diamond closed down the mill after a heavy loss. The mill lay idle from 1882 to 1884, when it was again operated by Louis Knapp for a short time; this ended the sawmill business on Hubbards Creek.

The third venture in the sawmill business was in 1884 when Joe Nay built a mill on Elk River below where the highway bridge now crosses the stream. The Schooner *Mose* took on a full load of cedar June, 1884, and failing to clear the harbor, struck Hells Gate and was a total loss. This was a sad blow to Joe Nay and he never recovered financially.

The Crawford and Wilbur Mill was built in 1886. The first mill was built about one mile in on the Cape Blanco Road. This was a small mill to cut lumber to build a larger mill and at the same time they started a foundation for a mill on Hughes' ranch and this was washed away. Then they built their mill on the north end of what is now the Knapp Ranch. A tramway was built from there to the wharf which they built in 1885. This was the first wharf ever built in Port Orford and stood for 28 years. The tramway crossed the north end of the lake, where the present bridge crosses it. Crawford had a store at Port Orford and was the uncle of Al Marsh.

The Crawford and Wilber Mill failed after a loss to the owners.

In 1940, we find a saw mill at Port Orford that cuts more lumber at one shift than the old mills cut in a month, and they do not depend on the ox teams to carry their lumber to the wharf. Steam instead of sails takes the lumber to market. The Trans-Pacific Company ships more lumber in 18 months than was shipped from 1854 to 1887.

With harbor improvements, all the mill companies in the past would have been financial successes.

19

Swift And Company Cheese Factory

Neonta Hall contributed the following report on the cheese company which was located at Sixes, Oregon in 1943.

During World War II there was a shortage of help so many women had to work in the cheese factory. Among the management team were Wes Zumwalt, manager; Ralph Hall, head cheese maker; Keith Miller, Joe Hayward, Crissy Miller and Beatrice Zumwalt and Neonta Hall. Stanley Quigley formerly was head cheese maker.

This factory contained three large vats, 10,000 pounds capacity each, of milk. May and June were high milk production months of the year. A large steam boiler, which used lots of wood, provided steam and hot water (a very necessary item). Ray Mills, Sam Hull and many others in the community supplied slab wood from small mills around at that time. Boxes were made at the factory to ship the cheese in. The Swift & Company brands and dates were on the cheese and boxes. They were five pound loaves, 28 pound longhorn and 15 pound wheels. All cheese was dipped in paraffin at the plant, using as much as 100 pounds of melted paraffin a day. Farmers brought milk to the factory in ten gallon milk cans which was weighed and a sample taken for a butterfat test. Farmers washed their cans in a can washer, the steam boiler providing hot water and steam. The larger dairy ranches would have more than 100 cans of milk in May and June, the peak months of the season.

Twenty or more ranches supplied milk to this factory, including Zumwalt Brothers, John Fromm, Virgil Libby, Kay Nodine, Raymond Capps, Ralph Hall, Stanley Quigley, Jessie Henry Welch, Davy Crockett, Farrier Brothers, George Horner, Joe Blanchard, Bill Bennett, William Tyson, the Hughes Ranch, The Piercy Sweet Ranch, the Knapp Ranch, the March Ranch, the Wagner Ranches, Harry White, Don McKenzie,

George Woodworth, Bob McKenzie, Bill Sweet Ranches of Sixes and Elk River areas. The factory had inspections by the State Health Department for cleanliness and for the quality of cheese being made.

Wes and Beatrice Zumwalt, with their children Bruce, Patricia and Arnold, lived in a house provided by the company at Crystal Creek near the bridge with the factory situated just north of the house. Both the factory and the house have since burned. Wes was well qualified for cheese making as the Zumwalt Ranch had been in the dairy business for many years prior to this time, making cheese for the markets.

20

World War II

The first days of December, 1941 were laden with the excitement of a maritime disaster, the sadness of the passing of a controversial but popular community leader and the shock of the attack by the Japanese Imperial Navy upon the naval base at Pearl Harbor, Hawaii.

The beginning of a period of uncertainty, well founded fear and isolation for the community of Port Orford followed on the shipwreck of the *S. S. Willapa* which foundered near Humbug Mountain; the death of Gilbert Gable and the Japanese air attack.

Following Pearl Harbor the Japanese invasions of the Philippines and Pacific Islands would ensnare two local men who were subjected to the infamous Bataan Death March. Everett Quigly, working as a civilian, was captured at Wake Island and while permanently disabled survived the horrible ordeal. Curly Tribby was taken at Corregidor … he did not survive the march.

Dozens of the Port Orford area's men and women would subsequently answer the patriotic call to arms serving in practically all theatres of war as fleet marines, submariners, foot and ski troopers, fighter, bomber and transport air crews and pilots, cat skinners and drivers for the "Sea Bees," communication and code decypherers, nurses, paratroopers, merchant mariners and defense plant workers. Able bodied men were at a premium during the duration for ranching, logging and fishing. They were busy fighting a war.

In Memorium

Jesse Sturdivant   Lost in submarine disaster just before war.
Curly Tribby   Died on Bataan Death March, 1942.
Huck Malloy   Lost in airplane crash.

The Saga Of The *I-25*

On station at the entrance of Pearl Harbor on December 7th, 1941, the 350-foot submarine *I-25* was assigned the task of destroying any vessel attempting to clear the harbor during the air strike. Although the sub spotted the *U. S. S. Enterprise,* the huge carrier easily outran the undersea marauder. The *I-25* then proceeded to the west coast of the United States where it patrolled from the Columbia River to Monterey, California. It was on the first of its three missions to the west coast and was one of nine "I-Boats" assigned to patrol the Pacific Coast. The *I-9,* later sunk in the Aluetians, was the first submarine stationed off Cape Blanco during the early days of the war.

These boats were the cream of the crop of Japanese navy subs. Over 350-feet long with a crew of 100 men they could easily range along the entire west coast of the United States from their supply base at Kwajalein in the Marshal Islands. These subs continued their patrols from December of 1941 until October 1942, sinking eight surface vessels and one Russian submarine while damaging six other ships. Although the subs were ordered to shell major west coast mainland targets on Christmas Eve in 1941, the plan was scrapped due to increased defensive operations along the coast. On February 23, 1942 the submarine *I-17* surfaced in the Santa Barbara channel and lobbed several rounds toward oil storage tanks at Galeta from its 5.5 inch deck gun, while on June 21 the *I-25* fired 17 rounds at Fort Stevens near the mouth of the Columbia River. (Both subs escaped but their daring raids unnerved the population, the military and of course headline writers.)

The author had an opportunity to interview an ex-mariner who recalled a submarine attack in 1942:

"My first visit to Port Orford was under much different circumstances," related Bob Adams of Salt Lake City, "and most people just don't believe it happened." His first trip was made on the Richfield Oil Company's tanker *Larry Doheney* in 1942. The voyage was abruptly interrupted when the Japanese submarine *I-25* slammed a torpedo home about 25 miles southwest of Port Orford.

"It was Monday, October 5th. I was working as an oiler and was just starting to get ready to take the midnight to four a.m. watch. I was resting in my bunk which was aft when around 10:30 the explosion occurred. The tanker raised up about two feet and then was literally bent amidships. After the initial shock and confusion we managed to lower the boats. The navy gun crew stayed at their station which was on the stern ... hoping to get a round off if the sub surfaced. Fire then broke out and the sea became a raging inferno ... it was as bright as high noon. The navy crew had to jump from the stern and several were badly burned.

"Our skipper was the last to leave the ship and unfortunately as he attempted to descend the oil slickened safety line he lost his grip. He fell near the lifeboat but never reappeared. He was our only fatality. A short time later the Navy's *Q-boat,* or Mystery Ship as we called her, came to our rescue." (This vessel, the *Anacappa,* was a converted Olsen lumber schooner with holds jammed with logs and armed to the teeth with four inch guns.) "She sailed, lit up like a Christmas tree, trying to lure the sub from hiding," Adams recalled, "but the sub didn't show. We circled the stricken tanker most of the night or until she sank. Late in the afternoon of the sixth, we were transported to Port Orford. The people were very helpful by providing beds and bedding, personal items and such. We were put up at the Legion Hall and the Coast Guard's barracks.

"There was never much publicity on the sinking. In the early days of the war no one knew for sure how many subs were operating. Things were pretty scary ... and the mystery ship added a little intrigue to the excitement.

"I sailed several more times, but after another shelling and a trip to Australia on a tanker loaded with high octane fuel, I looked for other work.

"I almost missed the Port Orford trip," Adams concluded, "I missed the boat at San Pedro and the Long Beach Coast Guard took me by launch past the sea buoy to catch the *Doheney.* I can't tell you how glad I was to see the old dock at Port Orford." Adams and his wife Jeanne were on their way to Boise and decided to relive their experiences at Port Orford.

Nubue Fujita

Most of the I-boats carried small "erector-set" observation float planes tucked away in watertight hangers just forward of the conning tower. Although designed for reconnaissance duties Chief Flying Officer Nubue Fujita on the *I-25* envisioned another more productive activity ... actually bombing the West Coast. While his plan was accepted the targets ordered hit were disappointing to his ego, for instead of the Panama Canal or Golden Gate Bridge he was ordered to bomb the forest of Southern Oregon in hopes of starting major forest fires. Two such flights were completed. The first on September 9, 1942, and the second on the 29th during which four 76 kilogram incendiary bombs were dropped, none of which did any noticeable physical damage. The little aircraft which Clyde Wagner, a local dairyman overheard at his ranch on Elk River, was described as sounding like a "Model-T Ford."

The first mission nearly proved disastrous to Commander Tagami and the crew of the *I-25* as the sub was spotted by a coast patrol Hudson bomber which made a bombing run on the then surfaced raider inflicting minor but frightening damage to the boat. Tagami crept into the harbor at Port Orford and lay on the bottom until damage could be repaired. Both Tagami and Fujita survived the war but the *I-25*, nearly hit at Yokosaka by a Doolittle Raider and again at Kwajalein by U. S. S. Enterprise dive bombers ran out of luck in the fall of 1943, and was lost with all hands in the Western Pacific.

Fujita's name will survive historically as the first man to pilot a plane which dropped bombs on the American mainland. Let's hope he shall be the last.

21

U.S. 101 Or The Roosevelt Coast Military Highway

Early day travelers along the Southern Oregon Coast were faced with extremely hazardous road conditions. Most traffic was limited to horse and pack animals following ancient Indian and game trails that followed high ground and beaches where possible. Attempts at road and bridge building by the county were expedited by the formation of road districts which levied a road tax to finance construction and repair. This method was subject to widespread abuse by supervisors who tended to collect the money and pay themselves for work done. Curry County supervisors were faced with different problems than the valley or Eastern Oregonians. Lack of available help and adverse terrain, coupled with harsh weather, made road construction and maintenance practically impossible during the winter months and the pioneers endured long periods of bridge washouts, slides, and quagmires which limited travel to hardy horsemen. In 1901, a reform law was passed which placed a general tax of up to 10 mills on the dollar of all taxable property in the county (a dollar per year poll tax), and empowered the County Court to appoint a Roadmaster who would lay out the engineering and construction work. This was the initial step in development of market roads statewide.

B. F. Jones, a Lincoln County legislator, introduced a bill in the 1919 legislature calling for the state to appropriate 2.5 million dollars for the construction of the Coast Highway from Astoria to the California state line providing the federal government funded a like amount. This bill was referred to the people and received overwhelming voter support. The 1923 legislature empowered the governor to sell bonds for the project and by 1924 the highway was opened for traffic through Curry County. This project was undoubtedly the most influential cause for the opening up of the Southwestern Oregon Coast. Although still rather primitive by today's standards, one could finally "get there from here." (See Roosevelt Highway Number, *Curry County Reporter,* 8/7/24.)

The first county road survey in the north end of Curry County was done in 1865 by Edson, Hughes, Wilson and Dyer as recommended by the county court. This survey went from New Lake to the wharf at Port Orford. Today the alignment follows, for the most part, the same path as the 1923-24 road although several relocations have occurred from Port Orford to Humbug and of course the Gold Beach-Brookings relocation which eliminated the Carpenterville Hill section between Pistol River and Brookings in the 1960s.

The 1923 road was constructed with horsepower, picks and shovels resulting in the following of contours rather than fills, cuts and structures. The finished product was one of the most crooked stretches of roadway in Oregon (between Port Orford and Gold Beach). Early truck drivers were all excellent arm wrestlers and all the natives can remember "Toilet Tissue Twist" among the stretch's 128 curves; Linville Hill's infamous grade and Humbug canyon's treacherously narrow passage. But if you were patient, the road offered some of the most spectacular scenery in the United States.

22

Coos-Curry Electric Cooperative, Inc.

History of the Utility

The story of Coos-Curry Electric Cooperative, Inc. was developed for the author by W.A. Cook, general manager and represents an informal history of the utility. According to Cook, Ivan Laird was the driving force to get the company started and was the first and only president for 25 years. Through the efforts of Ivan Laird with the help of George Jenkins, Coos County Agent, a small group of men became interested in procuring power for the small community of Sitkum about 20 miles northeast of Myrtle Point. Laird, who has been president of the board since organization, was chairman of a committee to meet with representative of REA and outline the procedure necessary to get an organization started.

The Coos Electric Cooperative was incorporated under the laws of the State of Oregon on June 1, 1939, and its first REA allotment of $119,500 was made in November 1939. In July 1940, construction started on the initial 84 miles of line to serve 255 members. This initial line was energized on November 4, 1940 with power purchased from Mountain States Power Company through a connection near Norway.

A second REA allotment of $107,000 was made in November 1940 to construct 95 miles of line to serve an additional 247 members. In August 1941, another loan was approved to build and acquire 152 miles of line to serve another 588 members in Coos and Curry Counties. With the approval of this loan, negotiations were started to purchase the properties of the Port Orford Light and Power Company.

In February 1942, the purchase was completed and lines were extended into the rural areas around Port Orford and up the coast to Bandon. Power for this system was supplied from a small hydro plant at Denmark owned by the City of Bandon, and a 120 horsepower diesel plant at Port Orford.

During the early stages in the formation of the cooperative, local groups in the southern portion of Curry County became interested in obtaining electric service and began a study to determine the feasibility of forming a People's Utility District. After several public hearings in the area early in 1940, the Hydroelectric Commission of Oregon recommended against the formation of a P. U. D. After it became evident a P. U. D. could not be developed, representatives of the area met with the Coos Electric Cooperative Board to request that the possibility of extending the cooperative's lines into the southern portion of Curry County be investigated.

By this time it was becoming apparent that a more adequate source of power would be necessary to keep up with the demand for electric service to this area. Therefore, in June 1940, an application was made to BPA for delivery of 300 kilowatts of firm power. In October 1941 another application was made for an additional 350 kilowatts. As BPA had no transmission facilities in the area, negotiations were started for transfer of power over Mountain States Power facilities at Norway and California Oregon Power Company's facilities for the Brookings area.

It wasn't until February 1947, however, that BPA power was first available to the cooperative. The five-year period between 1942 and 1947 was an exceptionally rough period for the cooperative with hundreds of potential customers clamoring for service, existing customers demanding better service, and no adequate source of power available.

In January 1945, the Brooking Light and Power Company was purchased and a small area in the extreme south portion of Curry County was served by a diesel generating plant until February 1946, when some power was purchased from Copco through an 11,000 bolt connection at the California State line.

The name of the cooperative was officially changed to Coos-Curry Electric Cooperative in October 1946. In December 1947 the cooperative began service in the Gold Beach area with the purchase of a part of the Gold Beach Utilities System.

It was also about this time that preliminary plans were being formulated for BPA to build into the area and relieve the serious shortage of available power. In February 1947, BPA power was made available at Norway by transfer and by the summer of 1948 plans were studied to continue the Eugene-Mapleton 115 kv line into Coos Bay and then build from McKinley to Norway and Bandon.

These sections were finally constructed in 1950 and service by BPA to the cooperative began at the Norway and Bandon substations early in 1951. Energy was furnished for several years by transfer from the Copco system through an interconnection at the McKinley switching system. The BPA 115 kv line was extended to Port Orford and

Gold Beach by October 1952, and by this time the cooperative had constructed a 69 kv transmission line from Gold Beach to Brookings to serve the lower portion of Curry County. The portion of Copco's line 20 from Coos Bay to McKinley was purchased from Copco about 1954 by BPA.

In September 1955, a new point of delivery was established at the 115 kv line at Geisel Monument, and in October 1957 the area between Port Orford and Bandon was served by a new substation near Langlois.

During the period 1957/58, the Cooperative constructed new substations at Gold Beach, North Brookings and Harbor. New 10,000 kva transformers were installed at Gold Beach; the transformers removed were installed at North Brookings and Harbor, and are 2,500 kva each.

In connection with other BPA substations, new switching structures for additional circuits were constructed at Port Orford and Geisel.

A new transmission line was constructed from the BPA substation at Gold Beach to Brookings to provide for load growth in that area.

In Coos County, which is supplied mostly from the BPA substation at Norway, the feeder to Sumner was converted from 12.5 kv to 24.9 kv. This was done during the first of 1960, to provide for increased usage.

In 1961, Bonneville Power Administration was scheduled to serve the Cooperative with 115 kv at Gold Beach. This power was to be transmitted to Brookings over the new transmission line now being operated at 69 kv, which was constructed for future operation at 115 kv. Other developments that were happening in the early 60s involved new 115 kv to 69 kv, 30,000 kva transformer to be placed at Brookings in conjunction with the 115 kv cutover, a new 10,000 kva transformer for North Brookings. Under construction then was a new feeder to the community of Agness. Also in the Agness Illahe area, exploration on the Illinois River for a generation site was progressing slowly. At the present time and an application was pending for a license to construct a dam on the Illinois River in the Bald Mountain and Buzzards Roost vicinity. Aerial mapping and core drilling at the dam site had been completed, and generation cost figures were expected by late 1961.

The Port
Of Port Orford

Tichenor's original townsite plat, drafted by V. Wakenruder, laid out the plat much differently than the one used today. The southeast corner was located nearly halfway down the beach toward Hubbards Creek near the large rocks below "Cabbage Rock" and extended on a line west southwest to a point near the present dock. Tichenor envisioned a levee built along the southern boundary from "Fort Point" eastward and extending from near the center of the levee he proposed a "T" dock which would extend south 500 feet into 30 foot deep water. Landings at this time were made on the beach west of Battle Rock.

The drawing made by Col. Joseph Mansfield in an 1854 report clearly shows a wharf constructed near the present dock and, in all probability, the army constructed it for service to the fort. This site was utilized over the years and the principle facility although two other projects were developed at "Mill Rock" and "Fort Point."

Prior to the formation of the Port of Port Orford, four other projects were attempted to facilitate loading of lumber and other goods ... namely Frankport-Corbin, the Port Orford Cedar Company pier at Hubbards Creek, the Pacific Furniture and Lumber Company apparatus at Fort Point and Port Blacklock north of the Sixes River.

After the loss of the *Brother Jonathan* in 1865, pressure was put on the government to establish a "Harbor of Refuge" between Cape Mendocino and the Columbia River to enable commercial and military vessels seeking anchorage (a safe haven) for repairs and protection from the violent seas. While the engineers made cursory inspections every townsite, bay and roadstead vied for the plum. William Tichenor pushed hard for the Port Orford site and in a lengthy article in the *Alta Californian* in the 70s he presented a well thought-out discourse that pointed out the favors and faults of all the potential harbors and bays along the coast. He discussed weather, currents, depths and obstructions of each site, based on his long experience in the maritime trade along the coast. He had, in fact, been the first captain to visit and inspect many of the locations. In the 1880s the engineers set aside $80,000 in their budget for a feasibility study on the project but Congress failed to provide the necessary funds.

After his death in 1883, his son, Jacob, and grandson, Frank, continued the cause and as late as 1912, the first Port Commission at Port Orford sent a letter of protest over the work done at Crescent City by the engineers. The lack of interest by the government didn't fool "Whisker" the last chief of the Sixes River band of Quo-to-mahs, however. He advised Jacob Tichenor in the mid-1880s not to take government promises too seriously, referring, no doubt, to the unratified treaties, broken promises and a host of other problems that the Indian people faced trying to deal with the "Great White Father."

Blacklock - 1885

The Frank Company of San Francisco developed the Three Sisters as a shipping pier in the 1890s although no specific date was ever found. Renamed Frankport, this facility was used to load tan oak bark used in the firm's large tannery in San Francisco. Harvesting was accomplished by felling the tree and stripping the bark. The tree was left on the ground and needless to say, it didn't take long to devastate the area around Mussel Creek. In April of 1901, the Pacific Coast Lumber and Manufacturing Co. leased the property from the Frank Company and began an ambitious project which included a sawmill, townsite and pier located on Mussel Creek. The existing narrow gauge tramway was abandoned and a 1,500 foot pier was constructed directly into the tidelands near the mouth of Mussel Creek (May 1901). The "Company" printed up a booklet which described their timber holding and vastly exaggerated timber volumes and values in an attempt to market a stock issue of $400,000. Walter Sutton, editor and publisher of the *Port Orford Tribune* pointed out the fallacies of the booklet and engaged in a heated exchange of newspaper articles in May and June of 1901. In September of that year, the pier which had been pushed out 1,300 feet, collapsed. Only one person was injured as the crew was on a dinner break, but a donkey, pile driver and other equipment was lost. The Corbin Mill continued to operate for several years and in March 1902, a post office was established "… some miles off the main route."

In the mid-1880s, a 500 foot pier was constructed near Hubbards Creek by the Port Orford Cedar Company. This structure was anchored to the rocks and you can see traces of the concrete piling casements at extreme low tide near Mill Rock today. The rocks were terraced and leveled to accomplish the project and this alteration is still evident. In 1880, the outer pier was destroyed by a storm and coupled with the loss of several steam schooners at sea, the fortunes of Port Orford Cedar Company went sour. In 1882, Crawford and Wilbur purchased this mill and lands and moved the mill to a site north of Port Orford just west of Silver Butte. The old Hubbards Creek mill site occupied the old Indian village at the mouth of the creek and the field just north of the present day bridge held a large mill pond created when the creek was dammed up. The sand pile on the south side of the creek represents the remains of the old barrier or dike.

In the early 1900s, the Pacific Furniture and Lumber Company constructed a loading apparatus on Fort Point designed to carry bundles of ties down a cable anchored to the large rock just below the point. This worked fairly well as there was enough water for the old schooner *Bandon* to lie in beneath the cable and load. The old vessel did survive a soft grounding there once, but it had survived many a mishap. Some of the crew of the ill-fated ship said, "... she was aground more times than she was afloat."

A narrow gauge tramway was constructed to connect the loading device at Fort Point to the mill at Elk River. The tram right-of-way went out Arizona Street, crossing the lake on a piled bridge where the fill is now and continuing north on or near the present road to the sanitary landfill. This tram eliminated the hardships of hauling the ties in by team and wagon. The survey for this project began February 11, 1903.

The Lakeport scheme at Floras Lake had as its main selling point the opening of a channel between the ocean and the lake which it was purported would enable the largest of ocean going vessels to enter the land and Lakeport would rival San Francisco as a deep water harbor. A townsite was surveyed and platted and hundreds of lots sold. The town sprang up almost overnight, complete with a large hotel, newspaper, stores and a freight line. The channel was never cut, as to do so would lower the level of the lake at low tides without a lock system and the effort was abandoned. The promoters "took the money and ran."

The next attempt at formation succeeded and in 1919, the first bonds were sold for the construction of a wharf and the district was well on the way towards prosperity ... or so it seemed. The first commissioners were C. W. Zumwalt, J. H. Miller, S. P. Pierce, J. W. McKenzie and Hardy Stewart. Collier H. Buffington was retained for legal counsel. They bought the Port Orford Wharf Company from Will T. White for $1,662.50 and the right-of-way for $1,500.00. Twenty-eight men were immediately employed at the dock site, including the Limpach brothers, E. White, C. White, F. Nordberg, C. Wilson, Mel Johnson, R. Leutwyler, J. Star, G. Quigley, R. Smith, W. Jamieson, C. Baldwin, D. Jenks, A. Hoggatt, V. Boyer, E. Lynch, J. Fromm, Jess Sutton, George Sutton, George Fromm, L. Johnston, G. Johnson, Harry Strahan, George Forty,

Bert Dean and Axel Erikson. Henry Adolphsen cut the timbers and N. H. Larson cut the lumber.

At mean low water, the depth at the end of the wharf was 22 feet with seven feet, four inches at the north end of the structure. Moore Mill and Lumber Company leased a 50' x 100' section of the dock for lumber storage. By October 21, 1921, the district was in debt to the tune of $45,000, and George Sutton was appointed Wharfinger. The Western White Cedar Company brought in the *S. S. Frogner* to load Port Orford cedar logs for export. This steamer was 410 feet long with a beam of 52 feet and displaced over 9,300 tons, making it the largest vessel ever to call at Port Orford.

On May 19, 1926, the Corps of Engineers toured the facility and were given the red carpet treatment by the ladies of the town with a hearty lunch. John Gillings requested the survey be made "not for the purpose of a harbor of refuge but rather for an additional 300 feet of wharf." The commissioners agreed that the criticism of the "1912 letter was adverse to their cause." Hopes for assistance were not based on the fact of deep indebtedness but rather on the positive aspects for what had been accomplished by the district. In the year 1923, 61 steamers had called there, delivering 1,085 tons of freight while loading 35,585 tons of logs, lumber and freight. Two redwood reservoirs, holding 10,000 gallons of water for fire protection and supplying ships had been built while mooring, wire and manila hawsers were purchased. Add to that the huge inventory of Port Orford Cedar standing in Coos and Curry Counties, (nearly a billion board feet!) and the newly constructed Roosevelt Highway,and the port commissioners thought they had the necessary ingredients for a slice of the federal pie. However, on October 5, 1926, the Corps regrettably rejected the proposal. From then on the fortunes of the district began to fade.

Several attempts were made by private interests to purchase or lease the port property; in 1922 and 1926 by Kronenberg and Inman, and again in 1927 by Inman Lumber and Development Company. The port rejected the first two offers and the third was blocked by litigation. In September 1927, a petition, signed by 250 district property owners calling for the port district to sell the wharf property, was presented to the commissioners. The taxpayers had had enough. The dock was used for fish and crab landings but the lumber and log shipments dried up. In the summer of 1932, Ed Skog operated the Port Orford Fish Company with several boats selling to him. The wharf was eventually sold on December 31, 1934 to the Gable interests.

Gilbert Gable proved to be a tireless worker who fell in love with Northern Curry County. His first endeavor was a mining venture up Sixes River, but he envisioned an East-West railroad terminating at the deep water port at Port Orford. He set out, in the depths of the Depression, to finance the railroad, a jetty and a sawmill. He hustled the wealthy, cajoled the meek and badgered the bureaucrats while he attained two of the three goals. The railroad was surveyed but never approved and the route of the Gold Coast Railroad can be seen in an impressive volume at the Port Orford City Hall. The jetty was constructed but failed to hold up against the awesome power of the sea, washing out the first year of its existence. The mill, Trans-Pacific Lumber Company, located at what is now Buffington Park prospered into the early 1940s, shipping millions of board feet of high grade clear fir and cedar lumber. Mr. Gable died in early December, 1941, bringing to an end a colorful and productive era in the history of Port Orford.

Ed Kaakannin, a Finnish fishmonger from Westport Washington, bought the dock facility and operated a cannery for many years. Although he allowed the dock to deteriorate, he kept the cannery going and provided employment for the community. Donna Robourge, Crawford Smith, Harry Strahan, Clyde Estabrook, Fred, Cecil and Howard Jamieson, Bill Durant, Bert Dean, Ray Menke, George Collins, George Corkin, Frank Thorpe, "Digger" Bales ... all fished for him, when the crabs were huge and the salmon thick. (When the crab price broke a dollar a dozen the boys were "... in 'em!")

The port commission bought back the facility from Kaakannin in 1956 for about $75,000. Ed was somewhat hard to deal with and the commissioners sent Ray Nowlin, with an olive branch and a top price to Westport, and after several trips Ray brought back the bacon ... the deed to the dock which he immediately sold to the port commission.

Much needed improvements were made to the structure and in the early 1960s, Herb Crook utilized the facility to ship lumber via Chamberlain and Foss ships and barges. Disaster struck in 1961, and the dock collapsed with nearly a million board feet of lumber stacked on it. The beaches and coves were clogged with beautiful dimension lumber and local salvors had a field day once the insurance companies released their claims.

In the mid-1960s, the Corps of Engineers designed and constructed a jetty to protect the dock. At first, the project was hailed by all as a wonderful improvement, but it didn't take long to recognize that its design was to have an adverse effect on the water depths at the dock. The entire area, from Fort Point to the dock, filled with sand as the jetty, while taking pressure off the dock from westerly and southwesterly surge, was restricting the natural ebb and flow or wave action that heretofore had maintained a constant depth of water at the dock site. (The "curse" of 1856 was apparently still in force!) The shoaling has, at this writing, severely restricted the fishing fleet. Periodic dredging of a basin adjacent to the dock by the Corps of Engineers provides some relief but falls far short of a permanent solution. The Corps, undergoing massive cutbacks in funding, finds it more difficult each year to find monies to dredge at Port Orford. The fact that the construction of the jetty caused considerable damage to the value of the port facility has not yet been seriously considered and, at this point, may be a dead issue due to the statutes of limitations. A suit filed by the patrons of the district based upon the premise that the faulty design of the jetty did indeed cause a devaluation of the port facilities would make an interesting case.

Today, the hardy fishermen at Port Orford struggle against an unpredictable supply of fish and crab, a deteriorating port facility (depth-wise) and bureaucratic regulations … but they continue to ply their trade, not perhaps for a comfortable living but rather because the Cobbs, Harrisons, Guerins, Crums, Wagners, Marshes, Smiths and all are an independent lot and seem to prevail come hell or low water.

What might lie in the future for the Port of Port Orford? New residents study the photos of the 1940s when large lumber schooners loaded at the dock with ease and wonder if this will ever happen again. Perhaps in 70 years when the timber lands that were clear cut in the 1950s and 1960s are ready to yield their precious and stately fir and cedar on a sensible and sustained basis lumbering will once again figure heavily on the local economy. In the days of the lumber boats, little or no concern was given to the prudent management of timberlands. If it stood tall and straight, cut it; or if it was in the way, cut it. Timber was translated into cost to acquire, harvest, transport, mill and sell. These policies have since proven disastrous to local, state and national resources. (The tear in the eye of the Indian suggested much more than river pollution.)

It is likely that the next generation of merchantable timber will spawn many more diversified small industries which in turn will have a stabilizing effect on local economy. Waste will become a punishable crime … hopefully. The future of the fishing industry in Port Orford will undoubtedly bring many changes. Restrictions will apply more severely than they do now … if that is possible. The burgeoning population will put more pressure on the resources and bring about advantageous technological breakthroughs in fish processing and marketing. The mock crab and shrimp appearing in the supermarkets are certainly a forerunner of this. While this product will never take the place of the delicious Dungeness crab, it must be remembered that millions of people are not connoisseurs and most have never tasted the real thing. The days of the three "Cs", catch, cook and can, are numbered.

24

Pioneers Of Port Orford

No history of Port Orford would be complete without paying tribute in print to the pioneers of Port Orford, the men and women who came from Europe and the Orient to settle in the United States, then trekked westward and arrived in Oregon either by boat from San Francisco or by wagon from other states. All had in common the conviction that Oregon, and Port Orford, spelled opportunity for them. They became saw mill owners, carpenters, farmers, telephone operators, pastors, timber cruisers, trappers, fishermen and surveyors. All of them individually contributed to the character and personality of Curry County and imprinted their achievements on the history of Port Orford.

P. J. (Pehr Johan) Lindberg: Born in 1851 in Sweden, Lindberg arrived in Port Orford in 1882. The Lindbergs had two children, Edward and John. Lindberg was active in the general contracting business and in the first 30 years he lived in Port Orford he built almost all of the business and residence structures there. He also constructed farm buildings and bridges throughout Curry County. At one time he served as County Commissioner, Road Supervisor and Constable of Port Orford. Mrs. Lindberg died in 1919 and her husband in 1920. The most famous of Lindberg's works are the Hughes House on Sixes River, the Lindberg house at Ninth and Washington, and the old Seaside Hotel, also known as the Masterson House on Highway 101 and Jackson. P. J. Lindberg's son Edward married Syneva Sorenson in 1913. Their children are Eddie, Marie (Barrington), Bill, Lucile (Douglas), Dora (Hooton), Rachel (Leopold), Helen (Richmond), and Jim. Lucile Douglas lives in the home her grandfather build in 1896.

Asmus and Anna Adolphson, with sons Hans and Henry, of Denmark, emigrated to Portland, and on to Battle Rock where he landed, hired a team and wagon, fording Elk and Sixes River to get to Denmark, Oregon. He built a sawmill and in 1900 purchased two sections of timber on Elk River. He built a home, cook house, bunk house, tank house and a steam mill with three boilers and three engines, and cut about 40,000 board feet of timber per day. He also started using donkey logging and the first highline logging in the West. Asmus died in 1922. Henry worked for his father until he retired, then moved to Seaview ranch and courted Florence McKenzie for 12 years, finally marrying her in 1919. They rode horseback to the dances in Port Orford, fording the creeks and changing clothes, then returned to help milk 60 cows — making butter that was shipped to San Francisco. Also the men at Seaview Ranch gathered sea gull eggs, packed them in barrels and shipped them to the Chinese cooks in San Francisco. Henry's logging operation at one time employed 65 men. Office in his pocket, he hired and fired and paid by check. He bought his first bulldozer in 1935. After Florence died in 1954, Henry married widow Mary (Ma) Woodworth. They traveled extensively. He was generous to 4-H, hospitals and other organizations.

Joseph L. Nay, born in New Hampshire, came to Port Orford in 1860 and took over the remains of the A. M. Simpson sawmill property on Elk River after the destructive fire of 1868. He rebuilt the mill and operated it for many years. One load of lumber went down in a shipwreck at Port Orford with a great loss to Nay. The original mill building still stands and is used as a hay barn at the Sweet Ranch on Elk River. Joe eventually went to Coos County and the Joe Nay Slough near Charleston is named for him.

Alfred J. Marsh, born in New York in 1861, came to Curry County in 1883, developing a dairy farm on Elk River. He married Rachel Kronenberg, and they had nine children. Marsh served as County Assessor for a time and as Road Supervisor. Son Louis Marsh was born in 1892 at the ranch. He served in World War I and was wounded and gassed. He married Francis (Frenchy) Timmons; they had two children, Gary and Barbara. Other Alfred Marsh children are Dorothy (Mansell), Beatrice (Zumwalt), Marge Kathryn (Niva), Fred, Donald, John, and Nicholas who married Catherine Wehrley; their children being Dolores Ann (Mayea), Blaine, and Judy (Jensen). Nick was a County Commissioner, served on the City Council and did logging, trucking and farming.

George and Sara Fitzhugh crossed the plains from Missouri to Oregon in 1872. They came to Curry County and purchased 160 acres of land from Capt. Benson for

$400. This was up Sixes River and since there were no roads the couple crossed the river several times in summer. They cleared the land, most of which was covered with Port Orford white cedar, which they felled and burned to clear land for pasture and other agriculture purposes. The Fitzhughs had nine children: Charles, George (married Luella Isenhart), Melvin, Francis (Ferrier), James, John, Mary Jane (Jamieson), Nancy (Hale), Lester (married Mary Wells), and Addie (Helmken). The children attended an early day school erected on their place called Cherry Grove School. One of the teachers was Grafton Tyler. The Fitzhugh family was well respected. Eldest son Charles was the Curry County Surveyor for 40 years. Lester and Mary Fitzhugh had three children, Florence, Lucinda and Charles, who married Norma Price. At one time the couple owned a restaurant in Port Orford, called "Norma's Place" which was famous for it's homemade pies. Charles was County Assessor for 22 years. Addie born in 1889, was a telephone operator in Bandon. Her husband, Ralph Helmken, was a timber cruiser; their only son Harry was a star basketball player at University of Oregon. He married Ray Capps and the couple owned the Sixes Store for a number of years.

George Dart, born in Pennsylvania in 1820, came to Curry County in 1854. He married Anna Tichenor at Port Orford in 1855. Their children were Elizabeth, born 1858; William, born 1860; and Harry, born 1868.

Charles H. Crew, born in England in 1814, came to Oregon and Port Orford in 1853. He had two sons, Charles and James. He applied for and received citizenship papers in 1873. Charles H. Crew was born at Port Orford in 1856, lived there and at Sixes all of his life. He was a miner, otter and seal hunter and a rancher. He married Clarinda Wilson. Two sons of the couple were James, born in 1890, married Essie Hofsess who was born in Langlois, and married in Port Orford at the Methodist Episcopal Parsonage in 1915. Charles was born in 1891, and married Myrtle Clarno in Port Orford in 1916. Their children were: Charles, Martha (Strain-Sweitz) and Bett.

Thomas Cornell, born in Ohio in 1843, came to Oregon in 1858. He did black sand mining at Cape Blanco with A. G. M. Dyer, then later mined up the Sixes River. He left, but came back later to settle on Crystal Creek.

Georgia Anna West, born in 1880 in Kansas to Mr. and Mrs. Albert Dunsar, came west in a covered wagon to John Day country. There she met John West and married. They came to Curry County and farmed on the Sixes River. Children: Albert, Oliver, Bradley, Dick and John. Grandchildren names were North West and South West.

James Crowley, son of John Crowley, came west from Missouri in 1886 and settled on the Sixes River. He purchased land from the Indians, paying $14.00 in four bit pieces. His farm became known as the "Crowley Homestead," later as the Helmken, and still later the Fred Lancaster Property. James was a logging contractor. The spot known as the "Crowley Hole" was the best swimming place on the Sixes River. Many picnics and swimming parties were held there by young and old over the years.

Steve Spoerl, born in 1880 in Wisconsin, came west with his mother Lucy Perkins and stepfather Erwin Baker. Nat Perkins, an uncle, came with the group and settled in Curry County in 1908. The family bought a 160-acre ranch near Brush Creek, and called it the Coast hills Ranch. They raised acorn-fed hogs, and made hams and bacon for sale. Steve worked for the forest service at Panther Mountain Area. The Coast Hills Ranch totalled 1,666 acres; also raised Romney sheep, receiving champion awards for wool at the Pacific International Livestock Exposition. Steve and Nat were both active in Port Orford community and school affairs. Steve was on the County Welfare Commission, the Port Orford Port Commission; he also helped reorganize the Curry County Bank after the depression. Adelaide Siegel is a survivor.

George Forty was born in England and came by ship to Port Orford in 1870. He married Maude Paskins who came to Port Orford with her parents, Mr. and Mrs. Robert Paskins of San Francisco by ship and landed at Battle Rock. Paskins, a carpenter and shoemaker, went to Gold Beach to work for R. D. Hume until he retired.

The George Fortys homesteaded on a ranch up Elk River which is now owned by the Marsh family. In 1889 the family moved to Port Orford. A son, Robert, was born there and attended some of the Port Orford schools, with teachers J. C. Logan (who had a wooden leg), Will Guerin, Jessie Warner, Rose Long and Abe Johnson. Robert was married to Myrtle McGill in 1915, at the home of his parents, by Justice of the Peace M. T. Wright and a wedding dinner was served guests at the Seaside Hotel. Myrtle was born in Wisconsin in 1896 to Mr. and Mrs. Douglas McGill who came to Port Orford in 1914. Douglas was a carpenter, building several homes: the Marsh house (now RV Park), Jack Guerin, Smith house (Sutton), Wallace and Robert Forty houses.

Robert worked for Jim Cowan, a timber cruiser, on Brush Prairie with a huge stand of timber, mostly cedar, which was continuously logged for 40 years. He also worked at logging for 22 years with Coos Curry Electric.

Robert and Myrtle celebrated their fiftieth wedding anniversary with many attending, including Robert's family: Bernal and Fernel (Porter) Forty, Lorrin and Josie

Forty, Lottie (Forty) Smith, Nesta (Forty) Johnson, and Myrtle's sister Inez McGill. The golden anniversary was hosted by daughters Shirley (Mrs. Court Boice) and Doris (Dode), (Mrs. George Woodworth).

Lorrin and Josie Forty had three sons; Kenneth, George and Myron. George's son, Bernal Forty, married Fernel (Porter). Bernal worked many years as a State Highway Supervisor. Their son Gordon, born 1923, married Alene (Hatcher). Gordon's sister is Elaine (Russell-Huffstetter).

George Stanley Quigley, Curry County native was born on his parent's (James and Jessie Quigley) homestead on Crystal Creek in 1907. This ranch bordered the Frank Cox (Susy White) ranch on the north and Raymond Capp's ranch on the south. It was by trail only that supplies came in. Later George lived at other ranch locations. He helped his father with a team doing freighting, hauling ties from the Sixes area to Port Orford. Much trapping was done in wintertime, and he also worked in the mines. Mines operating then were Madden Mine, and Pakk Mine, both black sand mines and wages were about $1.00 to $1.10 per cay. The Big Jewell Mine at the mouth of Dry Creek on the Sixes was a hydraulic mine and produced gold, but when gold was only $16.00 an ounce and wages of $3.00 per day, the mine shut down and never reopened. In 1933, George Stanley married Maxine Matheny in Port Orford. He continued farming and dairying. Lester Fitzhugh, Erney Matheny and George Stanley cut battery stock. Later they built a home on a half acre purchased from Lester Fitzhugh. George Stanley spent many years working in the woods; he also labored four years as first cheesemaker for Swift & Co. at Sixes. Then followed the woods working for Nick Marsh, Kerber Brothers, Moore Mill and Hall Logging. George Stanley's son, hosted a fiftieth wedding reception for his father and mother in 1983.

Robert Ellsworth Thomas was a descendent of an early pioneer family whose grandparents came from Illinois to Oregon in 1852. The family had eight yoke of oxen, four cows and wagons piled with all their possessions and was in constant danger of Indians, bad weather and poor roads. Robert married Noma (Quigley) in 1924, moved to Sixes in 1933 and took over the Cornwall ranch on Crystal Creek. Robert and neighbor Raymond Capps with Bob Knox, County Agent, set up the first farm irrigation system in Curry County. Later he was in the milk business at the Sweet Ranch on Elk River. He built a home at Silver Springs. The Thomases and their son-in-law's parents, Tracy and Margaret Corbin, celebrated their fiftieth wedding at the Masonic Hall. Daughters are : Adelle (Corbin), and Joan (Macy).

Willis T. White was born in Main in 1847. He came to Curry County in 1870. He married Margaret Curry and moved to Port Orford in 1912. He bought and sold considerable real estate, was Curry County Assessor for two terms, a Deputy Sheriff and Port Commissioner. Children were: Willis "Will" (married Susy Neer), Violet (married John Fromm). James, Leland and Magnolia, were the others. White's second wife was Alice.

Susy Neer White was born at Myrtle Point and attended school and became a teacher. Susy and Will White were married in a hose drawn buggy by Judge Wright in Port Orford in 1913. They lived first at Weddeburn where Will managed the MacCleay Estate. Three daughters were born to the Whites, and the family moved to Illahae where Susy taught school for five years. They moved to Port Orford where they owned and operated the Western Hotel and White's General Store and Meat Market on Main Street. All of the family worked at this operation of serving the public with meals and food stuffs. Will operated a slaughter house by the Sixes River bridge, and supplied meat for his market, which Bert Hoggatt took charge of. This operation was sold to R. C. Dunham and later Safeway. Will and Susy lived at their Crystal Creek ranch. Will died in 1949, then Susy sold real estate. In 1959, she directed the Port Orford Battle Rock Celebration for Oregon's Centennial. She invited Governor Mark Hatfield to be Grand Marshall. Later the Chamber of Commerce honored her for her leadership. Children of Susy and Will: Camilla "Polly" (Childers), Vivian (Arnold), and Melba (Lawrence.)

Charles W. Zumwalt who was born in Missouri in 1847, came to Curry County in 1869. He married Agnes Blacklock in 1887. They operated a large dairy farm at Sixes. He was a Curry County Commissioner, and Assessor, Justice of the Peace, and Deputy Collector of Customs at Port Orford. They had six sons: John Henry, Marion R., Raymond B., H. Weston, Clarence W. and Charles P. Raymond and Clarence continued to operate the farm until they died. The farm is now owned and operated by Herb and Euila Morrill and sons John and David. They have a large herd of Polled Herfords. Herb is the only stockman in Curry County raising Polled Herfords.

Robert Lee Wagner was born in North Carolina in 1871 and his family came to Coos county in 1873 to settle near Powers. He married Oma McCracken in 1897. Later the couple came to Curry County, buying a farm on Elk River in 1917. He served as a County Commissioner, the Port of Port Orford Commissioner and was president of the Curry County Fair Board for a period of time. Children include Gertrude (Zumwalt); Clyde, Paul, Vera and Clarence. Clyde married Erma, their children are Keith and Glenn. Paul, married Grace Fromm. Their children are Kent, Brice and Books. Vera married George Sutton and bore children, Maxine and Margaret. Clarence married Jewell Crow who had one child, Barbara. The Wagners are a very respected, hard working family.

Frank and Susan Nicholson lived north of Port Orford where they operated a grocery store, feed and hardware store for 35 years. They had one son, Francis Nicholson.

Hattie Whitworth, who was born 1882 in Philadelphia, came to Oregon in a covered wagon in 1905. She married Emory Whitworth in 1911. They lived at Silver Springs. Their daughter, Ellen, married Sam Hull. Her children are Lois Hohman and Scodina Dwek.

Mary Pugh was born 1890 in Salem, South Dakota, educated at the Hamlin University in St. Paul. She earned a pharmacy degree as well as teaching certificate. She married Dr. R. Pugh in 1927 and came to Port Orford. They operated a dental office and drug store in what was known as "The Centennial Building," the oldest building in town located on the corner where the Wheelhouse Restaurant now resides. Mary taught school at Ophir and Port Orford high schools after selling their business. The Pugh children were Lonna Lee and Richard.

Ed Maloy was born in 1884 at Brockton, Massachusetts and married Mildred Paulman in San Diego in 1915. They came to Port Orford in 1923. Ed drove for the Panter Freight Line and did carpenter work. The couple were married 64 years before he passed away in 1979. A son, Hewitt, was killed in a plane crash in World War II. A daughter, Ruth (Morris), died in a car accident in 1961. James Maloy lives in Portland, and his daughter, LaReine (Eckholm), a retired nurse, lives in Port Orford.

Rosa Lee Pfisterer was born at Port Orford in 1877. Her parents were Fredrick Pfisterer and Whilhelmina (Langensee) Pfisterer, from the province of Bavaria in Germany. Rosa Lee grew up on a ranch at Brush Creek with her older brother and sister, Fredrick Karl and Henreitta Pfisterer. The children attended a small country school for eight or 10 students at Brush Creek, then Rosa Lee worked for 10 years at the Knapp Hotel. Henreitta married Thomas Wooden in 1888 and moved to the Langlois vicinity. Rosa Lee married George Curry in 1907. His parents were James Curry and Frances (Coleman) Curry of Gold Beach, originally from Ohio. George and Rosa Lee resided on Elk River for many years. They had one daughter, Francis (White). Harry White came from Michigan where he worked for the auto industry. He purchased a new Chevrolet for $565.00. They were married in Carson City, Nevada in 1940. She and her husband still reside on Elk River.

J. S. Capps, Born in 1864, and wife Ona Capps, came to Curry county in 1888. Their children were Raymond, Edward, Eva (Donaldson), Edna (Zumwalt), and John. They lived at Ophir for a number of years, where the children were born. In 1915, Raymond Capps married Ada Bailey of Gold Beach. They moved to Sixes and purchased a ranch on Crystal Creek. Ada Taught school at Sixes for a number of years. Ray was the First Master of the Sixes Grange, a position to which he was elected many times. Ray and Ada were well liked and respected in the community. Their children were Helen (Fields), Ray (Hemken) (Rundberg), who served as Postmaster at Sixes for 41 years; and Bill Capps, U. S. Navy retired and U. S. Postal Service, retired.

Walter Sutton. born 1849 was married to Louisa Ann Sutton, who was born 1859. They came from Illinois at an early age and owned several newspapers, including *Port Orford Post, Curry County Post, Gold Beach Gazette,* and *Port Orford Tribune.* Walter served as Curry County Clerk three times, and also served a term in the state legislature. Children were: Linda (Guerin), Alta (Jamieson), Laura (Mann), James and George. James had two daughters, Audrey (Kreiger) and Phyllis (Woodward), one son, Frank Sutton. George was County Assessor for many years. He and Vera had two daughters, Maxine (McMillan) and Marjorie (Munday).

Robert George McKenzie, born 1835 in Scotland, and his wife Georgina Tullock, also born in Scotland, were married in Australia in 1863. Children born in Australia were Catherine, Eliza, John and Annie. They came to San Francisco where he met a Mr. Blacklock, who knew of the George Dyer pre-emption claim on Elk River filed in 1853, which was for sale. This was purchased by McKenzie in 1874.

The family lived on what is known as Seaview Ranch on lower Elk River and was engaged in dairying and stock raising. A post office was established in the McKenzie home in 1890, and disbanded in favor of Port Orford in 1892. Family members were educated by home schooling until later when they were sent to boarding schools or attended Port Orford schools. Children born in Port Orford were Isabella in 1875; Ena (Sheridan) in 1877; David in 1879; Florence (Adolphson) in 1885; R. G. (Bob) in 1883. The above family members are all deceased.

Bob McKenzie married Lucile Sorenson of Port Orford in 1918. Their children are: Roderick Tullock McKenzie, who married Grace Goucher of Boston in 1946. Rod was an Oregon State graduate in 1941, a member of the U. S. Marine Corp and served with Carlson Raiders in World War II. He served in the State House of Representatives. He engaged in sheep and livestock raising. Ted McKenzie, born 1920, married Bonnie

Lewis. He served in the U. S. Air Corps in World War II. Georgina, born in 1922, married John Wahl in 1946. John was school principal at Blanco for a number of years. Georgina is an accomplished sheep raiser, and manages her large ranch. Robert G. McKenzie, born 1924, married Beverly Mermilloid in 1951. Bob was in military service, later in sheep and stock raising and became one of the large cranberry growers in the area. Shirley was born in 1926 and married Corky Van Loo in 1950. Shirley and Corky were both teachers. For a time she served as a Curry County Commissioner. Corky became a commercial fisherman and sheep rancher. David McKenzie married Myrtle Axtel in 1911. Myrtle was a telephone operator in Port Orford for 20 years. Their children are: Donald, who married Hazel Woodworth of Sixes. Donald and Hazel had a large ranch on Elk River. Donna married George Churchill. Donna was a graduate of S. O. Normal School, and held a master's degree from University of Oregon. She taught school for over 30 years, much of that time in Port Orford Schools.

Arthur and Docia Sweet were married in 1914 at Bandon, and were engaged in store-keeping in Langlois for a period of years. They produced four children: Neonta (Hall); Effie (Parsons), Sidney, who married Phyllis Cope of Langlois, and Ralph who wed Caryl Vanderwall of Ashland. In 1924 the Sweet family moved to the Arizona Inn — now called the Arizona Ranch. They operated a dairy ranch and the Inn, plus a store and service station. They were active in Grange, 4-H and school affairs. The children attended school at Ophir. Docia Sweet was a talented musician and was soloist for the Community church in Port Orford, and sang for almost all of the funerals in Curry County. She was also the first woman appointed to the Curry County Fair Board, on which she served for more than 20 years. A hall at the fair grounds is named in her honor. In 1935, the Sweet family moved to the mouth of Sixes River into the old James Hughes house, where dairying was pursued. The children attended school in Port Orford, catching the bus after crossing the Sixes River by swinging bridge or boat and riding to school with the Masterson kids and others from the Cape Blanco Lighthouse families. Neonta (Hall); Effie went to SONS and became a teacher. She married Jim Parsons and moved to Ashland. Sidney and Ralph both joined the U. S. Navy and came home unscathed. Sid operated heavy equipment for years. Ralph was a forester and worked with Weyerhaeuser as a fire fighting specialist until retirement.

Neonta Sweet married Ralph Hall who arrived from Indiana during the Bandon fire. He lived with his uncle and aunt, Harry and Josephine Dewey, on their ranch in Sixes. He and Neonta met playing for barn dances, country dances and Grange dances. They were married in 1938. Ralph operated the Dewey ranch and was first cheese maker for Swift and Company at Sixes. Later, he did logging. Neonta was a 4-H livestock and forestry leader for over 20 years. She also wrote for local newspapers for 35 years. On their 50th wedding anniversary, they were grand marshalls for the Fourth of July parade, riding in a surrey, with the rest of their original wedding party in a second surrey.

W. J. Sweet purchased land on Elk River in 1914. Caretakers farmed the ranch for many years, but after the Bandon fire which burned the family home, he found it necessary to move to Elk River. Their children Bill, Don and Anne attended Port Orford schools for a while. A. W. (Bill) Sweet spend a few years at college, then returned to the ranch and started building a purebred Jersey herd of cattle. His herd ranked second in the nation in 1960, and also had the distinction of being the highest milk producing herd in the world. In 1941, he married Evelyn Perkins. He also bought the Harry Dewey ranch on Sixes River, the Art Sweet property on Cape Blanco Road and part of the Zumwalt ranch on Sixes River. The couple built a house on the Sixes River property. In time, Bill assumed leadership of Western Bank and the family moved to Coos Bay. At present, Bill is president of the "Friends of Cape Blanco" and was instrumental in getting *Port Orford, A History* published.

John Fromm, Sr., was born in 1855, wed Christina Nelson, born 1856, in Denmark and came to Curry County about 1880. The couple settled on a fine farm on Sixes River and had six children. Theron Fromm married May Anderson and had two daughters: Grace (Wagner) and Freda. Theron's second marriage was to Jessie Hoggatt. Theron worked as a fisherman and rancher. Later he moved to the Johannas Fromm ranch on Mussel creek. Anna Fromm Married Caughell and had two sons, Jack and Charlie Caughell. Robert Fromm married Nellie Anderson and had sons Ray, Orris and Kenneth Fromm. Kate Fromm married Fred Caughell and had three children.George Fromm married Francis Court and had a daughter, Francis Ann. John Fromm, Jr., born 1882, married Violet White, born 1884, in 1907. They operated a large dairy farm on the Sixes River and had four children, Lex, Clinton, Leland and Yvonne. Lex Fromm, born in 1909, married Georgia Hartue in 1932. Both Lex and Georgia were school teachers. Lex taught at the Sixes school and later at Gold Beach. He taught for 14 years. Lex built boats at Weddeburn, and was also a Rogue River Boat Pilot and guide. He made a second marriage to Grace Wagner. Georgia taught for 30 years; also was Curry County School Superintendent. Clinton Fromm was born in 1911. He was a star basketball player in school and later for the Trans Pacific professional team. He married Wanda Nodine. He was a dairy farmer. Leland (Hickey) Fromm, born in 1917, was a basketball star in school. He served in the U. S. Army during World War II. He married Sunny Leonard. He and Clint could catch more salmon from the Sixes River than anyone else. Ralph

Sweet and Bob McKenzie came in close seconds. Yvonne Fromm, born in 1925, was a Port Orford High School graduate. She worked for the fish processing plants at the Port Orford dock for over 30 years.

Rudolph Leutwyler first opened a blacksmith shop about 1920 in Port Orford. Later the shop was taken over by his brother, Paul. Paul was born in 1898 in Switzerland, and came to Port Orford in 1925. He was married to Agness Miller who had a son, Lawrence Miller. Paul took over a blacksmith shop and garage. There were no sidewalks. Paul was busy shoeing horses everyday, also working on Model-T cars. Later, he built the Battle Rock Garage, which opened in 1940 with a dance and party. Agness was a colorful person, a good business woman and the couple acquired a number of properties around town. She built the "Magnolia Gardens," a popular dance hall in town. Paul's second wife was Aletha Neely, mother of Thelma Foster. Bill Foster took over the operation of the garage when Paul retired.

C. C. and Mary (Ma) Woodworth came to Sixes in 1929 and purchased the Sixes Store. They had three children. Hazel was one who married Don McKenzie, and she and her husband ranched on Elk River. Elliot married Francis Moyer and operated the old Charlie Long Store (now Orfords), and lived in the apartment upstairs. George married "Dode" Forty and ranched on the Elk River, by the Elk River Bridge. C. C. Woodworth donated the land on which the Grange Hall at Sixes is located.

Robert Smith, born in Scotland, and Amanda Smith, born in Texas, came to the Sixes in early 1900. They lived at Dry Creek. Children are: Fritz Smith, a Curry County Sheriff for over 10 years; James Smith who married Irene McLelland in 1929; Calvin (Dolly) Smith who married Althea Conley and Crawford Smith who married Lottie Forty. Their children are Orris, who wed Francis Norton, and Jack, who wed Evelyn "Red" Billings. Orris is a commercial fisherman and Jack owns a sheep ranch.

Son, Robert Smith, married Elizabeth Price; Margaret Smith married Tracy Corbin and their sons are Allen and Clarence (Corky) Corbin; Catherine Smith married Roy Mills, a commercial fisherman, then wed Jessie Gilfillan.

Amaziah Jamieson was married to Eunice Corbin. In 1887, they came to Myrtle Point and later to Sixes, where he operated a saw mill. In 1912, they moved to Port Orford with their family: Fred, Ethel, Warren and Eunice.

Fred Jamieson, born in 1888, married Edna Richards. Fred worked in the woods and sawmills, also was a Deputy Sheriff for a while. Edna was Postmistress for 22 years.

Their children are Howard, Cecil and Hazel (Siegrist).

Ethel (Mather) (Buntin) (Anderson), lived up the Sixes River on a ranch. Warren, who wed Alta Sutton, worked in the woods and had a home on Hubbards Creek. Warren's children were: Vernon, Richard, Kenneth, Thelma (Coburn), Janice (MacManiman), Marceli (House), Gerald and Warren (Curly). Eunice (Mayea) (Aiken) had three children, Iris Mayea (Mrs. Alva Ingell), Warren Mayea and Jewell Mayea (Mrs. Lee Port), and she lived with her family in Port Orford and later at the Arizona Ranch on Mussel Creek where Buck Aiken worked in the woods. Eunice was born in 1898 and is still living in Eugene.

Tom Hatcher, born in 1892, married Nadda Barrington. He worked in the woods and the couple's children were: Alene, Clara and John. Alene (Mrs. Gordon Forty) was born in 1920. Clara (Mrs. Pat Miller) was born in 1921. During World War II Pat Miller was a major in the Army. He is deceased. John Hatcher was born in 1927. He married Joyce Bright and later Georgia Kalina. John operated logging trucks out of Port Orford.

E. B. Hall came to Grassy Knob in 1893 and lived there for many years. A son, Fred, married Leona and they had two children: Mildred Hall married Bob Farrier and lived many years at the Farrier ranch on the Sixes River. Fred Hall, born 1916 at Sixes, married Strellsa Farrier. They lived many years at the Hughes ranch on Lower Sixes, then later moved to the Farrier ranch up Sixes, where they still reside.

Louis Farrier, born in Humboldt County, California, came to Denmark, Oregon in 1887 and married Francis Irene Fitzhugh. He obtained land on Sixes River for stock and dairying. The couple's children are: Guy Edward, John, Robert (Bob) and Strellsa (Hall).

Ed Conley, born in 1914 at Port Orford, married Esther Diedrich in 1938. Both attended high school. Ed was an outstanding basketball player and member of the state champion Trans-Pacific team. They live up Elk River and Ed worked for Moore Mill in the woods. They have one son, David conley, a graduate of Oregon State University and U. S. Air Force veteran.

Ariel MacDonald was born in 1907 to parents Turner and Maude MacDonald. He was a minister, crippled with arthritis,and he came to Port Orford to minister to the community church. Ariel worked for Trans-Pacific Lumber Company helping to build a dock. Gable hired Ariel and Calvin Smith to build a dredge at Inman Mine on the Sixes

River. He became a caretaker for the Inman Mines, and mined the Sixes River. He tried his hand at baking in Port Orford and worked for Charlie Long in his general merchandise store. In 1935, he married Evelyn Garrett. They had three children. His widow married Everett Oscarson.

William Winsor, born in 1832 in New York, came to Port Orford in 1854 in Company K, of the Oregon Mounted Volunteers under Captain Bledsoe and General Lamrick. Winsor rented a sawmill, sawed and shipped the first white cedar to be put on the market as "Port Orford White Cedar," now a famous name for the timber. He married Charlotte White in 1858 and spend the next 40 years in Port Orford. He was Treasurer of Curry County one year, also had a hotel and general merchandise store along with the sawmill. His children were: Anna Gauntlett, Mary Gauntlett, Charles, Harvey, Nettie and Ruby.

Will Johnson, born in 1870 in Illinois, and his wife, Lilly (McBride), came to Port Orford in the early 1880s and landed on the beach at Paradise Point. They were farmers on Elk River. Their children: Harold, Arlin, Waneta, Velma, Loleta, Ima.

Ima married George Tribby. Children were Fay (Miles) and George "Curly" Tribby. After graduating from Port Orford High School, he joined the service and died in the baton Death March in the Philippines in World War II.

Ima married Harry Strain, a commercial fisherman. She cooked in many restaurants in Port Orford, also clerked for Norm's Grocery located on the corner near the theater. She was a member of five bowling leagues at the age of 75, still bowling at 85 and playing bingo.

Alfred Johnson was born in 1909 to Melvin Johnson who was born in 1875. Melvin worked in the sawmills in the Port Orford area and also on ranches. Alfred worked for the State Highway Department and had the first garbage truck route in Port Orford, selling out in 1954.

Daniel C. Oxley, born in 1903 to parents Eppa and Delpjia (Peek) Oxley, came to Port Orford in 1920. Brother Randall P. Oxley operated a garage and service station starting in 1924, which was located where the Shoreline Motel is presently situated. Dan and Violet (Hickox) of Port Orford married in 1926. Both were musicians and played for dances and community events.

Ruth E. Clark, born in 1893 in Illinois, was persuaded by her good friend Marry B. Rice, who was principal and teacher of the Port Orford Grade School, to come to Port

Orford and accept a teaching position at the high school. In 1921, Ruth Clark came and taught high school in one room at the old grade school.

A new high school and gymnasium was build in 1927, located on the hill at Sixth Street (North of the Castaway Motel.) Ruth was principal, teacher, boy's and girl's basketball coach — taking many district championships. In 1936 when the ship *Cottoneva* went aground on the beach in a storm, she told students they couldn't go watch, but when class change time came, there were only two students left in school. The other 50 were on the bank watching the shipwreck. She admitted later, she wished those two students had gone, so she could have joined the majority. She continued teaching until 1944 when she left for Montana and her favorite pastime of fishing and hunting. Later, she taught underprivileged children in St. Louis. She returned in 1976 for a large all-class high school class reunion and reception. She was grand marshall of the Fourth of July annual parade. A host of students returned for this once in a lifetime gala event. A teacher loved by one and all, she passed away in 1987.

The Knapp Family: Johann Knapp and Rachel Horn, born in the early 1800s in Germany, immigrated to the United States. They married about 1840. Louis Knapp Sr. was born in Maryland, and came to Port Orford in 1859 after the death of Johann in 1858. He got a job working at the Peter Ruffner Hotel. His mother arrived from San Francisco and was always known as "Mother Knapp." During the 1860s, after the start of the Civil War, the West Coast was very depressed. Ruffner moved away and turned the hotel over to the Knapps. They used to always keep a light in the window at night to guide ships, as there was no light house at Cape Blanco then. The great forest fire in 1868 burned all of Port Orford, except the horse stables at the Knapp Hotel. Louis Knapp, Sr. build a new home, then in 1883 he built a new updated hotel and this was used until 1945 when it was demolished to make way for Highway 101. In 1888, Mother Knapp died. Louis, Sr. married Ell Stag in 1893. They had three children: Louis Jr., Orris and Lloyd.

Louis Knapp, Jr. graduated from Portland University. He was a lifelong business man, historian, and was active in community affairs. He organized and was president of First Curry County Bank. A Port Commissioner, school board member, he served in the state legislature, operated a dairy and stock ranch on Elk River, then turned the operation over to his brother Orris. Orris married Hazel Brown; their children are Harold, Neil and June (Angell). Hazel was a professional dancer who had dance studios in Port Orford and Marshfield. Louis had acquired the Thrift Ranch in Langlois, where he built a new home and retired there. Lloyd Knapp married Laura Reed; they had one daughter, Marjorie. The family moved to Coos Bay, where Lloyd worked in the tug boat industry. Children of Orris and Hazel Knapp are: Harold, who married Mary Hale. Harold managed the

Knapp ranches and a gravel business after his father retired. His sons, David and Mike, now manage the ranches since Harold's death in an auto accident in 1993. Orris Neil Knapp married DeAudrey Scott, and now resides in Seattle, and June married Nathaniel Angel, captain of a shipping line. They live in Louisiana.

25

Historical Hilarities of Humbug Hollow

Nineteen Forty Two was a year of anxiety for the residents of the Oregon Coast due to the submarine activity of the Japanese Navy. The *I-25,* a 350 foot monster boat was assigned to the area of the Oregon and Washington coasts and although it did manage to torpedo four vessels; launch two bombing runs into the forests of Curry County and lob over a dozen shells near Fort Stevens in Clatsop County, its mere presence was disconcerting to the military and the civilian population alike. One evening Agnes Leutwyler mistook the wash rock near the dock for the conning tower of this vessel and immediately "made like Paul Revere" without a horse, alerting the poker players and customers of the Pastime Tavern (now Orford's) and every house in the downtown area that had smoke coming from the chimneys. "Douse the lights and the fires" she warned, "they're in the bay!" The alert was soon relaxed as several brave men armed with 30-30s crept up on Fort Point and noted the error.

Harvey Shindledecker swore he had "almost seen" hillside hodagers up near his claim at Bald Mountain Creek on Elk River. So adamant was the old prospector on this point that Pat Miller and Howard Boice, proprietors of the Pastime provided the "proof" of the existence of this elusive critter. Obtaining a bobcat from a local trapper they proceeded to reconstruct the carcass by shortening the legs of one side. "This allowed the vicious hodager to only go uphill and the object of an encounter was to stay on the downhill side of the brute." They placed the critter in the truck of a car and summoned Harvey. "That's one of 'em" Harvey said, and he was dispatched to obtain a camera to record the rare find. When he returned with a "Brownie" the critter was gone … "The damned thing came to life and attacked us," explained Miller, "we had to get inside to protect ourselves. The last we saw of him he was heading up the hill toward the cemetery, snarling and turning circles." 'Till the day he died Harvey was convinced that he had finally got to see his hillside hodager and no one told him any different.

Harvey Shindledecker swore that one time he fell off the dock and, unable to swim, walked toward shore. His favorite old briar pipe survived this feat and, according to Harv, was still lit when he crawled out of the breakers.

Sometimes Harvey got in the way of legitimate projects. One day when Pat Miller was attempting to inventory the Pastime, Harvey insisted on helping. "Go back and inventory the ice cubes," Pat instructed, "and I'll need an accurate count." Harvey disappeared into the back room and several hours later when the crew missed him he was located at the ice machine where he was carefully taking the cubes out and placing them in buckets on the floor saying, "How'll I count 'em when they melt?"

Curry's First Piano. The book *Then 'Till Now,* published by the Brookings Rotary Club in 1979, credits the first piano to the Driskells who settled that area in 1912.

Let us put the damper on that rumor! From an unpublished manuscript of an engineer working at Flores Lake in 1895 who purchased the salvage rights to the grounded British steam schooner *Bawnmore* for $500 we learn, "A grand piano crated in a hermetically sealed container came ashore without a scratch and was purchased by the lighthouse keeper on Cape Blanco (Frank Langlois). It had the distinction of being the first piano in Curry County."

Miss Jennie Malehorn advertised in the *Southwest Oregon Recorder* in February 1885 her business as a "resident music teacher ... lessons given on the piano or organ!"

The author's aunt, Mary Masterson, learned to play a piano prior to 1910 ... on Mrs. Nygren's piano brought to Port Orford in 1903 on the ship *Alta*.

The Driskell instrument rates a white ribbon for third place, and more probably, fourth.

Port Orford's Organ: In 1901, Mrs. Knapp, McKenzie, Leneve, Kerr and Masterson chipped in $5 apiece along with 47 other donors including Wong Cong ($1) to purchase a public organ. It rented for $1 for public pay dances, $2 to travelling shows and no charge for the public to practice.

The theatre building was constructed in 1925 by Mr. H. Axtel.

Port Orford Jakie, the last of the Sixes River Tyees, died at Port Orford in February 1908.

In November 1903 George Forty found an Indian canoe on the beach near Battle Rock and concluded it originated from the Smith River in California. It is probably the same artifact salvaged from Garrison Lake by Wayne Thomas in the 1950s, now stored at the Hughes House Museum.

A relic of the Battle of Battle Rock was found by Marion Zumwalt and Blanchard Caldwell in October of 1901 near Battle Rock. It was identified as a cold "five shooter" and was still in a sheath although covered with sea growth. It was given to a Mr. Bartelle who ran the Centennial Saloon. Kirkpatrick, the leader of the Battle Rock defenders, mentions a .38 caliber pistol in his narrative.

A movement was initiated in 1925 to construct a bronze statue of President Teddy Roosevelt astride his favorite horse up on Battle Rock to be dedicated in conjunction with the opening of the Roosevelt Military Highway (U.S. 101) in that year.

The first minister to preach at Port Orford was Rev. Alderson, a Methodist who made the trip from Empire City in February, 1858, conducting services at a Mr. Frank Ross's dining hall at a mining camp at Sixes and then, after considerable hardships crossing the rain swollen Sixes and Elk Rivers, managed to arrive intact at Port Orford.

Miner Dan's place on the north bank near the mouth of the Sixes was known for more than a hotel in the early 1850s. Two writers from New York found Dan in an irate mood as the Coos County Sheriff had just left after imposing Dan with a heavy tariff on his stock of spiritous liquor.

The knife dropped by an Indian scout when wounded by fire from a sentry at Port Orford in March, 1856 is in the Smithsonian Institution along with a sea otter hide and mineral samples sent by R. Dunbar in 1858.

Cape Blanco had the distinction of being the farthest west point in the U.S.A. from 1859 until 1889 when Washington became a state. Cape Alava is farther west but

Blanco is the farthest west you can drive to.

The movement to secede from the union was a serious matter in the late 1940s, but the attack on Pearl Harbor and subsequent declaration of war on the Japanese Empire necessitated those involved with the movement to send a certified testament to F. D. R. proclaiming allegiance to the Union ... secession during time of war is ... Treason!

"The first practical railroad in Curry County was constructed by P. J. Lindberg ... from Patrick Hughes's barn to the creamery some 150 feet." *Port Orford Tribune*, April 23, 1901.

In September, 1942, Captain Tagami and Nobu Fujita waited for ten days in the 350 foot submarine *I-25* to launch an airplane to set fire to the forests of Curry county. The reason for the delay ... unseasonable rainy, stormy weather. Plan ahead!

In 1902, the Post Office posted hours were from 5:00 a.m. until 8:00 p.m., six days a week, and Sundays from 9:00 a.m. to 10:00 a.m. Do you suppose they had time enough to get the mail in the right boxes in those days? Can some of you remember when Edna and Lela had it out by 9:30 a.m., first to fourth class inclusive when there were more people in town than there are now?
Star Route mail delivery was inaugurated in 1902.

The great air-sea battles in the Western Pacific during World War II (1941-'45) brought interesting flotsam and jetsam to the beaches around Port Orford. Life preservers, K and Sea Rations, life rafts, cases of spent ammunition cartridges, gun oil and other debris littered the beaches for several years. Globs of heavy oil, more accurately described as soft tar was commonplace along the beaches.

The Coast Guard maintained beach patrols during the early years of World War II and took over the Administration Building (later the Castaway) where dog kennels were constructed. The beaches were off-limits after dark. The U. S. Army backed this effort up with daily highway patrols. They dug a pit at the end of Fort Point which they used to set up a machine gun. This patrol was made up of several peeps, a jeep and an armored personnel carrier which carried about two squads of men.

Port Orford gained national attention after a visit by the widely read columnist for Scripps-Howard papers, Ernie Pyle, in January, 1942. On his way to Portland, Pyle spent an afternoon here and was given the grand tour by *Port Orford Post* Editor Frank Hilton. He later wrote articles with a Port Orford dateline that featured Gilbert Gable, the secession movement, and Jimmie Combs, the hero of the Willapa sinking. Pyle later gained fame as a war correspondent and was killed by a sniper at Guadalcanal.

The first movie was shown at Leneve's Hall in August, 1901, and was, of course, an Edison.

In 1942 the longshoremen of Port Orford elected Jim Sutton president, V. Boyer vice president, Harry Strahan treasurer, Grover Tichenor secretary, and Crawford Smith dispatcher of the ILWU. Bert Dean, Harry Strahan and George Inman made up the Labor Relations Board.

In March, 1942, Gene Mangini signed with the Brooklyn Dodgers. He pitched for the Curry County Savages of Port Orford and hailed from Southern California.

In February, 1890, a large slide occurred up Sixes River burying a house, killing three people and 21 head of stock.

In September, 1940, 6.1 million board feet of lumber was shipped from Port Orford eclipsing the old record of 4.8 million in August of that year.

Port Orford's bowling alley of the late 1930s, the Pot Of Gold, featured duck-pins and was owned by Charles and Lorraine Haines. Teams that enjoyed the facility were Trans Pacific Mill, the Marsh Loggers, Phillips Market and the Brookfield Dodgers.

The Port Orford Rod and Gun Club was organized by Pat Miller and Dolly Smith. The club sponsored fishing derbies and hunting awards as well as promoting tourism in the late 1930s.

Often along the South Coast an elderly whale decides not to make the long trip to Alaska or Baja and adopts an area to live out his or her life. Such was the case of Barnacle Bill, a 30 foot grey who became a resident in the late 1940s. Old Bill was immediately adopted by the locals who enjoyed his frequent visits to the dock area. His only bad habit was to use the pilings at the deep end as "scratching posts" and all